GLYPH I

GLYPH

JOHNS HOPKINS TEXTUAL STUDIES

THE JOHNS HOPKINS UNIVERSITY PRESS
Baltimore and London

The Johns Hopkins University Press, Baltimore, Maryland 21218
The Johns Hopkins Press Ltd., London
Library of Congress Catalog Card Number 76–47370
ISBN 0–8018–1930–X (hardcover)   ISBN 0–8018–1931–8 (paperback)

STATEMENT TO CONTRIBUTORS

The Editors of *Glyph* welcome submissions concerned with the problems of representation and textuality, and contributing to the confrontation between American and Continental critical scenes. Contributors should send *two* copies of their manuscripts, accompanied by return postage, to Samuel Weber, Editor, *Glyph*, Humanities Center, The Johns Hopkins University, Baltimore, Maryland 21218. In preparing manuscripts, please refer to *A Manual of Style*, published by the University of Chicago Press, and *The Random House Dictionary*. The entire text, including extended citations and notes, should be double-spaced.

Copies of *Glyph*, both hardbound and paperback, may be ordered from The Johns Hopkins University Press, Baltimore, Maryland 21218.

The illustration on the cover and title page, an Egyptian crocodile from the Ptolemaic period, is reproduced through the courtesy of the Walters Art Gallery, Baltimore.

CONTENTS

PROGRAM

To INITIATE a new serial publication by means of a program cannot but provoke reservations of the kind recently formulated by Northrop Frye:

I have a rooted dislike of the "position paper" genre. In all the arts, adhering to a school and issuing group manifestoes and statements of common aims is a sign of youthfulness, and to some degree of immaturity; as a painter or writer or other creative person grows older and acquires more authority, he tends to withdraw from all such organizations and become simply himself.

The statement of a series of principles or of positions which is intended to define the possibility or even necessity of a collective effort is thus to be regarded with suspicion: it is a sign of youthful immaturity on the part of those who must look to a *group* for the authority that they cannot find in themselves as *individuals*. The collective "statement of common aims" is, in this view, a symptom not of strength but of weakness. And how much more telling this diagnosis must be where the collective effort bears on the reading and writing of texts, in which "interpretation" and even "creativity" are held to be the decisive factors and, hence, in which general principles and positions, theories and methods, are only there to be transcended in the irreducibly individual *act* of criticism. However little general consensus there may be, therefore, concerning general concepts and categories, there does seem to be agreement on one question, and it is surely the decisive one: that such

VIII
Program

generalities are subordinate to and indeed have little influence upon criticism, which is, ultimately, all that counts.

When, therefore, a number of individuals come together in order to cooperate in a serial publication; when they proceed to write a *program*, which is intended to delineate the contours of that cooperation, the conditions which render it possible and the lines it is to take; when, finally, such a program seeks to articulate a certain historical configuration of theory and of practice as the point of departure for a collective effort which must necessarily, if it is effective, call the traditional dichotomy of "theory and practice" into question—then, the suspicions of critics like Northrop Frye can only appear confirmed. The program is clearly doomed from the start. The mature person will recognize the immaturity of the project, withdraw from all such organizations, and trust instead to time and his own labors to bring, ultimately, the authority that only comes from being, or becoming, oneself.

This would therefore be the time to stop, before it is too late; before we write the program that can only confirm the absence of the authority it presumably will proclaim. We can still avoid this surest sign of youthful immaturity, if only we refuse, now and henceforth, *to write the program*, to engage in the *organization* it implies. The choice is simple. Or so it would seem.

But can we refuse to write programs? Is this a choice we can freely make? The question is perhaps less simple than it seems. For to refuse the program is to refuse not just a certain form of statement, but *writing* as such. Not merely because all writing is inevitably informed by certain prior categories, notions, conceptions, and values—by a certain *program*, that is, which exists prior to the individual operations of reading and writing—but also because, in writing, we engage ourselves in a process that takes us beyond ourselves, to other texts and other readers. However personal, individual, or esoteric our writing may seem, it is ineluctably programmatic, at least in the original sense of the word, which denoted a writing, γράφειν, that was written *in and out front*, πρό, a matter of public interest and concern. And this is also an attribute of all writing, inasmuch as it entails necessarily a domain of otherness that is not merely exterior to its operation but constitutive of it. The "critical" text may appear to master this alterity in the text it criticizes; but the limits of that mastery are already at work, at least latently, in its "own" reading, and they become manifest in its destination as a text to be read by others, elsewhere, in another space largely beyond its control.

This other space, then, is the field of the program: its *alibi*. It is a space to be avoided by the "mature" critic, as Frye and others construe him, for in it the critic is inevitably displaced, outside of himself. And yet, although it exceeds the confines of the individual critic, in this sense, it is also difficult for him to avoid entirely, however mature he may be. For it is not simply an empty or vacuous space, "out there," but also, and above all, the space in which the texts the critic reads, and his "own" text as well, are situated. The situation of those texts is hardly arbitrary: it is determined by the distinct and distinguishable tendencies of a force-field, which, because it is the domain not merely of the writer as critic but of the general public, constitutes an alterity that only the *program* can begin to delineate.

But if the program is to begin this de-lineation, it can only do so by calculating, articulating the πρό of its γράμμα in all of its grahic ambivalence: the pro-grammatic text is "out front," not merely as a *prospectus*, with an eye to the future, nor does it majestically survey the past. It does not merely proclaim or plan what is to come, nor does it claim precedence over what has been. It is not merely a statement asserting something and enjoining someone, a pro- as opposed to a con-. For all this would only serve to reduce what is its ultimate resource: its singular eccentricity. The program is eccentric, for it is a text that takes the place of something else, it replaces or supplants, as a pro-noun replaces a noun. And this indicates why and how the program must be *collective*, even if it is written by an individual. The program must be collective because it collects. It collects individuals and articulates them as a collective. But this collective is not merely the sum or synthesis of its individual members: it is no Super-Individual, in and through which the Group speaks, as with a single voice. The collective, on the contrary, gathers individuals together without producing a positive, definitive synthesis. For what collects the individuals of the collective, what brings them together is the *co-legere* of common *readings*, readings which interact with one another to produce collective writing, not as writing written with several hands directly, but which seeks to chart a space of differences and to promote their articulation.

In this sense, then, the collective program, or programmatic collective, must begin—for there must be a beginning, whatever its ultimate status may be—by tracing the limits of the field in which it is collectively situated. That field, provisionally, may be designated as a *space of representation*. It is a space whose boundaries are perhaps as old as Western thought itself, inasmuch as this thought has constituted and consolidated its system of interpretation—"Metaphysics"—around the category of representation: thought being considered the representation of reality, and language the representation of thought. This system of Western Metaphysics has thus sought to install representational, referential discourse as the normative model of language, and this includes "poetical" or "literary" language no less than so-called non-fictional modes of discourse. The notion of "fiction" does not, in and of itself, call the category of representation into question; on the contrary, it has generally been structured by it. For a variety of reasons, this structure of representation—with its inevitable supposition of an extra-representational referent, existing independently of and prior to all representation —is being increasingly and from diverse directions called into question. The interrogation of this model of representation, its dislocation from its traditional status as a self-evident certainty to a problem to be investigated, marks the initial and preliminary coherence of the publication *Glyph* and the collective effort it involves.

It is the form which this interrogatory effort assumes, however, that contributes to delineating the specificity of the particular collective venture designated by *Glyph*. As its title indicates, this effort entails not only the elaboration of a *theory* of what has been called the "crisis of representation," because such a theory would still depend upon forms of discourse that are part and parcel of the representational system that is being questioned. The elaboration of a theory of this crisis of representation can only be effective if it is simultaneously the articulation of forms of reading and writing that are no longer entirely dominated by the referential discourse of representational Metaphysics. If, at this juncture, the text qua writing appears as the form of language that has been most resistant to the domination of referentiality and of representation, we may describe this process of articulation as the development of *practices of textuality*. The elaboration of such practices, no longer wholly governed by the schemata of representation, can hardly leave the traditional metaphysical distinction between theoretical, critical, expository discourse, on the one side, and poetical, literary, fictional language on the other, untouched. If the notions of "literature," "philosophy," "psychoanalysis," and the like cannot be used to delimit the field of our concerns, even though the concrete texts we will be reading are generally situated within such fields, it is not because of a desire to transcend such distinctions in an interdisciplinary synthesis but, rather, because of the necessity to rethink those divisions once the ontology of representation and its hierarchies are no longer self-evident.

And this brings us to a third aspect of our program. For the elaboration of non-representational practices of the text can only produce forms of reading and writing which drastically violate the traditional norms of scientific and scholarly discourse, particularly in the Anglo-American "universe of discourse," which is, let us recall, no mere geographic accident for us but, rather, the particular *public space* of our programmatic intervention. One of the most deeply rooted convictions prevailing in this space—and it is the one in which its appurtenance to a metaphysical tradition that it often criticizes is most effective—is the belief that anything worth saying can be said simply and clearly. "Wovon man nicht sprechen kann, darüber muß man schweigen—What we cannot speak about we must pass over in silence." But Wittgenstein's dictum does not exhaust all possibilities; with a slight modification, it can read: Wovon man nicht sprechen kann, darüber muß man *schreiben*: what we cannot say, we must *write*. But our writing, programmatic and collective, in the senses already indicated, is a writing *for* . . . in front and out front, for itself and also instead of itself. This pro- as *instead*, the structural operation by which a writing not governed by the category of representation is not only the surrogate of another but also of itself, defines such writing as inevitably a process of *grafting*. The collective effort of *Glyph* must therefore seek to reflect and to calculate its practice as a form of graft for reasons which are both "historical" and also "structural." The particular problematization of the representational framework of Western Metaphysics, which we take as our starting point, has been articulated by certain European thinkers—the names of Nietzsche, Marx, Freud, Heidegger, Derrida can serve here as indexes— who, however, were addressing themselves to a "universe of discourse" quite distinct from that prevailing in the English-speaking world. This continental form of Metaphysics, predominantly speculative, rationalist, and idealist, contrasts sharply with an Anglo-American tradition characterized precisely by a critique of such continental tendencies, from standpoints that can be described as nominalist, empiricist, functionalist, and syncretistic. Thus, if the sway of Metaphysics as a system of thought has also prevailed in the English-speaking world, the forms it has taken have been quite distinct from those of continental rationalism. To identify and challenge effectively the domination of representation here and today thus requires a transformation of investigative concepts and procedures consonant with the specific differences of the Anglo-American scene, in which, for instance, the critique of referential discourse, of the value of truth and of certain forms of subjectivity—all decisive blind spots of continental Metaphysics—have long been integrated into and appropriated by representational thought. Such specific differences and resources of the space in which we are situated are not obstacles to be overcome by a theory seeking to dethrone and replace it, and which as such could only become another version of what it is supplanting; rather, they are the provocation and possibility of a practice of transformation, transforming itself together with its "object."

SAMUEL WEBER

GLYPH I

ONE
THE DIVARICATOR: REMARKS ON FREUD'S *WITZ*
Samuel Weber

THE HISTORY of Freud's thought might well be approached in terms of the different polemical stances through which it successively defined and redefined its own position. In its early years, this stance was naturally directed at critics from without, who sought to deny psychoanalysis any kind of theoretical or therapeutical legitimacy. As Freud's work consolidated itself and won adherents, however, the object of his polemics shifted from without to the enemy within. The emergence of prominent apostates, such as Adler and Jung, as well as Freud's followers, such as Rank, presented a continuing series of challenges to the status of Freudian psychoanalysis and could not help but provoke varying responses from its founder. Despite the diversity of these responses, it is possible to discern a single trait characterizing Freud's defense of psychoanalysis, particularly in the years following 1910: against the revisions of renegades and disciples alike, Freud insisted that any attempt to reduce psychoanalysis to a single, causal factor must be considered as an unacceptable impoverishment of his theoretical efforts. In his essay published in 1914, "On the History of the Psychoanalytic Movement," for instance, Freud takes Adler to task for reducing the complexity of psychoanalytic theory to one of its elements—the ego's striving for power in its struggle for self-preservation—and thereby necessarily misconstruing the fundamental discovery of psychoanalysis: namely, that the ego is entirely unintelligible apart from the dynamics of unconscious

Samuel Weber

repression. Freud thereby compares Adler's conception to what he had termed "secondary revision" in "The Interpretation of Dreams": the process by which the manifest absurdities of the dream-text are made to conform, on the surface, with rational expectation: "The Adlerian theory was from the very beginning a 'system'—which psychoanalysis was careful to avoid becoming. It is also a remarkably good example of 'secondary revision,' such as occurs, for instance, in the process to which dream-material is submitted by the action of waking thought. In Adler's case the place of dream-material is taken by the new material obtained through psychoanalytic studies; this is then viewed purely from the standpoint of the ego, reduced to the categories with which the ego is familiar, translated, twisted, and—exactly as happens in dream-formation—is misunderstood."[1] Freud criticizes Adler for having "translated" the discoveries of psychoanalysis, which necessarily and essentially involve the unconscious, into "the categories with which the ego is familiar." And yet, the danger of such a reductive translation is perhaps more insidious, its temptation more potent, than Freud's polemic would seem to imply.

In its most general aspect, the problem involves the unique character of psychoanalytic *theory*, of psychoanalysis *as* a theory. The problem is in some sense *unique*, inasmuch as the "object" of psychoanalysis must be situated within the realm of the unconscious and its effects, which, by definition, never present themselves directly or in a pure form to the contemplation of consciousness; and yet, the very notion of *theory*, in the traditional sense at least, is unthinkable apart from a homogeneous and continuous space of perception or contemplation, as the etymology of theory, from *theoria*, indicates. Yet, it is precisely this homogeneous and continuous space of theoretical contemplation that psychoanalysis, with its structurally interrelated notions of the unconscious and of repression, calls into question.

Although this problem is never subjected to prolonged discussion by Freud, its effects are legible throughout his texts. They can be described as taking two forms, at least. In the first, the question is articulated as it pertains to "objects" that psychoanalysis has identified and *comprehended*; here, the tendency of psychoanalysis to *delimit* the space of theory is confined, as in the stricture against Adler, to objects of study, like the dream, which themselves appear to be situated *within* the scope of psychoanalytical theory itself. This delimitation of the problem, confining and comprehending it, serves, implicitly at least, to establish and to consolidate the authority and legitimacy of the comprehending theory itself, that is, psychoanalysis. Thus, in "Totem and Taboo," Freud elaborates his notion of secondary revision as "the prototype (*Vorbild*)" of all systematic thought, the manifestations of which he finds most clearly exemplified "in delusional disorders (in paranoia), where it dominates the symptomatic picture."[2] By thus defining systematic thought as a species of "secondary revision," Freud implicitly ascribes to psycho-analytical *thought* the power of distinguishing what is *secondary* from what is *primary*, and consequently, of comprehending systematic thought without being subject to the limitations of the latter. This implicit ascription becomes evident when Freud continues: "In all these cases [of secondary revision] it can be shown that a rearrangement of the psychical material has been made with a fresh aim in view; and the rearrangement may often have to be a drastic one if the outcome is to be made to appear intelligible from the point of view of the system. Thus, a system is best characterized by the fact that at least two reasons can be discovered for each of its products: a reason based upon the premises of the system (a reason, then, which may be delusional) and a concealed reason, which we must judge to be the truly operative and the real one."[3] The secondary, derivative nature of systematic thought in no way seems to impede the power of psychoanalytic theory to discern what, in each given case, is a "rearrangement" and what the original and anterior arrangement must have been.

If this is one of the two forms in which the problematical status of conscious, systematic thought is articulated in the texts of Freud, and if it is also the more conspicuous of the two forms, it is nonetheless the weaker and less interesting one. This is because it limits its own limitation of such thought to an *object*, which it can then comprehend, enclose in its own discourse, and in its own conceptual . . . *system*. This version of psychoanalytical epistemology is *critical*, dividing the wheat from the chaff, the secondary from the primary, the revision from the original. And yet, at the same time it is strangely uncritical, since it ignores the implications of its own critique, which, if it is to be valid for systematic thought in general, cannot help but involve psychoanalytical theory itself, inasmuch as this theory can hardly avoid systematic strivings.

If one views the development of Freud's theory from a diachronic perspective, this first, weak form of the question—posing the status of systematic thought as a general, but limited object—seems to prevail during the period extending to 1914, the year not only of "On the History of the Psychoanalytic Movement," but also of the far more important "On Narcissism, An Introduction," (*Zur Einführung des Narziβmus*). During this time-span, which runs from "The Interpretation of Dreams" (1900) to the first general history and defense of the "movement" (1914), psychoanalytical theory received its first comprehensive formulation and elaboration. It would seem that, by ignoring the implications of the critique of systematic thought for his own developing system,

Freud exemplified—in the sense of *acting out*—exactly what he sought to confine and to attribute to the otherness of his object. For if it is true, as he wrote in "Totem and Taboo"—once again apropos of secondary revision as the paradigm of systematic thought in general—that "there is an intellectual function in us which demands unity, connection, and intelligibility from any material, whether of perception or thought,"[4] it is inevitable that such a function will be all the more powerful during the period in which a system is in the process of constituting itself and establishing its identity, and thus imposing "unity, connection, and intelligibility" upon its material, than need be the case once the system has been erected.

Whether or not such a diachronic perspective in regard to Freud's thought is ultimately valid or not, his essay on narcissism doubtless marks a turning-point. It ushers in the phase of extended "metapsychological" reflection, in which Freud addresses himself not so much to the implications of his "material" as such as to the consequences emerging from the psychoanalytical *concepts* he had hitherto used to organize and structure that "material." Freud's psychoanalytical theory had by now attained a degree of cohesiveness and systematicity which enabled, or rather compelled him to reflect "metapsychologically" upon the questions raised by that theory itself, and not simply by its "objects." Implicitly, some of the reservations earlier expressed concerning systematic thought now began to be extended by Freud to his own theoretical operation. Freud begins this extension by reiterating the distinction he had often drawn previously between "speculative theory" such as philosophy, and sciences such as psychoanalysis, that are grounded in the observation and interpretation of empirical reality:

It is true that notions (*Vorstellungen*) such as that of an ego-libido, energy of the ego-drives and so on, are neither particularly easy to grasp (*klar faßbar*) nor sufficiently rich in content; a speculative theory of the relations in question would begin by seeking to construct a clearly delineated concept as its foundation. In my opinion, however, that is precisely the difference between a speculative theory and a science erected upon the interpretation of empirical data. The latter will not envy speculation its privilege of having a smooth, logically unassailable foundation, but will gladly settle for nebulous, evanescent, scarcely imaginable (*kaum vorstellbaren*) basic thoughts, which it hopes to grasp more clearly in the course of its development, or which it is even prepared to exchange for others. For these ideas are not the foundations of science, upon which everything rests: that, on the contrary, is observation alone.[5]

The distinction of science from speculation seems straightforward and unequivocal. By contrast with speculation, science is ready to discard its concepts when they no longer aid in the "observation" and the "interpretation of empirical data." Science, therefore, would represent a triumph over a mode of thought which, despite its sophistication cannot conceal its narcissistic origins. *Observation*, in this context, would represent the antipode of *speculation*. And yet, what allows us to read Freud's text here, despite its apparent simplicity, as an anticipation of a certain self-criticism, is the fact that it does not only speak of observation, but also of interpretation, not only of the *Beobachtung*, but of the *Deutung der Empire*. For these two words are by no means simply synonymous. The interpretation of a dream, for instance, is something very different from its mere observation. If observation, as an epistemological notion, is situated within the traditional continuum of theoretical space conceived as the neutral medium of contemplation, this is not necessarily so of interpretation.

Freud does not confront this problem here, in the essay on narcissism, directly. He still seeks to define the theoretical operation of psychoanalysis positively in terms of a science based upon empirical observation; and in so doing, he leaves himself open to the very critique he had addressed to Adler and other renegades: namely, of distorting the discoveries of psychoanalysis by "translating" them into the language and the categories of the ego. And yet, if the ego's language and categories render the operations of speculative, systematic thought inadequate for the articulation of psychoanalysis, are they any less prevalent in a scientific discourse based on observation? If observation, as opposed to speculation, is the foundation of the science of psychoanalysis, will the space that it thereby presupposes ultimately be any different from that of the system "perception-consciousness," which, in the Freudian topology, is ineluctably that of the ego?

This is why, in the passage cited and increasingly throughout his writings, the "observation" that Freud opposes to rationalistic speculation emerges as being of a most peculiar kind. For its medium is not clarity but obscurity, not light so much as shadow. The notions (*Vorstellungen*) developed from psychoanalytical "observation," as opposed to those of speculation, are *kaum vorstellbar*, hardly imaginable, fleeting and nebulous. If Freud appeals to observation, then, it is to establish the necessity of a certain theoretical *obscurity*.

This necessity is nowhere affirmed more strikingly than in what is probably Freud's last "metapsychological" essay, *Inhibition, Symptoms and Anxiety*. Here, again, it is the philosophers who provide Freud with the apparently simple foil against which he seeks to delineate the specific contours of psychoanalytical thought as one that deliberately and essentially resists the temptation of reducing the alterity and ambivalence of its objects in order to comprehend them. And again, it is surely pertinent if the particular object here is none other than the *ego*, which in this text is no longer simply the instance of consciousness and perception, but also and more significantly, *the site of anxiety* and *the agent of repression*: "Many writers have laid much stress on the weakness of the ego in relation to the id and of our rational elements in the face of the daemonic forces within us; and they display a strong tendency to make what I have said into a cornerstone of a psychoanalytical *Weltanschauung*. Yet surely the psychoanalyst, with his insight into the way in which repression works, should, of all people, be immune to such extreme partisanship."[6] If the mechanism of *repression* excludes any univocal determination of the ego—for instance, in terms of its "weakness" with regard to the id—and if it furthermore excludes in principle the use of psychoanalysis as a *Weltanschauung*, this still presupposes that repression, however ambiguous it may be, is still accessible to the *Einsicht*, the insight of the psychoanalyst. And yet, if this is so, it is only because that insight, as Freud goes on to describe it, is no less complex than the observation upon which it is based:

I must confess that I am not at all partial to the fabrication of *Weltanschauungen*. Such activities may be left to the philosphers, who avowedly find it impossible to make their journey through life without a Baedeker of that kind to give them information on every subject. Let us humbly accept the scorn with which the philosophers look down upon us from the standpoint of their more elevated needs. But since we, too, cannot deny our narcissistic pride, we shall seek solace in the reflection that such "guide books to life" soon grow obsolete, that it is precisely *our shortsighted, provincial, and microscopic work (unsere kurzsichtig beschränkte Kleinarbeit)* which makes their revised editions necessary, and that even the most modern of these Baedekers are nothing but attempts to replace the venerable, highly convenient, and exhaustive catechism. We know exactly *how little light* science has hitherto been able to spread upon the enigma of the world, and all the fulminations of the philosophers will not change this a bit. Only patient, persistent work, subordinating everything to the one demand of certitude, can gradually bring about change. The wanderer who sings in the darkness may deny his fear, but he will not see any better for it (*er sieht um nichts heller*).[7] (Italics mine)

If the insight of the analyst is to be preferred to the world-view of the philosopher, it is because of a certain *shortsightedness*, with which the analyst learns to live and to work. Thus, the Cartesian demand of *certitude*, that Freud appears here to make his own, is deceptive: for what kind of certitude can there be for the nearsighted, myopic Wanderer, except, perhaps, the certainty of the darkness in which he wanders. And yet, however modest, such certitude is not entirely empty: "It is almost humiliating that, after such long work, we should still encounter difficulties in our conception of the most rudimentary and fundamental matters

(*Verhältnisse*), but we have resolved not to simplify or to conceal anything. If we cannot see clearly, we shall at least try to see distinctly what is unclear."[8] From the affirmation of psychoanalysis as a positive science, based on observation and induction, to his description of the analyst as the wanderer, Freud's path has obviously been long and tortuous, and has led him away from the conviction that perception, qua observation, can provide an unshakeable foundation for psychoanalysis, and at the same time an impermeable shield against the narcissistic lures of speculation. Instead of seeing clearly, Freud hopes only "to see what is unclear." What is it, then, that he thus hopes to glimpse? As we have already read, such obscurity involves not merely peripheral questions, but "the most rudimentary and fundamental matters." Later in the same text, Freud gives us an instance: "In other words, we inadvertently find ourselves confronted by the riddle we have met so often: where does neurosis come from, what is its ultimate and particular driving force (*Motiv*)? After decades of analytical effort, this problem rises before us (*erhebt sich . . . vor uns*), untouched, as at the beginning."[9] The riddle or enigma that "rises up before us, untouched, as at the beginning," to baffle the eyes of the observer, reminds us that psychoanalysis, even as the science Freud described, was based not on observation alone, but also on *interpretation*; and also that "at the beginning," when Freud was concerned precisely with the question of interpretation, similar figures rose up out of a similar obscurity, this time to baffle not merely observation, but also interpretation itself.

Early in the seventh and final chapter of "The Interpretation of Dreams," Freud attempts to elaborate some of the more speculative consequences of his previous analysis of the structure and functions of dreams. "Hitherto," he writes, "we have been principally concerned with the secret meaning of dreams and the method of discovering it and with the means employed by the dream-work for concealing it. The problems of dream-interpretation have hitherto occupied the center of the picture."[10] Now, however, Freud sees himself constrained to set out along a new and more difficult path: "For it must be clearly understood that the easy and agreeable portion of our journey lies behind us. Hitherto, unless I am greatly mistaken, all the paths along which we have travelled have led us towards the light—towards enlightenment (*ins Lichte, zur Aufklärung*) and full understanding. But once we attempt to penetrate more deeply into the psychic processes involved in dreaming, every path will end in darkness."[11] Freud's previous journey—"unsere Wanderung," as he calls it—has been in and towards the *light*, uncovering both the "secret meaning" that the dream articulates even while dissimulating it, and the mechanisms by which the dream-work accomplishes that task. Now, however, Freud stands, as it were, on the edge of darkness, before the *unknown*: "There is no possibility of *elucidating* the dream as a psychical process, since to explain something means to trace it back to what is familiar, and there is at present no psychological knowledge under which we could subsume what the psychological examination of dreams enables us to infer as the basis for their explanations (*Erklärungsgrund*)."[12] The "unknown," the obscurity which confronts Freud, is apparently a not-yet-known, a hitherto uncharted terrain, but one which may one day be mapped out and "familiar." The darkness may only be *provisional*. If it is not yet open to the light of theory, to *Aufklärung*, it may still be explored with the aid of *suppositions, Annahmen*: "We shall, on the contrary, be constrained to set up a series of new suppositions (*eine Reihe von neuen Annahmen aufzustellen*) involving certain suspicions which concern the structure of the psychical apparatus and the forces active in it, while at the same time we take heed not to extend (*auszuspinnen*) these suppositions beyond their first logical nexus, lest their value dissolve in the indeterminable."[13]

The passage with which we will be concerned, then, is situated on the border between the brightly lit analysis of the dream and the uncertain obscurity of its theoretical implications which only a certain speculation, groping slowly forward with the help of hypotheses, can even begin to "penetrate."

But before he sets out on this new way—which, of course, will be that of "metapsychology"—Freud pauses, in the first section of the final chapter of "The Interpretation of Dreams," to discuss the status of this *interpretation* itself. And it is here that he addresses himself to the question of its *limits*:

Even in the best interpreted dreams, there is often a place (*eine Stelle*) that must be left in the dark, because in the *process* of interpreting, one notices a tangle of dream-thoughts arising (*anhebt*), which resists unravelling but has also made no further contributions (*keine weiteren Beiträge*) to the dream-content. This is then the dream's navel, the place where it straddles the unknown (*dem Unerkannten aufsitzt*). The dream-thoughts, to which interpretation leads one, are necessarily interminable (*ohne Abschluß*) and branch out on all sides into the netlike entanglement (*in die netzartige Verstrickung*) of our world of thought. Out of one of the denser places of this meshwork, the dream-wish rises (*erhebt sich*) like a mushroom out of its mycelium.[14]

Here, on the borderline between light and darkness, Freud, reflecting upon the limits of interpretation, apparently distinguishes a place which, for all of its impenetrable obscurity, hides no real mysteries; an obscurity which, because it can be clearly seen and recognized, can also be securely *put in its place*, and moreover, left there. For even though its various strands resist unravelling, there seems no question that "it has made no further contributions to the dream-content." No *further* contributions, *keine weiteren Beiträge*—does Freud, then, mean to imply that it has made *any* contributions? If the "tangle" is so inextricable, how can we know whether or not its strands contribute to the dream at all?

The tone of the passage is so resolute and reassuring, the obscurity is described with such apparent clarity, its interminable inconclusiveness is comprehended so conclusively, that readers have felt obliged to retain nothing but the striking formula with which Freud appears to name and to master the difficulty in a single gesture: *the navel of the dream*. And if the navel is itself shrouded in darkness, it still marks the place from which the *dream-wish*, which gives the dream its *meaning* as a wish-fulfillment, surges into view. In this perspective, which certainly appears, at first reading, to be that of Freud, the obscurity of the navel need concern us only as the final moment of darkness in a dialectic which immediately transcends it with the emergence of the dream-wish, as the "meaning" of the dream and hence, as the end of interpretation, but also as its definitive achievement.

Or so it might seem, in particular, to those readers of the Standard Edition who lack access to Freud's German text. They would be liable to read quickly over Freud's *description* of the interminable nature of the dream-thoughts without stopping to consider its *ramifications*. For these ramifications are rendered far more harmless in the Strachey translation than they are in Freud's text. For Strachey, the dream-thoughts "branch out in every direction *into the intricate network* of our world of thought." If my translation reads differently (see above), it is because Freud's "net" is not merely *intricate*, in a sense of being infinitely complex: it is also, and perhaps above all, a snare. As with snares in general, and with those of the unconscious in particular, they are rarely less effective for being ignored.

The words of Freud's text, which the Standard Edition chooses to translate as "intricate network," are, in German, literally inverted: "netzartige Verstrickung." If I have retained their literalness, by translating them as "netlike entanglement," it is because, even more than the *network*, it is the *net* and the *entanglement* that count. For what is crucial here, beyond the complexity of the network, is the "trick" hidden in the *intricacy* of Freud's net: in his text—and surely not only there—this net catches, entraps, and paradoxically arrests what appears to be the reassuringly expansive movement of infinite ramification, the endlessness of our thoughts. And if we can be sure of never being able to arrive at the end, this would seem more of a solace than a cause for concern, especially because it permits us to assume that, at all times, we know *where* we are, within the inexhaustible "world of thought" which is ours. And yet, if we take the trouble to *read* Freud's description, we discover something quite different: inscribed in this text is not simply the irresistible and inexhaustible *expansion* of thought, but rather its abrupt *entanglement* in something *netlike* (*netzartig*). And, as we can read in any modern German Dictionary, "from times immemorial nets have been used to catch things: first fish, then birds and game, and shortly thereafter, figuratively," humans.

Yet it is Freud's second word, the substantive, *Verstrickung*, which literally and necessarily imposes the notion of entanglement, or more precisely, of becoming entangled (*sich verstricken*) in the snares (*Stricken*) of the net. Intricacy is thus involved here, but in a decisively double sense: first, as the complexity of a fabric, tissue, or text, without which no net can be conceived. But more radically, also in its etymological meaning, as involving the entangling "tricks" and difficulties that inevitably envelope the intention of the interpreter, inasmuch as he seeks to arrive at an ultimate meaning. It is simply the unattainability of an ultimate meaning, however, that is involved? For if that were the case, if the "over-determination" of the dream simply indicated an inexhaustibility of meaning in the sense of an infinite richness, the interpretative intent would be confronted by the limits of its own finitude which would restrict, but not undermine, the value of its insight. And yet, if we reread this passage, nothing seems less certain. Indeed, after our literal translation of *netzartige Verstrickung*, we will be led to another equally literal and apparently inaccurate translation of that interminability of thought, which Freud describes as being "ohne Abschluß." Instead of designating an intellectual movement "without end," Freud confronts us with one that is literally *in-conclusive*. To discover this, we need only (attempt to) retrace the movement of his description.

If, in the "best interpreted" of dreams, we must nonetheless leave one area shrouded in darkness, it is, first of all, because we *see*, or *notice* "man . . . *merkt*" that dark place in a certain way. Namely, we perceive, in the shadow, "a tangle (*ein Knäuel*) of dream-thoughts." If we are able to discern it, despite the darkness of the place, it is because that tangle *rises* above the rest (*anhebt*, which can also signify, *begin*). This protruding tangle of thoughts, although inextricable, can, according to Freud, not only be distinguished as such, but also comprehended, allowing the interpreter to be certain that "it has supplied the dream-content with no further contributions." I have already emphasized the peculiarity, or even paradoxicality of this assertion, which assumes a kind of intuitive grasp of the unanalyzable knot of thoughts. A grasp, which—

however paradoxical—enables Freud to proceed to *name* that tangled knot "the navel of the dream." If this navel, as its name implies, is located more or less at the center of the *corpus* of the dream, and if it also marks the spot where the dream "*straddles* the unknown" (*dem Unerkannten aufsitzt*), it also marks the point in Freud's text where his attempt to describe and, indeed, to circumscribe the limits of interpretation, in and through the figure of the dream-navel, begins to get out of hand. For the naming of that dark, entangled spot as the navel, instead of *fixing* the center, within the framework of the described figure, *dislocates* it decisively. Assuming, of course, that one does not simply persist in *regarding* the text as the verbal representation of a visualizable image, but instead, submits to its curious and strangely unrepresentable movement.

That movement, in the opening sentence, which sets the scene, as it were, describes both the emergence and ensuing recognition of the umbilical tangle of thoughts, and also its confinement to a site which, if it resists penetration by interpretation, is still sufficiently marginal to avoid becoming an obstacle to the elucidation of the dream. Thus, if the interpreter need not involve himself in the hopeless task of trying to unravel the strands of this shadowy knot, it is because he *knows* that its only importance resides in the single strand that has led him to it, and consequently, to the dream-wish. Aside from this, the dream-navel, Freud assures us, has made "no further contribution" to the content of the dream.

And yet, the one contribution it does make is obviously decisive, since it is nothing less than the dream-wish itself. Indeed, this is what allows Freud to name the place out of which it springs as the *navel* of the dream. But if the navel suggests a location not on the periphery of the dream, but close to its center—indeed, to its origin, as wish-fulfillment—how can we, or Freud, be so certain that its *shadowy* area is, in fact, so very marginal?

Can the navel of the dream be both at its core, and also on its fringe? Are there, perhaps, *two* navels: one, bright, erect, and central, the others, entangled, obscure, and peripheral? Uncertainty increases as Freud's description progresses. The "dream-thoughts," which lead us into the entanglement of the dream-navel, are said by Freud to "branch out on all sides," suggesting an expansive, outward-bound movement, *away* from the dream as such and out into the endless "world of thought." And somewhere within this expansive ramification of thought—within what Freud intriguingly calls "*this* meshwork" (*dieses Geflecht*)—the dream-navel and dream-wish arise. But where precisely is *this* place located? *Within* the dream, or *outside* of it, in our general

Samuel Weber

world of thought? If we are to leave this place in the dark, must we not first know *where* it is? If not, can we ever be quite certain that we have, indeed, *left* it?

In this quandery perhaps what we really need is: a guide.

"I believe that when you go to read the texts of Freud, you will be able to feel yourselves guided by the terms I introduce," Jacques Lacan announced at the beginning of his lectures of 1964, now published as *The Four Basic Concepts of Psychoanalysis*.[15] And there can be no doubt that the terms introduced by Lacan have indeed guided many of those who heeded his appeal for a "return to Freud," and a rethinking of his work. Today, with the fecundity of the Lacanian *"retour"* evident for all who care to see, the time has perhaps arrived where it is necessary to come to terms with the terms of Lacan, and this means, with the discourse in which they are articulated. That this articulation has always been one of unusual complexity testifies to the extreme attention that Lacan has devoted to this question. In the lectures of 1964, he remarks on the specific resistances that a discourse concerning the unconscious—whether Freud's or his own—must necessarily provoke. And this leads him to "touch" (on) the navel of the dream:

No discourse can, in this respect, be inoffensive—the very discourse that I have been able to conduct for these past ten years derives at least some of its effects from this fact. It is not without consequences when, even in a public discourse, one aims at subjects, and when one touches what Freud called the navel—the *navel of dreams*, he writes, in order to designate, in the final analysis *(au dernier terme)*, the center of the unknown—which, like the anatomical navel itself, its representative, is nothing but that abyss *(béance)* of which we are speaking.[16]

Whether or not this passage leads us, as Lacan claims, to the "center of the unknown," we shall have to discuss. What is beyond all doubt, however, is that it does involve the center of the Lacanian terminology, in which words such as *"béance," "fente"* (split), *"rupture"* (break), *"manque"* (lack) are offered to guide us through the implications of the Freudian unconscious and its "effects." All the more significant, therefore, that Lacan authorizes those terms, here, by an appeal to "what Freud called the navel of dreams," which Lacan situates univocally and definitively: first, at "the center of the unknown," and then, as "nothing but that *béance* of which we have been speaking." *Au dernier terme*, in the final analysis, Lacan repeats the gesture we have retraced in the description of Freud, but at its manifest level: the obscure and tangled place is identified, situated, and *named*. If it remains unfathomable, its *site* is definitively determined, at the *center* of the unknown, as *béance*. And this gesture is absolutely necessary, if the terms that Lacan introduces are indeed to serve as *guides*, as something that we can *keep in hand*: "If you keep this initial structure in hand . . . you will see that, more radically, it is in a dimension of synchrony that you must situate the unconscious . . . in short, at the level where everything that suffuses the unconscious is diffused, like the mycelium, as Freud says with regard to the dream, *around a central point*" (italics mine).[17]

Were it simply a question of what Freud *said*, or wished to say, we might, indeed, as Lacan seems to say and to wish, have something that we might *keep in hand*, to guide us along the way. Were it, indeed, only a question of what *both* Lacan *and* Freud seem *to want to see*: the meaning of the dream *rising* out of its mycelium, *la signification du phallus*, Lacan's Baedeker might suffice.

But Freud did not, could not, and probably would not *say* what he *meant*. For instance, that the mycelium was diffused around a central point (which could only be the dream-wish, rising phallically out of it). Or, that the dream-navel "designates the center of the unknown."

What Freud *wrote* is quite different: namely, that the dream-navel marks the spot where the dream *straddles* the unknown, dem Unerkannten *aufsitzt*. If we don't know much about the unknown, are we sure we know what it means to straddle it?

Let us begin with what we do know, with what Freud tells us. If the dream-wish rises out of the dream-navel like the mushroom out of its mycelium, then the navel itself, where the dream straddles the unknown, must be something like a mycelium:

Mycelium, (f. Gr. *mykes* mushroom, after *epithelium*.) Bot. The vegetative part of the thallus of fungi, consisting of white filamentous tubes (*hyphae*); the spawn of mushrooms. *(O.E.D.)*

But this only confronts us with a new question: that of *la signification du thallus*, of a meaning which, remarkably, seems to exist entirely in negations:

Thallus, (Gr. *thallos*, green shoot, f. *thállein* to bloom.) Bot. A vegetable structure without vascular tissue, in which there is no differentiation into stem and leaves, and from which true roots are absent.

Whatever its etymology, it is already clear that the question of the thallus cannot be confused with that of the phallus. For how can we ever, as Lacan promises, *see more radically*—"You will see, more radically, that . . ."—if the essence of the unknown, qua thallus and not phallus, is to be a vegetative structure, *without* vascular tissue, *without* differentiation, and "from which *true roots* are absent"? Small wonder that Freud stopped at the mushroom and its mycelium, without mentioning the thallus. For what could he have told us about it, except what we now know and also don't know? That the thallus, without vascular tissue, undifferentiated, and lacking true roots, is obviously something

Samuel Weber

very different from the phallus and/or the dream-wish. And yet also very different from a whole, hole, gap, break, lack, or abyss.

The dream-wish rises out of the mycelial tangle of thoughts, where the dream straddles the unknown. That unknown, we now know, can only be *thallic*. What, however, does it mean for a dream *to straddle* . . . the thallus, or anything else for that matter? The question is obviously not simply lexical—and it is all the more complex, involving not simply one word, in one language, but two. But putting aside, at least for the moment, the question of *translation*, let us nevertheless begin, as before, by consulting the dictionary. According to the *O.E.D.*, the word *straddle*, coming from the verb, *to stride*, includes the following meanings: "1. *intr.* To spread the legs wide apart in walking, standing, or sitting. b. Of the legs: To stand wide apart. c. Of a thing, esp. of a thing having legs; also, to sprawl. 2. to walk with the legs wide apart. 3. To set (the legs) wide apart (in standing or walking). 4. To sit, stand, or walk with one leg on either side of; to stride over; to bestride. b. To stand or lie across or on both sides of (something). 5. *U.S. colloq.* To occupy or take up an equivocal position in regard to; to appear to favour both sides of. 6. *Poker.* To double (a stake, bet). 7. *Gunnery.* To find the range of (an object) by placing shots first to one side of it and then on the other." And in conclusion, as synonym: "Bot. divaricate."

Just when we may think we have finally arrived at the end, *au dernier terme*, at the last word of the meaning(s) of *straddle*, a final, puzzling reference. And so, just to make absolutely certain that nothing relevant escapes us, we turn to:

Divaricate: (fr. Dis- + *varicare*, f. *varicus*, straddling.) 1. *intr.* To stretch or spread apart; to branch off or diverge; in *Bot.* and *Zool.* to diverge widely. 2. *trans.* To stretch or open wide apart or asunder. 3. To cause or spread out in different directions.

And since we shall soon be concerned not only with the verb, but with the noun, under *Divaricator*: "a muscle which draws parts asunder, as that which opens the shells of Brachiopods."

Whatever else emerges from this brief recourse to the dictionary, one thing is now certain: the *ramifications* of Freud's description of the dream-navel can hardly be confined to or comprehended as the "center of the unknown." That is, unless it is a center which straddles, and hence, divaricates. And to divaricate, as Freud's text does, is also to prevaricate, to diverge both from the right line and from its center, and to be a *béance*.

Yet, if all this seems only a caprice of translation, we need only turn to Freud's German, in order to discover the same prevarication, and the same divaricator at work. For when Freud writes that the navel is the

Remarks on Freud's *Witz*

"Stelle, an der er (der Traum) dem Unerkannten aufsitzt," he does not merely signify that it is "the place where it *straddles* the unknown," and even less, "reaches down into" it, as the *Standard Edition* (and also Lacan) would have it. In German, *jemandem aufsitzen* means "to be duped or deluded by someone" (or thing). And where that someone or something is, as here, nothing other than the unknown—*das Unerkannte* —the possibility of being 'had' is all the more difficult to dismiss.

We begin to sense that what is involved here, at the very limit of interpretation, and—if we are to follow the connotations of "navel"— also at its very origins is a certain kind of calculated deception, concerning the relation not only of dream and interpretation, but of both to the unconscious and the unknown. Or, to put it even more generally, we sense that what is involved in this question is the relation of *meaning*— which always implies the possibility of *consciousness*—to a discourse which seeks to derive consciousness from processes that are necessarily unconscious.

From the point of view of a rigorous and logical epistemology, such an undertaking can only appear as something of a bad joke; or, less generously, as a calculated bluff. For no theory or theoretical discourse, involving necessarily the categories of consciousness, can hope to comprehend something as radically heterogeneous as Freud claimed the unconscious to be. And in this sense, Freud's delimitation of interpretation—the navel of the dream—can be regarded as concerning not just a special case within psychoanalysis, but the status of its discourse in general. From this standpoint, a recent joke of Lacan assumes its full import: taking up a problem central to his discussion of "the symbolic," involving the question of the "Name-of-the-Father," the *Nom-du-Père*, he renamed it, *Les non-dupes errent*. If the joke is pertinent, above and beyond its particular meaning, it is because it is in his study of jokes that Freud most directly confronts the problematic relation of meaning and the unconscious. And this, inevitably, will lead him—and us—to the questionable act of *aufsitzen*, or, more precisely, to the *Aufsitzer*.

The theory of the *Witz* developed by Freud, although far too complex to be adequately summarized here, turns upon the question of *meaning*, of its function in regard to the structure of the joke and its mode of operation. Put simply, the question is: does meaning constitute *an* or even *the* essential dimension of the joke? Freud's first and insistent response is negative: the essential structure of the joke involves not its content, but its (verbal or conceptual) *form*. And if this is so, it is because the joke represents the attempt of the mature psyche to retain the childish pleasure of pure play, which Freud conceives as being intrinsically independent of the constraints of meaning and its logic.

Samuel Weber

Where meaning does enter into the joke, it is only to pacify or to divert the critique of reason, which otherwise inhibits the adult from indulging the desire to play. Thus, if meaning has a role to play in jokes, it is purely instrumental, helping to remove the obstacle which the inhibitions of reason place in the way of the pleasures of play.

And yet, if this is Freud's first and most conspicuous response to the problem of meaning in the *Witz*, it is one that the movement of his text is constantly putting into question. For instance, in his genealogy of the joke, he distinguishes certain phases in its evolution. First, there is the play of the child, who derives pleasure from the recognition of what is already familiar. Second, once the child has begun to develop its critical faculty, the sphere of play, especially where it violates the rules of reason, is progressively diminished. In the jest (*Scherz*), which he sees as a first response to the new situation, Freud finds the prototype of the authentic joke. The jest, although not yet a full-blown joke, nevertheless already displays its essential qualities, inasmuch as it brings about a temporary suspension of rational criticism and thus allows one to indulge in play. And yet, although already incorporating the essence of the joke, the jest is not yet the joke itself, "der eigentliche Witz," as Freud writes.[18] Whatever it is that distinguishes a jest from a joke will constitute the latter in its full authenticity.

And yet, when we discover what this distinguishing difference is, which transforms the jest into the joke proper, it turns out to be nothing but the very meaning which—Freud insists—is precisely *not* involved in the essence of the joke: "If what a jest says possesses substance and value, it turns into a joke. A thought which would deserve our interest even if it were expressed in the most unpretentious form is now clothed in a form which must give us enjoyment on its own account."[19] What makes a joke a joke, as opposed to a jest, is thus its meaning, the substance and value of its statement, which, however, is precisely supposed to be extraneous to the joke as such. If meaning only enters into the joke as an instrument, "to protect that pleasure (of play) from being done away with by criticism,"[20] and if its intrinsic content is therefore entirely foreign to the joke as such, it is nonetheless this very content which is responsible for making the joke a joke, and not a mere jest. The peculiar fact is, that meaning, though alien to the joke, still distinguishes the "good" joke from the "bad" one:

If I may be allowed to anticipate the exposition in the text, I can at this point throw light on the condition which seems to determine whether a joke is to be called a 'good' or a 'bad' one. If, by means of a word with two meanings or a word that is only slightly modified, I take a short cut from one circle of ideas to another, and if there is not at the same time a link between those circles of ideas which has a significant sense, then I shall have made a 'bad' joke. In a bad joke like this the only existing link between the two disparate ideas is the one word—the 'point' of the joke. . . . A 'good' joke, on the other hand, comes about when what children expect proves correct and the similarity between the words is shown to be really accompanied by another, important similarity in their sense.[21]

The good joke thus depends on the fact that the "external" relation established at the level of language is also accompanied by an "internal" relation at the level of the ideas concerned: as, for instance, in the witticism, *Traduttore-Traditore*, cited by Freud. And yet, "as soon as we take into consideration the peculiar pleasure derived from jokes, we find that the 'bad' jokes are by no means bad as jokes—that is, unsuitable for producing pleasure."[22] Indeed, Freud could have added that it is only in "bad" jokes, or jests, that the true and unadulterated essence of the joke comes to the fore, since only here does meaning function entirely as an instrument in alleviating rational inhibitions.

Thus, if the joke consists of two elements, a negative and a positive one, and if the negative one involves the use of meaning to allay the critique of reason, while the positive factor inheres in nothing but verbal play itself, then the empty, meaningless word-play of the jest or 'bad' joke comprises the essence of the Witz, engaging the pleasure of play in its purest form. On the other hand, it is precisely the necessity of an *impure* form of play and of pleasure—the *Aufhebungslust* involved in the relaxation and relief from inhibitions—that makes the joke proper, and good.

It is only with all this in mind that we can now approach a phenomenon so peculiar that Freud admits there to be "no appropriate name" for it. This nameless phenomenon is inscribed at the very end of the chapter we have been discussing, entitled "Pleasure and the Genesis of Jokes," which tails off with a long footnote, in which "nonsense jokes, which have not had due attention paid to them in my account" are given "some supplementary consideration."[23] In this footnote, Freud makes the point that the kind of play which is at the heart of jokes does not necessarily involve nonsense. Nonsense, he continues, relates only to the play with thoughts: that is, to the direct transgression of the logic and laws of meaning. Verbal play, however, while being intrinsically independent of sense, need not involve nonsense. Although Freud does not use the term, what he seems to imply is that such play is inherently *senseless*, not *nonsensical*; indifferent to meaning, but not necessarily in opposition to it. In recapitulating his argument in this footnote, however, Freud again emphasizes that the joke must consist both of a playfulness, which is tendentially indifferent to meaning, and of an appeal to

Samuel Weber

reason with the sole intention of suspending its sway, thus eliciting a certain pleasure—the *Aufhebungslust*—out of this temporary lifting of its inhibitive power. The specificity of nonsense-jokes involves the fact that they remain within the sphere of this *Aufhebungslust*.

It is at this point, in what can only be described as a belated supplement to this supplement on nonsense jokes, that Freud adds a remark (first published in the edition of 1912) concerning certain "productions resembling jokes" for which there is no adequate name and which he calls "silliness in the guise of wit" (*witzig scheinender Blödsinn*). These "productions," which are "witzähnlich"—similar to jokes without necessarily being one—are, in fact, the joke of the joke. What they do is "to rouse the expectation of a joke, so that one tries to find a concealed sense behind the nonsense. But one finds none: they really are nonsense."[24] And yet, they are not entirely nonsensical, for they have a "purpose," an intent (*Tendenz*); namely, to fool the listener and thus "give the person who tells them a certain amount of pleasure in misleading and annoying his hearer." The *name* that Freud assigns to these hitherto anonymous productions is: *Aufsitzer*. For the listener, who is tricked into expecting a *good* joke, the *Aufsitzer* is the worst of all possible jests; it "really is nonsense." The listener has been had, the joke . . . is on him, and his only recourse is to "vent his annoyance by resolving himself to become a joke-teller" (*ein Erzähler*).[25]

The *Aufsitzer*, who totally dupes the expectation of the listener, depriving him of the "sense in nonsense" he has learned to expect of the joke-teller—the *good* joke-teller, that is—must clearly be the best joke of all, because it is the worst. And in duping the listener, it leaves him no choice but to assume his duplicity, by ceasing to listen and beginning to tell: another story, another *Aufsitzer*.

Is the *Aufsitzer*, the simulacrum of the joke, merely a marginal form of the *Witz*? Is the pleasure it produces, involving not simply the "lifting" of the inhibition of reason, but moreover, the tendentious, aggressive deception and duping of the listener, as peripheral to the *essence* of the joke as its place in Freud's text—a belated addition to a supplementary consideration—might seem to suggest?

If the question is crucial, above and beyond its specific import for Freud's *theory* of the *joke*, it is because it engages the more general problem of the mutual involvement and relationship of theory and joke in the writings of Freud. If the interpretation of dreams is delimited, and even organized, by its peculiar proximity to an unknown it can never fathom but to which it is linked as an *Aufsitzer*; if the *Aufsitzer*, in all of its duping duplicity, implies a relationship that can no longer be confined to the homogeneous space of the traditional subject of theory, consciously contemplating—representing—its "object"; and if *this* joke-teller *has* no "object," except for the calculated deception of another subject, who has only the possibility of recouping his losses by himself repeating the tale and becoming an *Erzähler*—then certain consequences for the status of psychoanalytic theory begin to emerge. And above all, the traditional theoretical model of contemplation, of perception or representation of an "object" by a "subject," cannot simply be replaced by a hermeneutic model of *interpretation* if this entails merely the substitution of an impenetrable Unknown for the translucid object of theory. For this would mean, as in the case of Lacan, ignoring the powerful effects of the *Aufsitzer*, as it functions in the texts of Freud (and for that matter, in those of Lacan as well). The most conspicuous effect would be to reinscribe the subject of theory, and of interpretation, in the charged context of an operation of story-telling, which splits the unified subject of theory into the duplicity of the narrator and the delusion of the listener; each, in some sense, a mirror-image of the other and each engaged in a most ambivalent game.

In order to situate this ambivalence within Freud's theory of jokes, we must first return to his description of play, which, we recall, is supposed to be both the origin and the end of the *Witz*: "Play—let us keep to that name—appears in children while they are learning to make use of words and to put thoughts together. This play probably obeys one of the drives (*Triebe*) which compel children to practice their capacities (*Groos*). In doing so they come across pleasurable effects, which arise from a repetition of what is similar, a rediscovery of what is familiar, similarity of sound etc., and which are to be explained as unsuspected economies in physical expenditure."[26] Play is pleasurable for the child because it involves the *recognition* of the familiar, and this in turn involves a reduction of psychic energy, an "economy" or saving (*Ersparung*). This notion of *Ersparung* plays a curious role in Freud's joke-book: indeed, it is probably the biggest (theoretical) joke in the book. For it implies a conception of pleasure which literally has nothing to do with the notion that Freud had already begun to elaborate in "The Interpretation of Dreams." What characterizes the Freudian notion of pleasure, the *Lustprinzip*, from its very inception and beyond all equivocation, is that it is *conflictual* in nature, involving not absolute quanta of energy—as implied by the notion of *Ersparung*—but a relation of forces, a state of tension (a *Spannungsverhältnis*).

Thus, the notion of "economy," which Freud employs throughout his book on the *Witz*, has nothing to do with his economical theory of pleasure as the moving force of psychical activity. And this is clear from an attentive reading of this text itself, where Freud himself moves from

Samuel Weber

a notion of economy as *Ersparung* to one of *relief* (*Erleichterung*), but without fully abandoning the former concept or discussing the equivocation involved in these utterly heterogeneous terms. Yet, the determination of *Spiellust* as the pleasure of sheer recognition, of "das Erkennen an sich," remains predicated upon this notion of psychic economy which equates the absolute reduction in effort or expenditure with pleasure.

If Freud never fully discusses the implications of this notion, he does something more important, and perhaps more appropriate in this particular context: he makes jokes at the expense of the theory of expenditure and of its "economies." "And let us, further, have the courage to admit that the economies made by the joke-technique do not greatly impress us. They may remind us, perhaps, of the way in which some housewives economize when they spend time and money on a journey to a distant market because vegetables are to be had there a few farthings cheaper. What does a joke save by its technique? . . . Is not the economy in words uttered more than balanced by the expenditure of intellectual effort."[27] And Freud concludes by posing what is doubtless the decisive question: And who saves by that? Who gains by it? Indeed, the question of the "subject" of the joke-pleasure, and of its origin and essence, *Spiellust*, overshadows this entire text. Freud's description of the joke's *social* nature, involving not merely a subject and a subject-matter or object— which Freud calls the "second person"—but *three* "persons," is a response to this question of the subject of the joke's pleasure. And this is what makes his conception of play not simply untenable, but also, in a certain way, symptomatic. Freud's description of the pleasure involved in play is untenable as the "origin" of the joke, because it bears no relation to the *conflict*, in whose force-field the joke is necessarily situated. The rational critique, in Freud's description of the "genesis" of the joke, its evolution from play, appears to be wholly external to play, which, on the other hand, itself seems to involve nothing other than the pleasure of re-cognition, cognitive pleasure itself, the repetition of the same and its apprehension by the child. Behind the semblance of unmediated exteriority, therefore, Freud's notion of play reveals itself to be the mirror-image of its apparent other: rational cognition. And if this is so, it is because both cognition and play, as Freud describes them, involve the solitary activity of a subject engaged in the process of developing its consciousness as self-consciousness. The cognitive pleasure of play, in this version, far from being the simple antithesis of critical reason, is its purest manifestation: its pleasure is the pleasure of consciousness. And more precisely, that of the ego in ascertaining its own *identity*.

Yet it is precisely this identity that the theory of the *Witz*, as a *narrative* operation, excludes. What distinguishes the joke, or jest, from mere play (as well as from related forms, such as the *comic*, and *humor*) is precisely the necessity of there being not one or two persons who participate, but three.

The most graphic example that Freud gives of this is his discussion of the *Zote*, or the development of the dirty joke. Smut, he asserts, involves "the exposure of the sexually different person to whom it is directed."[28] Freud traces this back to an "original" or infantile desire "to touch the sexual parts." In the course of development, original desire is sublimated into the "desire to see the organs peculiar to each sex," something that Freud here describes as "one of the original components of our libido." The fact that "a high degree of this tendency persists" within the adult libido is at the origin of smut. When the object of this desire to *see—Schaulust—*makes herself inaccessible and refuses to respond to the overtures of the "first person," the viewer takes his revenge by making her the object of obscenities, in which "the sadistic components of the sexual drives" are mobilized. This, however, is still not a dirty *joke*. The absence of the desired woman (or heterosexual 'object') and the resulting transformation of an erotic into an aggressive impulse, must be joined by a third factor in order for obscenity to become a *Witz*: namely, the *third* person, who replaces the second as object of the first: "So that gradually, in place of the woman, the onlooker, now listener, becomes the person to whom the smut is addressed."[29] From this point on, it becomes clear that, where the *Witz* is concerned, the pleasure of the first person will be mediated by, and dependent on, that of the third: "namely, that it is not the person who makes the joke who laughs at it and who therefore enjoys its pleasurable effect, but the inactive listener."[30]

If this description of the structure and evolution of the dirty joke, which is paradigmatic for the joke in general, demonstrates the gap that separates it from the simplistic notion of *Spiellust* as the origin and core of the *Witz*, it also points to another and more celebrated discussion of the phenomenon of play in "Beyond the Pleasure Principle," which, although written some fifteen years after the study of *Jokes*, seems far more suited to the claim of its title: ". . . in relation to the Unconscious." The story of this game involves some of the same elements we have just seen at work in the genesis of smut: the absence of the woman, as object of desire, and the transformation of erotic into aggressive impulses.

But here is how Freud tells the story:

This good little boy, however, had an occasional disturbing habit of taking any small objects he could get hold of and throwing them away from him into a corner, under the bed, etc., so that hunting for his toys and picking them up was often quite a business. As he did this he gave vent to a loud, long-drawn-out "o-o-o-o," accompanied by an expression of interest and satisfaction. His mother and the writer of the present account were agreed in thinking that this was not a mere interjection, but represented the German word *"fort"* (gone). I eventually realized that it was a game and that the only use he made of any of his toys was to play "gone" with them. One day I made an observation which confirmed my view. The child had a wooden reel with a piece of string tied round it. It never occurred to him to pull it along the floor behind him, for instance, and play at its being a carriage. What he did was to hold the reel by the string and very skilfully throw it over the edge of his curtained cot, so that it disappeared into it, at the same time uttering his expressive "o-o-o-o." He then pulled the reel out of the cot again by the string and hailed its re-appearance with a joyful *"da"* (there). This then was the complete game, disappearance and return.[31]

The game, like that described in the book on *Jokes*, involves the use of language and a certain pleasure in repetition. Yet, it is no longer a question of the pure pleasure of cognition and of consciousness, although this is also involved. What is more important, however, is the problem posed by the absence of the mother, the child's primary love-object; for the game, as Freud now interprets it, is a means of dominating that absence, which in turn involves nothing less than the "great cultural achievement" involved in accepting and assuming "instinctual renunciation" as such. This acceptance and assumption of what can only have been experienced as a situation of distress, necessarily involves an element of aggression: "Throwing away the object," Freud writes, "might satisfy an impulse of the child's, which was suppressed in his actual life, to revenge himself on his mother for going away from him," a suspicion which he sees confirmed in an observation made of the same child a year later, who now accompanied his gesture of throwing with the words, "Go to the front": "He had heard at that time that his absent father was 'at the fwont,' and was far from regretting his absence; on the contrary, he made it quite clear that he had no desire to be disturbed in his sole possession of his mother."[32] Nor, in this particular case, did the aggression stop here, at the father, in the classical oedipal stance. For, "when this child was five and three-quarters, his mother died. Now that she was really 'gone' ('o-o-o'), the little boy showed no signs of grief. It is true that in the interval a second child had been born and had roused him to violent jealousy."[33] This game, although it also involves language and repetition, can hardly be explained in terms of the simple saving of psychic energy, for what is involved is a conflictual situation of desire which places the subject at odds with *itself*, and not merely with *others*. But what, then, of the pleasures of revenge and of "mastery," in this new, and yet not so new context; and of the play with *language*, which remains, here as in the earlier study of *Jokes*, one of the distinguishing characteristics of the pleasure of play?

The question of language is, in fact, crucial for an understanding of this passage, as has been rightly stressed by Lacan, whose interpretation of this text has been largely responsible for the renewed attention it has received in recent years. According to Lacan, Freud's story marks nothing less than the moment of initiation of the human subject into the "symbolic" dimension of its (unconscious and conflictual) desire. The disappearance of the mother compels the child to come to terms, as best it can, with the loss of object that defines the structure of desire. Desire, in this reading, is concerned not with objects, whether real or imaginary, but with "signifiers," in the Saussurian sense of semiotic elements whose signification is determined by the place occupied within a chain of other signifiers, and by the differential relations entertained with the other members of the chain—and *not* by the *signified*, i.e. *semantic* elements. Lacan interprets the language of the child in this game as exemplary of that play of signifiers, within the dimension of void left by the absence of the mother, and hence, as the emerging articulation of unconscious desire.

As with Lacan's reading of the dream-navel, it is a certain and central *absence—loss* or *lack*—that is decisive in compelling the subject to "assume" its unconscious desire. And yet, this reading can only be sustained if the words of the child are, indeed, signifiers, in the sense that Lacan adapts from Saussure. Yet if the signifier, according to Saussure, is determined strictly by the relations of difference from other signifying elements, the child's language, as reported, or at least interpreted, by Freud, does not involve simply signifiers. For the opposition, o-o-o-o/a-a-a-a, is constituted by abbreviations of what Saussure calls "total signs," which do not merely consist both of a signifier and a "signified," but which are ultimately defined by their semantic function. Unlike the function of the signifier, which is purely differential and negative—and which Lacan uses to distinguish the *"symbolic"* sphere of unconscious desire from the *"imaginary"* realm of the ego, in which not the signifier but the signified governs articulation—the "positive totality of the sign," taken as a whole, articulates itself by determinate opposition, and involves what linguists today would call "morphemes," minimal units determined by meaning. And this is confirmed by the fact that the child in Freud's story is, indeed, articulating not a difference, but a determinate *opposition*: disappearing/return, or, ultimately: absence/presence.

Is this a "difference without a distinction"? Hardly. For the entire interpretation of this story depends upon the distinction of this differ-

Samuel Weber

ence. If Lacan's reading is correct, the child's game involves the articulation of unconscious desire, as opposed to the "imaginary,"
representational, and ambivalent sphere of the ego. And yet, if the play
with *fort/da* involves not simply the *difference* of signifiers, but the
opposition of already constituted verbal signs, with a distinct and determinate meaning, then this play, however much unconscious desire
and its conflicts are involved, will also concern the development of the
ego and of a certain narcissism.

And here we stumble upon a curious "fact." As is well-known, the
development of Lacan's rereading of Freud first appeared, in 1936, with
a theory of the ego, the *moi*, as constituting itself in what Lacan called
"the mirror-stage." The formation of the child's ego, according to this
theory, which Lacan has expanded and reworked, but certainly never
repudiated, depends upon the fact that the perceptive faculties of the
human being develop in advance of its motor control, so that the first
and decisive experience of conscious, personal identity which becomes
the foundation of the ego is related to the (narcissistic) experience of
the child seeing its own image in a mirror. From this image, which he
perceives as embodying that unity and wholeness that he experiences
only negatively in his lack of motoric coordination, the child, by a process of identification, develops the sense of its own identity. But this
identity, because it remains tied to the identification with another, remains alienated and ambivalent, and the more it asserts itself, the more
aggressive it is bound to become.

In later years Lacan elaborated this theory, not systematically but
rather allusively, in order to bring it more into conformity with the
Freudian oedipal structure, so that the perception of the mother, which
in Freud functions as the first apprehension of a total and unified being,
becomes the matrix of the specular—shall we say, *speculative?*—identification of the child with its image. And he has linked that process of
"identification," itself mysterious enough, to the web of desire that involves the subject not merely with determinate persons—mother, father,
etc.—but with an irreducible Other, or more precisely, an unattainable
Elsewhere. Yet, despite these modifications of the original theory of the
mirror-stage, what has remained constant has been a structural and
structuring *opposition* posited by Lacan's theory, between the narcissistic ambivalences of an ego deriving from that stage, and the movement
of unconscious desire, in turn constituted by the "symbolic" articulation
of purely differential signifiers.

It is this opposition—which in the writings of Lacan generally
takes the form of a valorization of the Symbolic as opposed to the
Imaginary, and a correlative polemic against the reification of the ego in

contemporary Anglo-American psychoanalysis—that explains what would otherwise seem either an astonishing oversight or a case of simple repression. For although Lacan repeatedly cites the game of *fort/da* as Freud's insight into the nature of the symbolic dimension, and the initiation of the subject into it, he constantly ignores a remark of Freud that would seem to be an anticipation of his own theory of the mirror-stage. For, in a footnote to his story of the child's play, Freud tells of the following supplementary observation: "One day the child's mother had been away for several hours and on her return was met with the words, 'Baby o-o-o-o!' which was at first incomprehensible. It soon turned out, however, that during this long period of solitude the child had found a method of making *himself* disappear. He had discovered his reflection in a full-length mirror which did not quite reach to the ground, so that by crouching down he could make his mirror-image 'gone.' "[34] Here, indeed, is Lacan's "mirror-stage" already in Freud. And if Lacan himself has avoided taking notice of it, it is probably because the context of this remark, within the text of "Beyond the Pleasure Principle," would seem to exclude the kind of sharp and polemical opposition between the *symbolic* and the *imaginary* that Lacan appears to have needed in order to justify his own position after he had been excluded from the international psychoanalytic establishment. In any case, what is beyond doubt in Freud's discussion of the child's game of *fort/da* is that such play, involving both *mastery* and *aggression*, can only be situated within the narcissistic development of the ego, which alone derives "pleasure" from such play.

And, it is in this sense that the play of the child may, indeed, mark the origin and the nucleus of the pleasure of the *Witz*: a pleasure which, being inherently narcissistic, would necessarily have to include aggression as one of its decisive elements, as well as mastery, and which, like that play, would inevitably depend upon *verbal discourse* to achieve its ends. At the same time, the ambivalent status of narcissistic identification, which has been repeatedly and rightly emphasized by Lacan, also marks the relationship of teller and listener, first and third person in the joke: for the joke-teller, it is the *third* person who, although fundamentally "passive," is decisive. A joke is only jocular, *witzig*, if the listener laughs. And laughter is something which is difficult to calculate, eludes conscious control, and above all, excludes a certain cognitive consciousness. "We do not know what we are laughing at," writes Freud in his study of jokes, and the phrase returns with the insistence of a leitmotif. The third person, as listener, decides whether or not the joke is successful—i.e. whether it is a joke or not—and thus, whether or not the *first* person really is a first person, an ego, the author, or at least the teller of a true joke. And yet, this decisive action of the third person lies beyond all volition—one cannot will to laugh—and outside of consciousness, insofar as one never knows, at the moment of laughter, what one is laughing at. The "decision" of the third person, therefore, is in reality the decision of a *third person neuter*, of an *it* or an *id*, and not of a him or her. In the uncontrollable, explosive burst of laughter—and laughter is always, for Freud, a kind of explosion—it (id) decides and determines the status of the joke, and with it, that of the ego telling it.

This adds a new dimension to the process of narcissistic identification and the constitution of the ego; for what it indicates is that this process, far from being the result of an instantaneous and solitary *act*, presupposing the same theoretical space and time discussed earlier, would instead have to be conceived as *the (after-) effect of a story*: that is, of a diachronic narration, directed towards and culminating in a burst of laughter, which in turn functions less as the embodiment of the instant than as its effraction.

Perhaps we can now begin to understand the unique position and power of the *Aufsitzer*: as the joke of (on) the joke, it brings into play not simply a partial aspect of the *Witz*, such as the suspension of rational constraints, but rather demonstrates how *the desire of a certain rationality*—and not only the inhibition of reason—is the necessary precondition of the joke. This desire, the urge to know—what Freud elsewhere calls the *Wisstrieb*—and which he relates, genetically and structurally, to the desire to see, the *Schautrieb*—is the *theoretical Trieb* par excellence.

The *Aufsitzer*, by evoking the expectation of a (good) joke: that is, of a simulacrum of nonsense concealing an essence of sense—and then by revealing its "true" sense to be none other than the duping of the listener, the third person, by the teller, the first person—ego—thereby reveals the ineluctable complicity linking the theoretical urge of that ego to the ambivalent identity of the theoretical subject, as "first person" singular.

If the joke 'proper' is the naïve affirmation of that identity, the *Aufsitzer* involves the assertion of its ambivalence. And that assertion, which is now manifestly made at the expense of the listener, forces him, in turn, to become an *Erzähler.* . . .[35]

NOTES

1. S. Freud, "On the History of the Psychoanalytic Movement," *The Standard Edition of the Complete Psychological Work of Sigmund Freud*, ed. James Strachey et al., 23 vols. (London: Hogarth Press, 1953–66), 14, 52 (henceforth: *S.E.*). *Gesammelte Werke* (Frankfurt am Main: S. Fischer Ver-

Remarks on Freud's *Witz*

lag, 1967), X, 96 (henceforth: *G.W.*). I have retranslated where necessary throughout.

2. S. Freud, "Totem and Taboo," *S.E.*, 13, 65.

3. Ibid., pp. 95–96.

4. Ibid.

5. S. Freud, "On Narcissism: An Introduction," *S.E.*, 14, 77. *G.W.*, X, 142.

6. S. Freud, "Inhibition, Symptoms and Anxiety," *S.E.*, 20, 95. *G.W.*, XIV, 123.

7. Ibid., p. 96.

8. Ibid., p. 124. *G.W.*, XIV, 155.

9. Ibid., pp. 148–49. *G.W.*, XIV, 180.

10. S. Freud, "The Interpretation of Dreams," *S.E.*, 5, 510. *G.W.*, II/III, 515.

11. Ibid.

12. Ibid., p. 511.

13. Ibid.

14. Ibid., p. 525. *G.W.*, II/III, 530.

15. Jacques Lacan, *Les quatre concepts fondamentaux de la psychanalyse* (Paris: Editions du Seuil, 1973), p. 25.

16. Ibid., p. 26.

17. Ibid., p. 28.

18. S. Freud, "Jokes and their Relation to the Unconscious," *S.E.*, 8, 137. *Der Witz und seine Beziehung zum Unbewußten* (Frankfurt/Hamburg: Fischer Bücherei, 1963), pp. 107, 111.

19. *S.E.*, 8, 137.

20. Ibid., p. 121.

21. Ibid., pp. 120–21.

22. Ibid., p. 138.

23. Ibid., p. 139. *Der Witz*, p. 112.

24. *S.E.*, 8, 139.

25. Ibid., p. 128. *Der Witz*, p. 112.

26. Ibid., p. 128. *Der Witz*, p. 104.

27. Ibid., p. 44. *Der Witz*, p. 35.

28. Ibid., p. 98. *Der Witz*, p. 79.

29. Ibid., p. 99. *Der Witz*, p. 80.

30. Ibid., p. 100. *Der Witz*, p. 80.

31. S. Freud, "Beyond the Pleasure Principle," *S.E.*, 18, 14–15. *G.W.*, XIII, 12–13.

32. Ibid., p. 16. *G.W.*, XIII, 14.

33. *S.E.*, 18, 16.

34. Ibid., p. 15. *G.W.*, XIII, 13.

35. An elaborated version of this text will be included in my forthcoming book, *Die Legende Freuds* (Berlin: Ullstein Verlag).

TWO

THE PURLOINED RIBBON
Paul de Man

POLITICAL and autobiographical texts have in common that they share a referential reading-moment explicitly built in within the spectrum of their significations, no matter how deluded this moment may be in its mode as well as in its thematic content: the deadly "horn of the bull" referred to by Michel Leiris in a text that is indeed as political as it is autobiographical.[1] But whereas the relationship between cognition and performance is relatively easy to grasp in the case of a temporal speech act such as *promise*—which, in Rousseau's work, is the model for the *Social Contract*—it is more complex in the confessional mode of his autobiographies. By reading a central passage from the *Confessions*, I attempt to clarify the relationship between critical procedures that start out from the discourse of the subject and procedures that start out from political statements.

Among the various more or less shameful and embarassing scenes from childhood and adolescence related in the first three books of the *Confessions*, Rousseau singled out the episode of Marion and the ribbon as of particular affective significance, a truly primal scene of lie and deception strategically placed in the narrative and told with special *panache*. We are invited to believe that the episode was never revealed to anyone prior to the privileged reader of the *Confessions* "and . . . that the desire to free myself, so to speak, from this weight has greatly contributed to my resolve to write my confessions" (86).[2] When Rousseau returns to the *Confessions* in the later *Fourth Reverie*, he again singles out this same episode as a paradigmatic event, the core of his autobiographical narrative. The selection is, in itself, as arbitrary as it is suspicious, but it provides us with a textual event of undeniable exegetic interest: the juxtaposition of two confessional texts linked together by an explicit repetition, the confession, as it were, of a confession.

The episode itself is one in a series of stories of petty larceny, but with an added twist. While employed as a servant in an aristocratic Turin household, Rousseau has stolen a "pink and silver colored ribbon." When the theft is discovered, he accuses a young maid-servant of having given him the ribbon, the implication being that she was trying to seduce him. In public confrontation, he obstinately clings to his story, thus casting irreparable doubt on the honesty and the morality of an innocent girl who has never done him the slightest bit of harm and whose sublime good nature does not even flinch in the face of dastardly accusation: "Ah Rousseau! I took you to be a man of good character. You are making me very unhappy but I would hate to change places with you" (85). The story ends badly, with both characters being dismissed, thus allowing Rousseau to speculate at length, and with some relish, on the dreadful things that are bound to have happened in the subsequent career of the hapless girl.

The first thing established by this edifying narrative is that the *Confessions* are not primarily a confessional text. To confess is to overcome guilt and shame in the name of truth: it is an epistemological use of language in which ethical values of good and evil are superseded by values of truth and falsehood, one of the implications being that vices such as concupiscence, envy, greed and the like are vices primarily because they compel one to lie. By stating things as they are, the economy of ethical balance is restored and redemption can start in the clarified atmosphere of a truth that does not hesitate to reveal the crime in all its horror. In this case, Rousseau even adds to the horror by conjuring up, in the narrative of the *Confessions* as well as that of the *Promenade*, the dire consequences that his action may have had for the victim. Confessions occur in the name of an absolute truth which is said to exist "for itself" (*"pour elle seule,"* 1028) and of which particular truths are only derivative and secondary aspects.

But even within the first narrative, in Book II of the *Confessions*, Rousseau cannot limit himself to the mere statement of what "really" happened, although he is proud to draw attention to the fullness of a self-accusation whose candor we are never supposed to suspect: "I have been very thorough in the confession I have made, and it could certainly never be said that I tried to conceal the blackness of my crime" (86).

Paul de Man

But it does not suffice to tell all. It is not enough to *confess*, one also has to *excuse*: "But I would not fulfill the purpose of this book if I did not reveal my inner sentiments as well, and if I did not fear to *excuse* myself by means of what conforms to the truth," ("que je [ne] craignisse de m'*excuser* en ce qui est conforme à la vérité" [86, italics mine]). This also happens, it should be noted, in the name of truth and, at first sight, there should be no conflict between confession and excuse. Yet the language reveals the tension in the expression: *craindre* de m'excuser. The only thing one has to fear from the excuse is that it will indeed disculpate the confessor, thus making the confession (and the confessional text) redundant as it originates. *Qui s'accuse s'excuse*; this sounds convincing and convenient enough but, in terms of absolute truth, it ruins the seriousness of any confessional discourse by making it self-destructive. Since confession is not a reparation in the realm of practical justice but exists only as a verbal utterance, how then are we to know that we are indeed dealing with a *true* confession, since the recognition of guilt implies its exoneration in the name of the same transcendental principle of truth that allowed for the certitude of guilt in the first place?

In fact, a far-reaching modification of the organizing principle of truth occurs between the two sections of the narrative. The truth in whose name the excuse *has to be* stated, even at Rousseau's assumed "*corps défendant*," is not structured like the truth principle that governs the confession. It does not unveil a state of being but states a suspicion, a possible discrepancy that might lead to an impossibility to know. The discrepancy, of course, is between the "*sentiment intérieur*" that accompanied (or prompted?) the act and the act itself. But the spatial inside/outside metaphor is misleading, for it articulates a differentiation that is not spatial at all. The distinction between the confession stated in the mode of revealed truth and the confession stated in the mode of excuse is that the evidence for the former is referential (the ribbon), whereas the evidence for the latter can only be verbal. Rousseau can convey his "inner feeling" to us only if we take, as we say, his *word* for it, whereas the evidence for his theft is, at least in theory, literally available.[3] Whether we believe him or not is not the point; it is the verbal or nonverbal nature of the evidence that makes the difference, not the sincerity of the speaker or the gullibility of the listener. The distinction is that the latter process necessarily includes a moment of understanding that cannot be equated with a perception, and that the logic that governs this moment is not the same as that which governs a referential verification. What Rousseau is saying then, when he insists on "sentiment intérieur," is that confessional language can be considered under a double epistemological perspective: it functions as a verifiable referential cognition, but it also functions as a statement whose reliability cannot be verified by empirical means. The convergence of the two modes is not a priori given, and it is because of the possibility of a discrepancy between them that the possibility of excuse arises. The excuse articulates the discrepancy and, in so doing, it actually asserts it as fact (whereas it is only a suspicion). It believes, or pretends to believe, that the act of stealing the ribbon is both this act as a physical fact, (he removed it from the place where it was and put it in his pocket, or wherever he kept it), as well as a certain "inner feeling" that was somehow (and this "how" remains open) connected with it. Moreover, it believes that the fact and the feeling are not the same. Thus to complicate a fact certainly is: to act. The difference between the verbal excuse and the referential crime is not a simple opposition between an action and a mere utterance about an action. To steal is to act and includes no necessary verbal elements. To confess is discursive, but the discourse is governed by a principle of referential verification that includes an extra-verbal moment: even if we confess that we *said* something (as opposed to *did*) the verification of this verbal event, the decision about the truth or falsehood of its occurrence, is not verbal but factual, the knowledge that the utterance actually took place. No such possibility of verification exists for the excuse, which is verbal in its utterance, in its effect and in its authority: its purpose is not to state but to convince, itself an "inner" process to which only words can bear witness. As is well known at least since Austin,[4] excuses are a complex instance of what he termed performative utterances, a variety of speech act. The interest of Rousseau's text is that it explicitly functions performatively as well as cognitively, and thus gives indications about the structure of performative rhetoric; this is already established in this text when the confession fails to close off a discourse which feels compelled to modulate from the confessional into the apologetic mode.[5]

Neither does the performance of the excuse allow for a closing off of the apologetic text, despite Rousseau's plea at the end of Book II: "This is what I had to say on this matter. May I be allowed never to mention it again" (87). Yet, some ten years later, in the *Fourth Rêverie*, he tells the entire story all over again, in the context of a meditation that has to do with the possible "excusability" of lies. Clearly, the apology has not succeeded in becalming his own guilt to the point where he would be allowed to forget it. It doesn't matter much, for our purpose, whether the guilt truly relates to this particular act or if the act is merely made to substitute for another, worse crime or humiliation. It may stand for a whole series of crimes, a general mood of guilt, yet the repetition is significant by itself: whatever the content of the criminal act may have been, the excuse presented in the *Confessions* was unable to satisfy Rousseau as a judge of Jean-Jacques. This failure was already partly inscribed within the excuse itself and it governs its further expansion and repetition.

Rousseau excuses himself from his gratuitous viciousness by identifying his inner feeling as *shame* about himself rather than any hostility towards his victim: ". . . the presence of so many people was stronger than my repentance. I hardly feared punishment, my only fear was shame; but I feared shame more than death, more than the crime, more than anything in the world. I wished I could have sunk and stifled myself in the center of the earth: unconquerable shame was stronger than anything else, shame alone caused my impudence and the more guilty I became, the more the terror of admitting my guilt made me fearless" (86).

It is easy enough to describe how "shame" functions in a context that seems to offer a convincing answer to the question: what is shame or, rather, what is one ashamed of? Since the entire scene stands under the aegis of theft, it has to do with possession, and desire must therefore be understood as functioning, at least at times, as a desire to possess, in all the connotations of the term. Once it is removed from its legitimate owner, the ribbon, being in itself devoid of meaning and function, can circulate symbolically as a pure signifier and become the articulating hinge in a chain of exchanges and possessions. As the ribbon changes hands it traces a circuit leading to the exposure of a hidden, censored desire. Rousseau identifies the desire as his desire for Marion: "it was my intention to give her the ribbon" (86), i.e., to "possess" her. At this point in the reading suggested by Rousseau, the proper meaning of the trope is clear enough: the ribbon "stands for" Rousseau's desire for Marion or, what amounts to the same thing, for Marion herself.

Or, rather, it stands for the free circulation of the desire between Rousseau and Marion, for the reciprocity which, as we know from *Julie*, is for Rousseau the very condition of love; it stands for the substitutability of Rousseau for Marion and vice-versa. Rousseau desires Marion as Marion desires Rousseau. But since, within the atmosphere of intrigue and suspicion that prevails in the household of the Comtesse de Vercellis, the phantasy of this symmetrical reciprocity is experienced as an interdict, its figure, the ribbon, has to be stolen, and the agent of this transgression has to be susceptible of being substituted: if Rousseau has to be willing to steal the ribbon, then Marion has to be willing to substitute for Rousseau in performing this act.[6] We have at least two levels of substitution (or displacement) taking place: the ribbon substituting for a desire which is itself a desire for substitution. Both are governed by the same desire for specular symmetry which gives to the symbolic object a detectable, univocal proper meaning. The system works: "I accused Marion of having done what I wanted to do and of having given me the ribbon because it was my intention to give it to her" (86). The substitutions have taken place without destroying the cohesion of the system, reflected in the balanced syntax of the sentence and now understandable exactly as we comprehend the ribbon to signify desire. Specular figures of this kind are metaphors and it should be noted that on this still elementary level of understanding, the introduction of the figural dimension in the text occurs first by ways of metaphor.

The allegory of this metaphor, revealed in the "confession" of Rousseau's desire for Marion, functions as an excuse if we are willing to take the desire at face value. If it is granted that Marion is desirable, or Rousseau ardent, to such an extent, then the motivation for the theft becomes understandable and easy to forgive. He did it all out of love for her, and who would be a dour enough literalist to let a little property stand in the way of young love? We would then be willing to grant Rousseau that "viciousness was never further from me than at this cruel moment, and when I accused the hapless girl, it is bizarre but it is true that my friendship for her was the cause of my accusation" (86). Substitution is indeed bizarre (it is odd to take a ribbon for a person) but since it reveals motives, causes and desires, the oddity is quickly reduced back to sense. The story may be a rebus or a riddle in which a ribbon is made to signify a desire, but the riddle can be solved. The delivery of meaning is delayed but by no means impossible.

This is not the only way, however, in which the text functions. Desire conceived as possession allows for the all-important introduction of figural displacement: things are not merely what they seem to be, a ribbon is not just a ribbon, to steal can be an act of love, an act performed by Rousseau can be said to be performed by Marion and, in the process, it becomes more rather than less comprehensible, etc. Yet the text does not stay confined within this pattern of desire. For one thing, to excuse the crime of theft does not suffice to excuse the worse crime of slander which, as both common sense and Rousseau tell us, is much harder to accept.[7] Neither can the shame be accounted for by the hidden nature of the desire, as would be the case in an oedipal situation.[8] The interdict does not weigh very heavily and the revelation of Rousseau's desire, in a public situation that does not allow for more intimate self-examination, hardly warrants such an outburst of shame. More important than any of these referential considerations, the text is not set up in such a way as to court sympathy in the name of Marion's erotic charm, a strategy which Rousseau uses with some skill in many other instances including the first part of *Julie*. Another form of desire than the desire of possession is operative in the latter part of the story, which also bears the main performative burden of the excuse and in which the crime is no longer that of theft.

The obvious satisfaction in the tone and the eloquence of the passage quoted above, the easy flow of hyperboles (". . . je la craignois [la honte] plus que la mort, plus que le crime, plus que tout au monde. J'aurois voulu m'enfoncer, m'étouffer dans le centre de la terre . . ." [86]), the obvious delight with which the desire to hide is being revealed, all point to another structure of desire than mere possession and independent of the particular target of the desire. One is more ashamed of the exposure of the desire to expose oneself than of the desire to possess; like Freud's dreams of nakedness, shame is primarily exhibitionistic. What Rousseau *really* wanted is neither the ribbon nor Marion, but the public scene of exposure which he actually gets. The fact that he made no attempt to conceal the evidence confirms this. The more crime there is, the more theft, lie, slander, and stubborn persistence in each of them, the better. The more there is to expose, the more there is to be ashamed of; the more resistance to exposure, the more satisfying the scene and, especially, the more satisfying and eloquent the belated revelation, in the later narrative, of the inability to reveal. This desire is truly shameful, for it suggests that Marion was destroyed, not for the sake of Rousseau's saving face, nor for the sake of his desire for her, but merely in order to provide him with a stage on which to parade his disgrace or, what amounts to the same thing, to furnish him with a good ending for Book II of his *Confessions*. The structure is self-perpetuating, *en abîme*, as is implied in its description as exposure of the desire to expose, for each new stage in the unveiling suggests a deeper shame, a greater impossibility to reveal, and a greater satisfaction in outwitting this impossibility.

The structure of desire as exposure rather than as possession explains why shame functions indeed, as it does in this text, as the most effective excuse, much more effectively than greed, or lust, or love. Promise is proleptic, but excuse is belated and always occurs after the crime; since the crime is exposure, the excuse consists in recapitulating the exposure in the guise of concealment. The excuse is a ruse which permits exposure in the name of hiding, not unlike Being, in the later Heidegger, reveals itself by hiding. Or, put differently, shame used as excuse permits repression to function as revelation and thus to make pleasure and guilt interchangeable. Guilt is forgiven because it allows for the pleasure of revealing its repression. It follows that repression is in fact an excuse, one speech act among others.

But the text offers further possibilities. The analysis of shame as excuse makes evident the strong link between the performance of excuses and the act of understanding. It has led to the problematics of hiding and revealing, which are clearly problematics of cognition. Excuse occurs within an epistemological twilight zone between knowing and not-knowing; this is also why it has to be centered on the crime of lying and why Rousseau can excuse himself for everything provided he can be excused for lying. When this turns out not to have been the case, when his claim to have lived for the sake of truth (*vitam impendere vero*) is being contested from the outside, the closure of excuse ("qu'il me soit permis de n'en reparler jamais") becomes a delusion and the *Fourth Rêverie* has to be written.

The passage also stakes out the limits of how this understanding of understanding then is to be understood. For the distinction between desire as possession and desire as exposure, although it undeniably is at work within the text, does not structure its main movement. It could not be said, for instance, that the latter deconstructs the former. Both converge towards a unified signification, and the shame experienced at the desire to possess dovetails with the deeper shame felt at self-exposure, just as the excuse for the one conspired with the excuse for the other in mutual reinforcement. This implies that the mode of cognition as hiding/revealing is fundamentally akin to the mode of cognition as possession and that, at least up till this point, to know and to own are structured in the same way. Truth is a *property* of entities, and to lie is to steal, like Prometheus, this truth away from its owner. In the deviousness of the excuse pattern, the lie is made legitimate, but this occurs within a system of truth and falsehood that may be ambiguous in its valorization but not in its structure. It also implies that the terminology of repression and exposure encountered in the passage on shame is entirely compatible with the system of symbolic substitutions (based on encoded significations arbitrarily attributed to a free signifier, the ribbon) that govern the passage on possessive desire ("Je l'accusai d'avoir fait ce que je voulois faire . . ." [86]). The figural rhetoric of the passage, whose underlying metaphor, encompassing both possession and exposure, is that of unveiling, combines with a generalized pattern of tropological substitution to reach a convincing meaning. What seemed at first like irrational behavior bordering on insanity has, by the end of the passage, become comprehensible enough to be incorporated within a general economy of human affectivity, in a theory of desire, repression, and self-analyzing discourse in which excuse and knowledge converge. Desire, now expanded far enough to include the hiding/revealing movement of the unconscious as well as possession, functions as the *cause* of the entire scene (". . . it is bizarre but true that my friendship for her was the *cause* of my accusations" [86]), and once this desire has been made to appear in all its complexity, the action is understood and, consequently, excused—for it was primarily its incongruity that was unforgivable. Knowledge, morality, possession, exposure, affectivity (shame as the synthesis of pleasure and pain), and the performative excuse are all ultimately part of one system that is epistemologically as well as ethically grounded and therefore available as meaning, in the mode of understanding. Just as in a somewhat earlier passage of the *Confessions* the particular injustice of which Rousseau had been a victim becomes, by metaphorical synecdoche, the paradigm for the universal experience of injustice,[9] the episode ends up in a generalized economy of rewards and punishments. The injury done to Marion is compensated for by the subsequent suffering inflicted on Rousseau by nameless avengers acting in her stead.[10] The restoration of justice naturally follows the disclosure of meaning. Why then does the excuse fail and why does Rousseau have to return to an enigma that has been so well resolved?

We have, of course, omitted from the reading the other sentence in which the verb *"excuser"* is explicitly being used, again in a somewhat unusual construction; the oddity of "que je craignisse de m'excuser" is repeated in the even more unusual locution: "Je m'excusai sur le premier objet qui s'offrit" ("I excused myself upon the first thing that offered itself" [86]), as one would say "je me vengeai" or "je m'acharnai sur le premier objet qui s'offrit."[11] The sentence is inserted, it is true, within a context that may seem to confirm the coherence of the causal chain: ". . . it is bizarre but it is true that my friendship for her was the cause of my accusation. She was present to my mind, I excused myself on the first thing that offered itself. I accused her of having done what I wanted to do and of having given me the ribbon because it was my intention to give it to her . . ." (86). Because Rousseau desires Marion, she haunts his mind and her name is pronounced almost unconsciously, as if it were a slip, a segment of the discourse of the other. But the use of a vocabulary of contingency (*"le premier objet qui s'offrit"*) within an argument of causality is arresting and disruptive, for the sentence is phrased in such a way as to allow for a complete disjunction between Rousseau's desires and interests and the selection of this particular name. Marion just happened to be the first thing that came to mind; any other name, any other word, any other sound or noise could have done just as well and Marion's entry into the discourse is a mere effect of chance. She is a free signifier, metonymically related to the part she is made to play in the subsequent system of exchanges and substitutions. She is, however, in an entirely different situation than the other free signifier, the ribbon, which also just happened to be ready-to-hand, but which is not in any way itself the object of a desire. Whereas, in the development that follows and that introduces the entire chain leading from desire to shame to (dis)possession to concealment to revelation to excuse and to distributive justice, Marion can be the organizing principle because she is considered to be the hidden center of an urge to reveal. Her bondage as target liberates in turn the free play of her symbolical substitutes. Unlike the ribbon, Marion is not herself divested of positive signification, since no revelation or no excuse would be possible if her presence within the chain were not motivated as the target of the entire action. But if her nominal presence is a mere coincidence, then we are entering an entirely different system in which such terms as desire, shame, guilt, exposure, and repression no longer have any place.

In the spirit of the text, one should resist all temptation to give any significance whatever to the sound "Marion." For it is only if the act that initiated the entire chain, the utterance of the sound "Marion," is truly without any conceivable motive that the total arbitrariness of the action becomes the most effective, the most efficaciously performative excuse of all. The estrangement between subject and utterance is then so radical that it escapes any mode of comprehension. When everything else fails, one can always plead insanity. "Marion" is meaningless and powerless to generate by itself the chain of causal substitutions and figures that structures the surrounding text, which is a text of desire as well as a desire for text. It stands entirely out of the system of truth, virtue, and understanding (or of deceit, evil, and error) that gives meaning to the passage, and to the *Confessions* as a whole. The sentence: "je m'excusai sur le premier objet qui s'offrit" is therefore an anacoluthon,[12] a foreign element that disrupts the meaning, the readability of the apologetic discourse and reopens what the excuse seemed to have closed off. How are we to understand the implications of this sentence and what does it do to the very idea of understanding which we found to be so intimately bound up with and dependent upon the performative function itself?

The question takes us to the *Fourth Rêverie* and its implicit shift from reported guilt to the guilt of reporting, since here the lie is no longer connected with some former misdeed but specifically with the act of writing the *Confessions* and, by extension, with all writing. Of course, we always were in the realm of writing, in the narrative of the *Confessions* as well as in the *Rêverie*, but the thematization of this fact is now explicit: what can be said about the interference of the cognitive with the performative function of excuses in the *Fourth Rêverie* will disseminate what existed as a localized disruption in the *Confessions*.

Paul de Man

With the complicity of the casual, ambling, and free-associating mode of the *Rêverie*, the text allows itself a puzzling lack of conclusiveness. Cast in the tone of a pietistic self-examination, it sounds severe and rigorous enough in its self-accusation to give weight to the exoneration it pronounces upon its author—until Rousseau takes it all back in the penultimate paragraph which decrees him to be "inexcusable" (1038). There is also a strange unbalance between the drift of the argument, which proceeds by fine distinctions and ratiocinations, and the drift of the examples, which do not quite fit their declared intent. The claim is made, for example, that, in the *Confessions*, Rousseau left out several episodes because they showed him in too favorable a light; when some of these incidents are then being told in order to make the disfigured portrait more accurate, they turn out to be curiously irrelevant. They do not show Rousseau in all that favorable a light (since all he does is *not* to denounce playing companions who harmed him by accident and from whose denunciation he would, at the time, have stood to gain very little) and they are, moreover, most unpleasant stories of physical assault, bloody mutilation, and crushed fingers, told in such a way that one remembers the pain and the cruelty much better than the virtue they are supposed to illustrate. All this adds to the somewhat uncanny obliqueness of a slightly delirious text which is far from mastering the effects it pretends to produce.

The implications of the random lie in the Marion episode ("je m'excusai sur le premier objet qui s'offrit") are distributed, in the *Fourth Rêverie*, over the entire text. The performative power of the lie as excuse is more strongly marked here, and tied specifically to the absence of referential signification; it also carries, in this literary context, a more familiar and reputable name since it is now called *fiction*: "To lie without intent and without harm to oneself or to others is not to lie: it is not a lie but a fiction" (1029). The notion of fiction is introduced in the same way that the excuse of randomness functions in the *Confessions*. Within the airtight system of absolute truth it produces the almost imperceptible crack of the purely gratuitous, what Rousseau calls "un fait oiseux, indifférent à tous égards et sans conséquence pour personne . . ." ("a fact that is totally useless, indifferent in all respects and inconsequential for anyone" [1027]). There is some hesitation as to whether such "perfectly sterile truths" are at all conceivable, or if we possess the necessary judgment to decide authoritatively whether certain statements can be to that extent devoid of any significance. But although the text vacillates on this point, it nevertheless functions predominantly as if the matter had been settled positively: even if such truths are said to be "rares et difficiles," it is asserted that the "truth" of such "useless facts" can be withheld without lying: "Truth deprived of any conceivable kind of usefulness can therefore not be something due [*une chose due*], and consequently the one who keeps it silent or disguises it does not lie" (1027). Moreover, "I have found there to be actual instances in which truth can be withheld without injustice and disguised without lying" (1028). Some speech acts (although they might better be called silence acts) therefore escape from the closed system in which truth is property and lie theft: ". . . how could truths entirely devoid of use, didactic or practical, be a commodity that is due [*un bien dû*], since they are not even a commodity? And since ownership is only based on use, there can be no property where there can be no use" ("où il n'y a point d'utilité possible il ne peut y avoir de propriété" [1026]). Once this possibility is granted, these free-floating "truths" or "facts," utterly devoid of value ("*Rien* ne peut être dû de ce qui n'est bon à *rien*" [1027]) are then susceptible of being "used" as an excuse for the embellishments and exaggerations that were innocently added to the *Confessions*. They are mere "détails oiseux" and to call them lies would be, in Rousseau's words, "to have a conscience that is more delicate than mine" (1030). The same paragraph calls these weightless, airy non-substances fictions: "whatever, albeit contrary to truth, fails to concern justice in any way, is mere fiction, and I confess that someone who reproaches himself for a pure fiction as if it were a lie has a conscience that is more delicate than mine" (1030). What makes a fiction a fiction is not some polarity of fact and representation. Fiction has nothing to do with representation but is the absence of any link between utterance and a referent, regardless of whether this link be causal, encoded, or governed by any other conceivable relationship that could lend itself to systematization. In fiction thus conceived the "necessary link" of the metaphor has been metonymized to the point of catachresis, and the fiction becomes the disruption of the narrative's referential illusion. This is precisely how the name of Marion came to be uttered in the key sentence in the *Confessions*: "je m'excusai sur le premier objet qui s'offrit," a sentence in which any anthropomorphic connotation of seduction implied by the verb "s'offrir" has to be resisted if the effectiveness of the excuse is not to be undone and replaced by the banality of mere bad faith and suspicion. Rousseau was making whatever noise happened to come into his head; he was saying nothing at all, least of all someone's name. Because this is the case the statement can function as excuse, just as fiction functions as an excuse for the disfigurations of the *Confessions*.

It will be objected that fiction in the *Rêverie* and the denunciation of Marion are miles apart in that the former is without consequence whereas the latter results in considerable damage to others. Rousseau himself stresses this: "whatever is contrary to truth and hurts justice in any conceivable way is a lie" (1030), and also "the absence of a purposefully harmful intent does not suffice to make a lie innocent; one must also be assured that the error one inflicts upon one's interlocutor can in no conceivable way harm him or anyone else" (1029). But the fiction, in the *Confessions*, becomes harmful only because it is not understood for what it is, because the fictional statement, as it generates the system of shame, desire, and repression we described earlier, is at once caught and enmeshed in a web of causes, significations, and substitutions. If the essential non-signification of the statement had been properly interpreted, if Rousseau's accusers had realized that Marion's name was "le premier objet qui s'offrit," they would have understood his lack of guilt as well as Marion's innocence. And the excuse would have extended from the slander back to the theft itself, which was equally unmotivated: he took the ribbon out of an unstated and anarchic fact of proximity, without awareness of any law of ownership. Not the fiction itself is to blame for the consequences but its falsely referential reading. As a fiction, the statement is innocuous and the error harmless; it is the misguided reading of the error as theft or slander, the refusal to admit that fiction is fiction, the stubborn resistance to the fact, obvious by itself, that language is entirely free with regard to referential meaning and can posit whatever its grammar allows it to say, which leads to the transformation of random error into injustice. The radical irresponsibility of fiction is, in a way, so obvious that it seems hardly necessary to caution against its misreading. Yet its assertion, within the story of the *Confessions*, appears paradoxical and far-fetched to the point of absurdity, so much so that Rousseau's own text, against its author's interests, prefers being suspected of lie and slander rather than of innocently lacking sense. It seems to be impossible to isolate the moment in which the fiction stands free of any signification; in the very moment at which it is posited, as well as in the context that it generates, it gets at once misinterpreted into a determination which is, *ipso facto*, overdetermined. Yet without this moment, never allowed to exist as such, no such thing as a text is conceivable. We know this to be the case from empirical experience as well: it is always possible to face up to any experience (to excuse any guilt), because the experience always exists simultaneously as fictional discourse and as empirical event and it is never possible to decide which one of the two possibilities is the right one. The indecision makes it possible to excuse the bleakest of crimes because, as a fiction, it escapes from the constraints of guilt and innocence. On the other hand, it makes it equally possible to accuse fiction-making which, in Hölderlin's words, is "the most innocent of all activities," of being the most cruel. The knowledge of radical innocence also performs the harshest mutilations. Excuses not only accuse but they carry out the verdict implicit in their accusation.

This other aspect of radical excuse is also conveyed by the text of the *Rêverie*, though necessarily in a more oblique manner. In telling another instance of a situation in which he lied out of shame—a less interesting example than the ribbon, because there is nothing enigmatic about a lie which, in this case, is *only* a defense[13]—Rousseau writes: "It is certain that neither my judgment, nor my will dictated my reply, but that it was the automatic result [*l'effet machinal*] of my embarrassment" (1034). The machinelike quality of the text of the lie is more remarkable still when, as in the Marion episode, the disproportion between the crime that is to be confessed and the crime performed by the lie adds a delirious element to the situation. By saying that the excuse is not only a fiction but also a machine one adds to the connotation of referential detachment, of gratuitous improvisation, that of the implacable repetition of a preordained pattern. Like Kleist's marionettes, the machine is both "anti-grav," the anamorphosis of a form detached from meaning and capable of taking on any structure whatever, yet entirely ruthless in its inability to modify its own structural design for nonstructural reasons. The machine is like the grammar of the text when it is isolated from its rhetoric, the merely formal element without which no text can be generated. There can be no use of language which is not, within a certain perspective thus radically formal, i.e. mechanical, no matter how deeply this aspect may be concealed by aesthetic, formalistic delusions.

The machine not only generates, but also suppresses, and not always in an innocent or balanced way. The economy of the *Fourth Rêverie* is curiously inconsistent, although it is strongly thematized in a text that has much to do with additions and curtailments, with "filling holes" (*remplir les lacunes*, 1035) and creating them. The parts of the text which are destined to be mere additions and exemplifications acquire autonomous power of signification to the point where they can be said to reduce the main argument to impotence. The addition of examples leads to the subversion of the cognitive affirmation of innocence which the examples were supposed to illustrate. At the end of the text, Rousseau knows that he cannot be excused, yet the text shelters itself from accusation by the performance of its radical fictionality.

The literal censorship and curtailment of texts appears prominently in several places. A quotation from Tasso provides a first example: Rousseau compares his own resolve not to denounce his playing companion to Sophronie's sacrificial lie when, in order to save the life of the Christians, she confessed to a crime (the theft of a religious icon) that did not take place. The comparison borders on the ludicrous, since Rousseau's discretion is in no way equivalent to a sacrifice. But the quotation which Rousseau now inserts into the text serves a different function. It is a passage which he had omitted, without apparent reason, from the translation he made of the Second Canto of Tasso's epic[14] at an earlier date. Any mention of Tasso, in Rousseau, always carries a high affective charge and generates stories clustering around dubious translations, literary falsifications, textual distortions, fallacious prefaces as well as obsessions of identification involving erotic fantasies and anxieties of insanity.[15] Limiting oneself, in this context, to the obvious, the insertion of the quotation must be an attempt to restore the integrity of a text written by someone of whom Rousseau himself had said "that one could not suppress from his work a single stanza, from a stanza a single line, and from a line a single word, without the entire poem collapsing. . . ."[16] But the restoration occurs as an entirely private and secretive gesture, not unlike the citizen stealing "en secret" the word "chacun" and thinking of himself when he votes for all.[17] Such a secretive reparation enforces the shamefulness of the crime as well as destroying any hope that it could be repaired. The mutilation seems to be incurable and the prothesis only serves to mark this fact more strongly. The accusation that hangs over the entire *Fourth Rêverie* and against which the excuse tries to defend itself seems to have to do with a threat of textual mutilation, itself linked to the organic and totalizing synechdocal language by means of which Rousseau refers to the unity of Tasso's work.

The omission and surreptitious replacement of the Sophronie passage is at most a symptom, all the more so since "Tasso," in Rousseau, implies a threat as well as a victim, a weapon as well as a wound. The mutilation is not just the excision of one specific piece of text. Its wider significance becomes more evident in another literary allusion in the *Fourth Promenade*, the reference to Montesquieu's conventionally deceptive preface to *Le Temple de Gnide*. By pretending that his work is the translation of a Greek manuscript, the author shelters himself from the possible accusation of frivolity or licentiousness, knowing that the reader who is enlightened enough not to hold his levity against him will also be sufficiently informed about literary convention not to be taken in by the phony preface. Rousseau treats Montesquieu's hoax without undue severity ("Could it have occurred to anyone to incriminate the author for this lie and to call him an impostor?" [1030]), yet behind this apparent tolerance stands a much less reassuring question. As we know from the "Préface dialoguée" to the *Nouvelle Héloïse*, the preface is the place in the text where the question of textual mastery and authority is being decided and where, in the instance of *Julie*, it is also found to be undecidable. With this threatening loss of control the possibility arises of the entirely gratuitous and irresponsible text, not just (as was apparently the case for Montesquieu or for naive readers of *Julie*) as an intentional denial of paternity for the sake of self-protection, but as the radical annihilation of the metaphor of selfhood and of the will. This more than warrants the anxiety with which Rousseau acknowledges the lethal quality of all writing. Writing always includes the moment of dispossession in favor of the arbitrary power play of the signifier and from the point of view of the subject, this can only be experienced as a dismemberment, a beheading or a castration. Behind Montesquieu's harmless lie, denying authorship of *Le Temple de Gnide* by the manipulation of the preface that "heads" the text, stands the much more dangerous ambivalence of the "beheaded" author.[18]

But precisely because, in all these instances, the metaphor for the text is still the metaphor of text as body (from which a more or less vital part, including the head, is being severed), the threat remains sheltered behind its metaphoricity. The possible loss of authorship is not without consequences, liberating as well as threatening, for the empirical author, yet the mutilation of the text cannot be taken seriously: the clear meaning of the figure also prevents it from carrying out what this meaning implies. The undecidability of authorship is a cognition of considerable epistemological importance but, as a cognition, it remains ensconced within the figural delusion that separates knowing from doing. Only when Rousseau no longer confronts Tasso's or Montesquieu's but his own text, the *Confessions*, does the metaphor of text as body make way for the more directly threatening alternative of the text as machine.

Unlike the other two texts, where the distortion had been a suppression, the *Confessions* is at first guilty of disfiguring by excess, by the addition of superfluous, fictional embellishments, "I have never said less, but I have sometimes said more . . ." (1035), but a few lines later it turns out that this was not the case either, since Rousseau admits having omitted some of his recollections from the narrative merely because they showed him in too favorable a light. There is less contradiction between the two statements when it turns out that what he omitted are precisely stories that narrate mutilations or, in the metaphor of the text as body, suppressions. Both stories have to do with mutilation and beheading: he nearly loses a hand in the first and comes close to having his brains knocked out in the other. Thus to omit suppressions is, in a sense (albeit by syllepsis), to preserve an integrity, "ne jamais dire moins." If the stories that have been omitted threaten the integrity of the text, then it would be even easier to excuse him for not having included them than to excuse him for the superfluous ornaments he added to the recollection of his happier memories.

But in what way are these narratives threatening? As instances of

Rousseau's generosity they are, as we already pointed out, more inept than convincing. They seem to exist primarily for the sake of the mutilations they describe. But these actual, bodily mutilations seem, in their turn, to be there more for the sake of allowing the evocation of the machine that causes them than for their own shock-value; Rousseau lingers complacently over the description of the machine that seduces him into dangerously close contact: "I looked at the metal rolls, my eyes were attracted by their polish, I was tempted to touch them with my fingers and I moved them with pleasure over the polished surface of the cylinder . . ." (1036). In the general economy of the *Rêverie*, the machine displaces all other significations and becomes the raison d'être of the text. Its power of suggestion reaches far beyond its illustrative purpose, especially if one bears in mind the previous characterization of unmotivated, fictional language as "machinal." The underlying structural patterns of addition and suppression as well as the figural system of text all converge towards it. Barely concealed by its peripheral function, the text here stages the textual machine of its own constitution *and* performance, its own textual allegory. The threatening element in these incidents then becomes more apparent. The text as body, with all its implications of substitutive tropes ultimately always retraceable to metaphor, is displaced by the text as machine and, in the process, it suffers the loss of the illusion of meaning. The deconstruction of the figural dimension is a process that takes place independently of any desire; as such it is not unconscious but mechanical, systematic in its performance but arbitrary in its principle, like a grammar. This threatens the autobiographical subject not as the loss of something that once was present and that it once possessed, but as a radical estrangement between the meaning and the performance of any text.

In order to come into being as text, the referential function had to be radically suspended. Without the scandal of random denunciation of Marion, without the "faits oiseux" of the *Confessions*, there could not have been a text; there would have been nothing to excuse since everything could have been explained away by the cognitive logic of understanding. The cognition would have been the excuse, and this convergence is precisely what is no longer conceivable as soon as the metaphorical integrity of the text is put in question, as soon as the text is said not to be a figural body but a literal machine. Far from seeing language as an instrument in the service of a psychic energy, the possibility now arises that the entire construction of drives, substitutions, repressions, and representations is the aberrant, metaphorical correlative of the absolute randomness of language, prior to any figuration or meaning. It is no longer certain that language, as excuse, exists because of a prior guilt but just as possible that since language, as a machine, performs anyway, we have to produce guilt (and all its train of psychic consequences) in order to make the excuse meaningful. Excuses generate the very guilt they exonerate, though always in excess or by default. At the end of the *Rêverie* there is a lot more guilt around than we had at the start: Rousseau's indulgence in what he calls, in another bodily metaphor, *"le plaisir d'écrire"* (1038), leaves him guiltier than ever, but we now have also the two companions of his youth, Pleince and Fazy, guilty of assault, brutality or, at the very best, of carelessness.[19] Additional guilt means additional excuse: Fazy and Pleince now both have to apologize and may, for all we know, have written moving texts about the dreadful things they did to Jean-Jacques who, in his turn, now has to apologize for having possibly accused them arbitrarily, as he accused Marion, simply because their names may have happened to occur to him for the least compelling of reasons.[20] No excuse can ever hope to catch up with such a proliferation of guilt. On the other hand, any guilt, including the guilty pleasure of writing the *Fourth Rêverie*, can always be dismissed as the gratuitous product of a textual grammar or a radical fiction: there can never be enough guilt around to match the text-machine's infinite power to excuse. Since guilt, in this description, is a cognitive and excuse a performative function of language, we are restating the disjunction of the performative from the cognitive: any speech act produces an excess of cognition, but it can never hope to know the process of its own production (the only thing worth knowing). Just as the text can never stop apologizing for the suppression of guilt that it performs, there is never enough knowledge available to account for the delusion of knowing.

The main point of the reading has been to show that the resulting predicament is linguistic rather than ontological or hermeneutic. As was clear from the Marion episode in the *Confessions*, the deconstruction of tropological patterns of substitution (binary or ternary) can be included within discourses that leave the assumption of intelligibility not only unquestioned but that reinforce this assumption by making the mastering of the tropological displacement the very burden of understanding. This project engenders its own narrative which can be called an allegory of figure. This narrative begins to vacillate only when it appears that these (negative) cognitions fail to make the performative function of the discourse predictable and that, consequently, the linguistic model cannot be reduced to a mere system of tropes. Performative rhetoric and cognitive rhetoric, the rhetoric of tropes, fail to converge. The chain of substitutions functions next to another, differently structured system that exists independently of referential determination, in a system that is

Paul de Man

both entirely arbitrary and entirely repeatable, like a grammar. The intersection of the two systems can be located in a text as the disruption of the figural chain which we identified, in the passage from the *Confessions*, as anacoluthon; in the language of representational rhetoric, one could also call it parabasis,[21] a sudden revelation of the discontinuity between two rhetorical codes. This isolated textual event, as the reading of the *Fourth Rêverie* shows, is disseminated throughout the entire text and the anacoluthon is extended over all the points of the figural line or allegory; in a slight extension of Friedrich Schlegel's formulation, it becomes the permanent parabasis of an allegory (of figure), that is to say, irony. Irony is no longer a trope but the undoing of the deconstructive allegory of all tropological cognitions, the systematic undoing, in other words, of understanding. As such, far from closing off the tropological system, irony enforces the repetition of its aberration.

NOTES

1. "De la littérature considérée comme une tauromachie," in Michel Leiris, *L'âge d'homme* (Paris: Gallimard, 1946). The essay dates from 1945, immediately after the war.

2. Page numbers are from J. J. Rousseau, *Oeuvres complètes, Les confessions, autres textes autobiographiques*, ed. Bernard Gagnebin and Marcel Raymond (Paris: Bibliothèque de la Pléaide, 1959), I. The passage concludes Book II of the *Confessions* and appears on pp. 85–87. Translations are my own.

3. This is so even within the immediate situation, when no actual text is present. Someone's sentiments are accessible only through the medium of mimicry, of gestures that require deciphering and function as a language. That this deciphering is not necessarily reliable is clear from the fact that the facial expression of, say, a thief at the moment he is caught red-handed is not likely to weigh heavily as evidence in a court of law. Our own sentiments are available to us only in the same manner.

4. See, for example, J. L. Austin, "Performative Utterances" and "A Plea for Excuses," in *Philosophical Papers*, ed. J. O. Urmson and G. J. Warnock (Oxford: Clarendon Press, 1961).

5. The usual way of dealing with this recurrent pattern in Rousseau's writings is by stressing the bad faith of his commitment to a *"morale de l'intention,"* the ethical stance for which he was taken severely to task by Sartre. In his commentary on the passage, Marcel Raymond, though less severe, takes the same approach: "By revealing his 'inner feelings' ['*dispositions intérieures*'] which were good . . . it appears that after having stigmatized his misdeed he gradually begins to justify it. The same gliding and swerving motion can be observed more than once in the *Confessions*, especially when Rousseau accounts for the abandonment of his children. He is always led to distinguish the intent from the act" (1273–74). It can, however, be shown that Rousseau's ethics is much rather a *"morale de pratique"* than a *"morale de l'intention,"* and that this analysis therefore does not ac-

count for the genuinely pre-Kantian interest of his ethical language and theory. The extensive possibilities of bad faith engendered by the distinction between the actual event and the inner feeling are abundantly present throughout Rousseau, but they don't govern the more puzzling and interesting movements and coinages of the text. Whether the link between "inner" feeling and "outer" action can be called intentional is precisely the burden of the interpretation and cannot be asserted without further evidence. If we are right in saying that *"qui s'accuse s'excuse,"* then the relationship between confession and excuse is rhetorical prior to being intentional. The same assumption of intentional apologetics, controlled by the narrative voice, underlies the recent readings of the *Confessions* by Philippe Lejeune in *Le pacte autobiographique* (Paris: Seuil, 1976) and "Le peigne cassé," *Poétique* 25 (1976), 1–30.

6. It is therefore consistent that, when the scheme ends in disaster, Marion would say: "Je ne voudrois pas être à votre place" (85).

7. "To lie for one's own advantage is deceit, to lie for the benefit of another is fraudulent, to lie in order to harm is slander; it is the worst kind of lie" (*Fourth Rêverie*, 1029).

8. The embarrassing story of Rousseau's rejection by Mme. de Vercellis, who is dying of a cancer of the breast, immediately precedes the story of Marion, but nothing in the text suggests a concatenation that would allow one to substitute Marion for Mme. de Vercellis in a scene of rejection.

9. See the episode of Mlle Lambercier's broken comb in Book I of the *Confessions*, especially p. 20.

10. "If this crime can be redeemed, as I hope it may, it must be by the many misfortunes that have darkened the later part of my life, by forty years of upright and honorable behavior under difficult circumstances. Poor Marion finds so many avengers in this world that, no matter how considerably I have offended her, I have little fear that I will carry this guilt with me. This is all I had to say on this matter. May I be allowed never to mention it again" (87).

11. The editor of the Pléiade Rousseau, Marcel Raymond, comments on the passage and quotes Ramon Fernandez (*De la personnalité*, p. 77): "He accuses her as if he leaned on a piece of furniture to avoid falling." Raymond speaks of "an almost dreamlike movement dictated by an unconscious which suddenly feels itself accused and by which he transfers the 'misdeed' upon the other, on his nearby partner" (1273).

12. Classical rhetoric mentions anacoluthon especially with regard to the structure of periodical sentences, when a shift, syntactical or other, occurs between the first part of the period (protasis) and the second part (apodosis). Heinrich Lausberg in *Handbuch der Literarischen Rhetorik* (Munich: M. Hueber, 1960), I. 459, §924, gives an example from Vergil: "quamquam anima meminisse horret luctuque refugit, incipiam" (*Aeneid* 2, 12). The following example from Racine is frequently quoted: "Vous voulez que ce Dieu vous comble de bienfaits/Et ne l'aimer jamais." Anacoluthon is not restricted to uninflected parts of speech but can involve nouns or inflected shifters such as pronouns. It designates any grammatical or syntactical discontinuity in which a construction interrupts another before it is completed. A striking instance of the structural and epistemological implications of anacoluthon occurs in Proust in the description of the lies used by Albertine ("La prisonniere," *A la recherche du temps perdu* [Paris: Pléiade, 1954], III, 153). For Rousseau's own description of an anacoluthon-like situation, see note 16.

Paul de Man

13. In this case he is being provoked into lying by the half-teasing, half-malicious questions of a woman inquiring whether he ever had children.

14. The translation is available in several of the early Rousseau editions, for example in *Oeuvres complètes de J. J. Rousseau* (Aux deux ponts: chez Sanson et Compagnie, 1792), IV, 215–47. It is printed in bilingual version and even the early editors had observed and indicated the absence of the passage which was later to be quoted in the *Fourth Rêverie* (ibid., 229).

15. On Rousseau and Tasso, one finds general observations, not very informative in this context, in several articles, mostly by Italian authors, mentioned by Bernard Guyon in his notes to the Pléiade edition of the *Nouvelle Héloïse* (II, 1339).

16. The statement is not a quotation from Rousseau but is reported by Corancez in *De J. J. Rousseau* (Extrait du Journal de Paris, # 251, 256, 259, 260, 261, An VI, 42–43). The sequel of the statement, in which Rousseau describes the one exception to the organic integrity of Tasso's work, is equally interesting for our purposes and could be read as Rousseau's description of an anacoluthon: ". . . sans que le poème entier ne s'écroule, tant (le Tasse) était précis et ne mettait rien que de nécessaire. Eh bien, ôtez la strophe entière dont je vous parle; rien n'en souffre, l'ouvrage reste parfait. Elle n'a rapport ni à ce qui précède, ni à ce qui suit; c'est une pièce absolument inutile. Il est a présumer que le Tasse l'a faite involontairement et sans la comprendre lui-même; mais elle est claire." Corancez could not remember the stanza Rousseau quoted, but it has been tentatively identified as stanza 77 of Canto XII of *Jerusalem Delivered*. See L. Proal. *La psychologie de J. J. Rousseau* (Paris: F. Alcan, 1923), p. 327 and Pléiade, I, 1386–87, which Rousseau chose to read as the prefiguration of his own persecutions. Corancez tells the story as an instance of Rousseau's growing paranoia and, in the same article, he reports Rousseau's death as suicide. His article is written in defense, however, of Rousseau's memory.

17. *Social Contract* (III, 306).

18. The same anxiety is apparent in another reference to prefaces in Rousseau, interestingly enough also in connection with Tasso. To deny authorship in a preface in the name of truth (as Rousseau did in the case of *Julie*) does not only mean that one's authorship of all texts can be put in question but also that all texts can be attributed to one. This is precisely what happens to Rousseau when a malevolent (or commercially enterprising) editor, in what reads like a transparent parody of the *"Préface dialoguée,"* attributes to him a poor translation of Tasso's *Jerusalem Delivered*, (see Pléaide, I, p. 1740 for the text of the editor's *préface*, and also p. 1386). Rousseau mentions the incident with some degree of paranoid anxiety in a letter to Mme. de Lessert of August 23, 1774 and among many other instances of false textual attribution, in the *Dialogues* (960). The chain that leads from Tasso to translation, to prefaces, to authorship, to beheading, and to insanity is ready to surface in any context of anxiety about truth and falsehood.

19. The description of the way in which Fazy injured Rousseau is ambiguous, since the narrative is phrased in such a way that he can be suspected of having done it with deliberation: ". . . le jeune Fazy s'étant mis dans la roue lui donna un demiquart de tour si adroitement qu'il n'y prit que le bout de mes deux plus longs doigts; mais c'en fut assez pour qu'ils fussent écrasés . . ." (1036).

20. For example, the fact that their names may have come to mind because of their phonic resemblance to the place names where the incidents are said to have taken place: the one involving Fazy occurs at Pâquis, the one involving Pleince at Plain-Palais.

21. The similarity between anacoluthon and parabasis stems from the fact that both figures interrupt the expectations of a given grammatical or rhetorical movement. As digression, aside, *"intervention d'auteur,"* or *"aus der Rolle fallen,"* parabasis clearly involves the interruption of a discourse. The quotation from Friedrich Schlegel appears among the formerly unavailable notes contemporary with the Lyceum and Atheneum Fragmenten. Friedrich Schlegel, *Kritische Friedrich-Schlegel-Ausgabe*, ed. Ernst Behler (Munich: F. Schöningh, 1963), XVIII, 85, §668. The use of the term parabasis (or parekbasis) by Schlegel echoes the use of the device especially in the plays of Tieck.

THREE

DISNEYLAND: A DEGENERATE UTOPIA
Louis Marin

MY REFLECTION on utopia was provoked by fascination with the signifier Ou-topia in which "something" was inscribed by Thomas More on a geographical chart; a name given by him at the beginning of the sixteenth century to a blessed island *between* England and America, *between* the Old and the New World.

The name Utopia is obviously written, through its Greek etymology, as a geographical referent; simultaneously in this writing, in this name, a play on words is also evident: Ou-topia is also Eu-topia, a play on words written by More in the margins of his book entitled *Utopia*. Sometimes, if not always, edges and borders have the precise and concealed function of indicating the center. Outopia can be written Eutopia by substitution of the first letters of the two words. I shall analyze such a play on words, through the play on spaces, as the core of the matrix of utopia. This play on words is also a play on letters which may be read as an indication of the utopian question: Nowhere, or the place of happiness.

Let me say, and this is my first step in another path toward utopia —a path leading my reading astray, a perverted path—that the topographical, political, social spaces articulated by the utopian text *play*, they shrink and swell, they warp, they do not fit exactly together: there are empty places between these spaces. The discourse held on utopia attempts, through the constructed reading of the text, to make the spaces signified by the utopian text coherent and consistent by filling them up with its own signifying substance. When the discourse on utopia dismantles the parts of the utopian totality in order to explain how utopia is functioning, it prohibits the utopian text to play. The quasi-system of the utopian construction becomes, by this metadiscourse, a real system, a structured whole where space no longer plays. This is the essential critique I make of my former study of utopia.[1] It did not leave the text playing and the only way to restore the utopian text is to displace its inconsistencies, its deficiencies, and its excesses, its quasi-system toward mere fantasy, mere ludicity, to take our pleasure without speculative or practical interest in order to inquire ultimately into the nature of the instantaneous manifestation of this pleasure.

I might say that, in my first attempts on utopia, I tried to formalize what its name indicates—ou-topia, no-where—with the notion of "neutrality" which was also approached by Blanchot and Derrida. Such a notion does not concern origin and *telos*; the question is not that of the neutrality of the institutionalized power, be this power that of the dominant truth. What is in question is not this imaginary representation where utopia unfolds its architectural perfection by fulfilling its wish of escaping the historical determinations. Neutral is the name given to limits, to contradiction itself. It seems that the fate of all theoretical knowledge and of the practice which derives from it is to dissolve contradiction, to solve it in a change that neutralizes it by overtaking it, a change by which the whole reconstitutes itself, in its identity, on every synthetic level it reaches. So the traces of contradiction, of differentiation are nothing else than the determinations of the totality which capitalizes them as its properties. All forms of dialectical thinking and knowledge are apparent in this description.

Is it possible to think of and to formulate the contradiction signified by that notion of neutral? And to keep it working? I try to discern in the utopian texts the traces of contradiction as its *fiction*, opposed to concept or image. Being such a fiction, utopia transforms contradiction into a representation and, in its turn, my own discourse about utopia transformed it into theory. A reading authority, an interpretive power settled down in the nowhere of the limits, occupied this no-place, possessed it in the name of truth, repeating the gesture already accomplished by utopia itself which endlessly recuperates the unbearable neutral with a logic joining together the contradictory terms. To take a paradigmatic example in More's *Utopia* at the very moment when wealth and poverty are negated—utopia is neither rich nor poor—More creates the harmonious image or representation of a society which is at the same time rich and poor, rich to corrupt and dominate its imaginary outside, poor to maintain virtue and to build with its citizens the ethico-religious monument of the State.

Moreover, a discourse on utopia can formulate the critical analysis of More's *Utopia* and discern, in the synoptic and totalizing image derived from the esthetic *affabulation*, the power of a scheme of pure imagination, to use Kantian language, and in the matrix of that scheme, the communication between concept and history. Without any doubt, a discourse on utopia can attempt to display the "vertical" relationships, formulated in terms of misreading and recognition, which allow the levels of the utopian text to generate each other and to sketch what Lyotard has called a figure in the discourse.[2] A figurative mode of discourse, utopia as the textual product of utopian practice or fiction is produced, in its turn, by the critical discourse as a possible synthesis of an historical contradiction. The critical-theoretical discourse will show, but always *post festum*, how a representation can have been produced from the negation of contemporary history; history that is the absent referent of the utopian representation. The utopian representation denotes a reality which is not signified by the utopian figure, but whose true signified is the critical discourse given at the end of the representation's own historical time.

To be effective, such a critical discourse on utopia has to lean back against the wall, [the thesis] of a final truth of history, a place from which it is formulated. But what would happen to its authority if the wall cracks and splits?

In other words and to conclude this introduction, I might say that in describing the utopian space in a critical way, my theoretical discourse was formulated in terms of a topic and its fabricated utopian figure consisted in making coherent the spatial inconsistencies which the utopian image structured as a whole. I would not emphasize the topic of the utopian fantasy, which is also a fantasmatic topic since the theoretical discourse about utopia operates [like in dreams, the screen memory] by filling up the gaps and the blanks of the utopian text, of the utopian space, by producing the systematic elements which are necessary to make the text intelligible. This production was possible only *après coup*, in a site supposed to be the true knowledge of the end of history that is the end of utopia as well. The topic of utopian fantasy as well as the fantasmatic topic of the critical-theoretical discourse on utopia rest on that basis.

In trying to analyse Disneyland as a utopian space, I aim at two targets.* First, I mean to show the permanence of some patterns of spatial organization which the history of ideas and myths allows us to call utopian. We find these patterns in the architectural schemes and the

---

* A more detailed version of this analysis originally appeared in *Utopiques, jeux d'espaces.*—Eds.

texts which can roughly be viewed as utopian, but which also fill a specific function with regard to reality, history, and social relationships. This function is a critical one: it shows, through the picture drawn by the utopian writer or designer, the *differences* between social reality and a projected model of social existence. But the utopian representation possesses this critical power without being aware of it; that is, unconsciously. In a sense, I apply to utopian texts (or spaces) what has been suggested by Lévi-Strauss' methodology of distinguishing models—the conscious representation built by societies to explain and legitimate their specific existences—and structures—the "unconscious" set of transformations that the anthropologist's analysis displays in the models themselves. The critical impact of utopia is not the fact of the model itself, but the differences between the model and reality; these differences being exhibited by the utopian picture. But this critical discourse, which is a latent characteristic of all utopias, is not separated from dominant systems of ideas and values: it expresses itself through the structures, the vocabulary of those systems by which individuals, a social class, decision-making groups represent the real conditions of their existence. It is this latent critique which is unfolded, *post-festum*, by a theory of society, a metadiscourse which, generally speaking, substitutes a rational understanding of the social reality for what it considers to be an ideological system of representation. Utopia is a social theory, the discourse of which has not yet attained theoretical status. In other words, utopia expresses a "possible" intervention of reason in the social field, but a "possible" which remains possible. Utopia is the real, iconic, or textual picture of this "possible." Therefore, utopia has a two-sided nature. On the one hand, it expresses what is absolutely new, the "possible as such," what is unthinkable in the common categories of thought used by the peoples of a given time in its history. So it employs fiction, fable to say what it has to say. On the other hand, utopia cannot transcend the common and ordinary language of a period and of a place. It cannot transgress completely the codes by which people make reality significant, by which they interpret reality, that is, the systems of representation of signs, symbols, and values which recreate, as significant for them, the real conditions of their existence. So Disneyland shows us the structure and the functions of utopia in its real topography and through its use by the visitor. From this vantage point, the possible tour which the visitor commences when he comes to Disneyland can be viewed as the narrative which characterizes utopia. The map of Disneyland he buys in order to know how to go from one place to another can play the role of the description; it performs the part of the representational picture which also characterizes utopia.

But Disneyland is more interesting from another point of view which is the second aim of our analysis: to show how a utopian structure and utopian functions degenerate, how the utopian representation can be entirely caught in a dominant system of ideas and values and, thus, be changed into a myth or a collective fantasy. Disneyland is the representation realized in a geographical space of the imaginary relationship which the dominant groups of American society maintain with their real conditions of existence or, more precisely, with the real history of the United States and with the space outside of its borders. Disneyland is a fantasmatic projection of the history of the American nation, of the way in which this history was conceived with regard to other peoples and to the natural world. Disneyland is an immense and displaced metaphor of the system of representations and values unique to American society.[3]

This projection has the precise function of alienating the visitor by a distorted and fantasmatic representation of daily life, by a fascinating picture of the past and the future, of what is estranged and what is familiar: comfort, welfare, consumption, scientific and technological progress, superpower, and morality. But this projection no longer has its critical impact: yes, to be sure, all the forms of alienation are represented in Disneyland, and we could believe Disneyland is the stage of these representations thanks to which they are known as such and called into critical question. But, in fact, this critical process is not possible in Disneyland in so far as the visitor to Disneyland is not a spectator estranged from the show, distanced from the myth, and liberated from its fascinating grasp. The visitor is on the stage; he performs the play; he is alienated by his part without being aware of performing a part. In "performing" Disney's utopia, the visitor realizes the models and the paradigms of his society in the mythical story by which he imagines his social community has been constructed.

THE LIMIT

One of the most notable features of the utopian picture is its limit: the utopian discourse inscribes the utopian representation in the imaginary space of a map, but at the same time, it makes this inscription in a geographical map impossible. We can make the survey of the blessed island described by Thomas More, but we cannot draw the geographical map in which this survey could take place. The utopian land belongs to "our world," but there is an insuperable gap between our world and utopia. More has given the paradigmatic example of this distance; he explains that when someone asked Raphael: "Where is the island of Utopia?" Raphael gave the precise information, but his words were hidden by a servant's cough. This mark in the discourse ironically designates the figurative process by signifying one of the conditions of the possibility of representation: it is a semiotic transposition of the frame of a painting.

This gap is a neutral space, the place of the limit between reality and utopia: by this distance which is a zero-point, utopia appears to be not a world beyond, but the reverse side of this world.

In Disneyland, the neutral space of the limit is displayed by three places, each of these having a precise function. (1) The outer limit is the parking area, an open, unlimited space, weakly structured by the geometrical net of the parking lot. The parking area, where the visitor leaves his car, is the limit of the space of his daily life of which the car is one of the most powerful markers. The fact of leaving his car is an over-determined sign of a codical change; for pragmatic utility, for his adjustment to a certain system of signs and behavior, the visitor substitutes another system of signs and behaviors, the system of playful symbols, the free field of consumption for nothing, the *passeist* and aleatory tour in the show. (2) The intermediary limit is lineal and discontinuous: the row of booths where a monetary substitution takes place. With his money, the visitor buys the Disneyland money, the tickets which allow him to participate in the Disneyland life. Thus, the Disneyland money is less a money than a language; with his real money the visitor buys the signs of the Disneyland vocabulary thanks to which he can perform his part, utter his "speech" or his individual narrative, take his tour in Disneyland. The amount of the exchange of real money for utopian signs determines the importance of his visit, the semantic volume of his tour, the number and the nature of its entertainments, in other words, it indirectly determines the number of syntactic rules which can be set working to coordinate the different signifying units. For example, with six dollars (four years ago), I received ten utopian signs—one A, one B, two C, three D, three E—and I was able to give utterance to a series of alternative narratives. (3) The inner limit is circular, linear, continuous, and articulated. It is the embankment of the Sante Fe and Disneyland Railway with its stations. This last limit is not a border line for the visitor or the "performer," since he does not necessarily use the train to go into Disneyland, but it is a limit for the utopian space which is encircled and closed by it. This limit belongs to the picture, to the representation, or to the map more than it appears as a limit to the traveller and to the tour he takes in the land. When he passes beyond the embankment, he is definitely in Disneyland. What I mean is that this element, the Railway, is a limit *in the map* for a dominant, all seeing eye; it is not a limit for the visitor, the consumer, or performer of

Disneyland; it is the first of the entertainments which he can consume. But, in fact, without being aware of it, the visitor is forced to spell the vocabulary in the right order. In other words, this structure which belongs to the map is a concealed *rule* of behavior for the visitor.

THE ACCESS TO THE CENTER

Disneyland is a centered space. Main Street USA leads the visitor to the center. But this route toward the central plaza is also the way toward Fantasyland, one of the four districts of Disneyland. So the most obvious axis of Disney's utopia leads the visitor not only from the circular limit or perimeter to the core of the closed space, but also from reality to fantasy. This fantasy is the trademark, the sign, the symbolic image of Disney's utopia. Fantasyland is made up of images, characters, animals of the tales illustrated by Disney in his animated films, magazines, books, and so on. This district is constituted by images; of particular significance is the fact that these images are realized, are made living by their transformation into real materials, wood, stone, plaster . . . and through their animation by men and women disguised as movie or storybook characters. Image is duplicated by reality in two opposite senses: on the one hand, it becomes real, but on the other, reality is changed into image, is grasped by the "imaginary." Thus, the visitor who has left reality outside finds it again, but as a real *"imaginaire"*; a fixed, stereotyped, powerful fantasy. The utopian place to which Main Street USA leads is the fantasmatic return of reality, its hallucinatory presence. This coming back of reality as a fantasy, as an hallucinatory wish-fulfillment, is in fact mediated by a complete system of representations elaborated by Walt Disney which constitutes a rhetorical and iconic code and vocabulary that have been perfectly mastered by the visitor-performer. So this coming back appears to be brought about through a secondary process which is not only the stuff of images and representations molded by wish, but which constitutes the very actuality of the fantasy where wish is caught in its snare. That snare is the collective, totalitarian form taken by the *"imaginaire"* of a society, blocked by its specular self-image. One of the essential functions of the utopian image is to make apparent a wish in a *free* image of itself, in an image which can play in opposition to the fantasy which is an inert, blocked, and recurrent image. Disneyland is on the side of the fantasy and not on that of a free or utopian representation.

Main Street USA is the way of access to the center, to begin the visitor's tour, to narrate his story, to perform his speech. From the center, he can articulate the successive sequences of his narrative by means

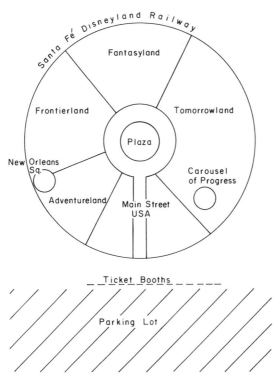

FIGURE 3.1. Disneyland Diagram

of the signs he has received in exchange for his money at the entrance. If we consider Disneyland as a text, Main Street USA is the channel of transmission of the story narrated by the visitor in making his tour. It allows him to communicate. Its function is phatic: it is the most primitive function of the communication since it only permits communication to take place without communicating anything. Thus, Disneyland can be viewed as thousands and thousands of narratives uttered by the visitors. Its text is constituted by this plurality of "lexies," to speak like Barthes, which are exchanged endlessly by the visitors according to the codes (vocabulary and syntax) imposed by the makers of Disneyland.

Now this semiotic function, the condition of possibility of all the messages, all the tours, all the stories told by the visitors, is taken into account structurally in a "lexie" belonging to a superior level, in the diagrammatic scheme of all the possible tours, an open and yet finite totality, the Disneyland map. When we look at this map (figure 3.1), we acknowledge a feature which we do not perceive when we recite the story in passing from the entrance to the center: the fact that Main Street USA is not only a street, but a "district," a land which separates and links Frontierland and Adventureland on the one hand, and Tomorrowland on the other. For the visitor-performer, Main Street USA is an axis which allows him to begin to tell his story. For the spectator, it is a place in the map which articulates two worlds; this place makes him look at the relations and at the differences between these worlds. But as a route to Fantasyland, it is the axis of the founding principle of Disneyland.

We can sum up this analysis in the following terms: Main Street USA is a universal operator which articulates and builds up the text of Disneyland on all of its levels. We have discovered three functions of this operator, (1) *phatic*: it allows all the possible stories to be narrated; (2) *referential*: through it, reality becomes a fantasy and an image, a reality; (3) *integrative*: it is the space which divides Disneyland into two parts, left and right, and which relates these two parts to each other. It is at the same time a condition by which the space takes on meaning for the viewer and a condition by which the space can be narrated by the visitor (the actor). These three functions are filled up by a semantic content. Main Street USA is the place where the visitor can buy, in a nineteenth-century American decor, actual and real commodities with his real, actual money. Locus of exchange of meanings and symbols in the imaginary land of Disney, Main Street USA is also the real place of exchange of money and commodity. It is the locus of the societal truth—consumption—which is the truth for all of Disneyland. With Main Street USA, we have a part of the whole which is as good as the whole, which is equivalent to the whole. The fact that this place is also an evocation of the past is an attempt to reconcile or to exchange, in the space occupied by Main Street USA, the past and the present, that is, an ideal past and a real present. *USA Today* appears to be the *term referred to and represented*; it is the term through which all the contrary poles of the structure are exchanged, in the semantic and economic meanings of the term, or, in other words, through which they are fictively reconciled. And by his narrative, the visitor performs, enacts reconciliation. This is the mythical aspect of Disneyland.

DISNEYLAND'S WORLDS: FROM THE NARRATIVE
TO THE SYSTEM OF READINGS

Let us now leave the narrator-visitor and his *énonciation* to the hazards of his possible tours. As we have seen, the syntax of his "discourse-tour" is defined first by his passing through the limits and by his journey to the center. The visitor has learned the codes of the language of Disneyland and has thus been given the possibilities to tell his individual story. Yet, his freedom, the freedom of his *parole* (his tour) is constrained not only by these codes but also by the representation of an imaginary history. This imaginary history is contained in a stereotyped system of representations. In order to utter his own story, the visitor is forced to borrow these representations. He is manipulated by the system, even when he seems to freely choose his tour. Now these remarks allow us to substitute the analysis of the map for a possible narrative and for its performative narration; the analysis of the map or the description not of a *parcours* in time (which is always a narrative) but of a picture, the parts of which coexist in the space of the analogue-model. Methodologically, we assume that the narrative tours constitute a total system and that the map is the structure of this total system. But we have had to justify this substitution by ascertaining that the possible tours in Disneyland are absolutely constrained by the codes which the visitors are given. The interplay of the codes is reduced to nothing. In a real town, in an actual house, there are some codes constraining the freedom or the randomness of the individual routes or passageways, but these codes do not inform the totality of the messages emitted by the inhabitants of the town or the house. By *realizing* a pure model, that is, by making an "abstract" model a reality, the makers of Disneyland have excluded any possibility of code interference, of code interplay. Not only are the different possible tours strictly determined, but the map of Disneyland can be substituted for a visit. In other words, Disneyland is an example of a *langue* reduced to a univocal code, without *parole*, even though its visitors have the feeling of living a personal and unique adventure on their tour. And since this *langue* is a stereotyped fantasy, the visitor is caught in it, without any opportunity to escape. This can be a definition of an ideological conditioning, or of a collective neurosis. But Disneyland provides us with a valuable lesson. If the substitution of the map for the narrative is somehow a necessary condition of the analysis of a town, a house, etc., we must remember not to jumble together the narrative processes by which people live, thus consuming their town or their house and the textual system which gives them the signs, the symbols, and the syntactic rules through which they display and perform these narrative processes. An architectural set is at the same time a set of places, routes, and pathways and a visible, "spectacular" totality. From this point of view, a progressive architecture seems to me to be defined as an attempt to build up a totality in which different codes are competing, are in conflict, are not coherent, in order to give to people living in

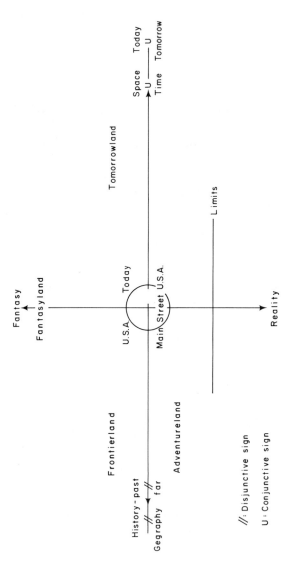

FIGURE 3.2. Semantic Structure of the Map

this totality, and consuming it, an opportunity to perform their specific *parole*, to use the town as a multicoded or overcoded totality, codes subverting each other to the benefit of a poetic *parole*. I mean a totality allowing for behaviors characterized by a factor of unpredictability. Viewed from this perspective, Disneyland is an extra-ordinary dystopia. It displaces the spatial habitability, what we have called its narrativity, into its spectacular representation; it reduces the dynamic organization of the places, the aleatory unity of a possible tour to a univocal scheme allowing only the same redundant behavior. So we are justified in viewing the map of Disneyland as an analogue-model which assimilates the possible narratives of its space.

On the left of the map, two districts: Adventureland and Frontierland. The first is the representation of scenes of wildlife in exotic countries which are viewed during a boat trip on a tropical river. The second is the representation of scenes of the final conquest of the West. The latter district signifies the temporal distance of the past history of the American nation, the former, the spatial distance of the outside geographical world, the world of natural savagery. The two left districts represent the two distances of history and geography, the distance represented inside America in the first, and the distance represented outside in the second.

The right of the map is occupied by a single district: Tomorrowland, which consists principally of representations of the Future-as-Space, Einsteinian Time-Space which realizes the harmonious synthesis of the two-dimensional world represented on the left part as time and space, time as historical, national past and space as strange, exotic primitivism. Tomorrowland is space as time, the universe captured by science and technology. In each of the two parts of Disneyland, we find an eccentric center, New Orleans Square on the left and the Carrousel of Progress, a gift of the General Electric Corporation, on the right. We can construct two models which are secondary representations of the map. The first is a purely analogous diagram, the second, a semantic structure (see figures 3.1 and 3.2).

Consideration of the center of these two models elicits the following remarks: (1) The center in the map is not the center in the semantic structure; in other words, the structure is not a simplified map. In the structure, the center is the sign of the numerous semiotic functions of Main Street USA as a route to the mapped center, an axis converting reality into fantasy, and vice versa, and an axis exchanging a scientific and technological conjunction of space and time for the historico-geographical distance.

(2) In the semantic structure, Main Street USA appears to be on

Louis Marin

different levels, formal and material, semiotic and semantic, a place of *exchange:* exchange of commodities and objects of consumption, but also of significations and symbols. The center of the structure functions at once inside and outside the structure. Inside, it is determined rigorously by the two main correlations of which it is made up—reality and fantasy: historico-geographical distance and space-time. But it is not only an intersecting point of these two semantic axes; somehow it produces them as well. Through it, the contrary poles of the correlations exchange their meaning: reality becomes fantasmatic and fantasy, actual. The remoteness of exotic places and of the American national past becomes the universal space-time of science and technology and this universality becomes American. In the semiotic theory of the narrative, the center is the representation of the dialectical mediation from which springs the narrative solution: it is the image of the inventions determined by the story on its different levels.

(3) It is not without significance that in this case, this image, this representation is named USA and is declined in the present tense. The ultimate meaning of the center is the conversion of history into representation, a conversion by which the utopian space itself is caught in the representation. This representational mediation makes it clear that in the utopian place, commodities are significations and significations are commodities. By the selling of up-to-date consumer goods in the setting of a nineteenth-century street, between the adult reality and the childish fantasy, Walt Disney's utopia converts the commodities into significations. Reciprocally, what is bought there are signs, but these signs are *commodities.*

(4) *The Eccentric Centers:* I shall just describe the Pirates of the Carribean attraction at the New Orleans Square center, in the left part of the map. This place reveals all of its semantic content only in its narration. So the visitor must begin to speak again in order to recite the underground tour, for the syntagmatic organization of his ride displays a primary and essential level of meaning. The first sequence of the narrative discourse is a place where skulls and skeletons are lying on heaps of gold and silver, diamonds and pearls. Next, the visitor goes through a naval battle in his little boat; then he sees off shore the attack of a town launched by the pirates. In the last sequence, the spoils are piled up in the pirate ships, the visitor is cheered by pirates feasting and revelling; and his tour is concluded. The narrative unfolds its moments in a reverse chronological order; the first scene in the tour-narrative is the last scene in the "real" story. And this inversion has an ethical meaning: crime does not pay. The morality of the fable is presented before the reading of the story in order to constrain the comprehension of the fable by a preexisting moral code. The potential force of the narrative, its unpredictability,

is neutralized by the moral code which makes up all of the representation. But if we introduce the story into the structural scheme of the map and especially if we do so by relating it to the structural center, another meaning appears beneath the moral signification. The center, you remember, is a place of exchange of actual products and commodities of *today*: it is a marketplace and a place of consumption. Correlated to the eccentric center of the left part, Main Street USA signifies to the visitor that life is an endless exchange and a constant consumption and, reciprocally, that the feudal accumulation of riches, the Spanish hoarding of treasure, the Old World conception of gold and money are not only morally criminal, but they are, economically, signs and symptoms of death. The treasure buried in the ground is a dead thing, a corpse. The commodity produced and sold is a living good because it can be consumed.

I do not want to overemphasize this point; but in Tomorrowland, on the right side of the map, the same meaning is made obvious by another eccentric center, the Carrousel of Progress. Here, the visitor becomes a spectator, immobilized and passive, seated in front of a circular and moving stage which shows him successive scenes taken from family life in the nineteenth century, the beginning of the twentieth century, today, and tomorrow. It is the *same* family that is presented in these different historical periods; the story of this "permanent" family is told to visitors who no longer narrate their own story. History is neutralized; the scenes only change in relation to the increasing quantity of electric implements, the increasing sophistication of the utensil-dominated human environment. The individual is shown to be progressively mastered, dominated by utensility. The scenic symbols of wealth are constructed by the number and variety of the means and tools of consumption, that is, by the quantity and variation of the technical and scientific mediations of consumption. The circular motion of the stage expresses this endless technological progress, as well as its necessity, its fate. And the specific organization of the space of representation symbolizes the passive satisfaction of endlessly increasing needs.

So the eccentric centers have powerful meaning-effects on Disneyland as a totality and on its districts.

We shall conclude our analysis with the following brief remarks. The left side of the map illustrates both the culture supplied by Americans to nineteenth-century America, and the one produced, at the same time, by adult, civilized, male, white people in exotic and remote countries. The living beings of Adventureland and Frontierland are only reproductions of reality. All that is living is an artifact; Nature is a simulacrum. Nature is a wild, primitive, savage world, but this world is only the appearance taken on by the machine in the utopian play. In

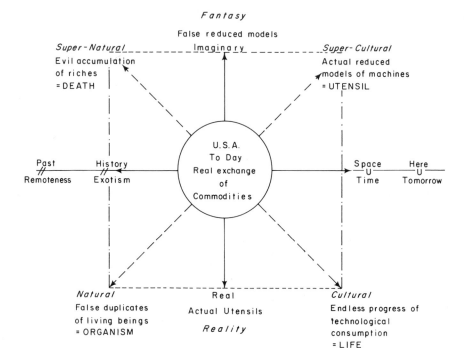

FIGURE 3.3. Semantic Structure of the Ideological Representation in Disneyland Utopia

other words, what is signified by the left part of the map is this assumption that the Machine is the truth, the actuality of the living. Mechanism and a mechanistic conception of the world, which are basic tenets of the utopian mode of thinking from the sixteenth century until today, are at work in Disneyland, no longer as a form of knowledge but as a disguised apparatus which can be taken for its contrary, the natural life.

On the right side of the map, the underlying truth of the left side becomes obvious. In Tomorrowland, machines are everywhere: from the atomic submarine to the moon rocket. The concealed meaning of the left side is now revealed thanks to the mediating center, Main Street USA. But these machines are neither true nor false; they are not, as in the left part, false reproductions. Instead, they are scaled-down models of the actual machines. We have false duplicates of living beings and concealed mechanistic springs on the left, obvious machines and true models on the right. Real nature is an appearance and the reduced model of the machine is reality. The ideology of representation and machine is all-pervading, and man is twice removed from Nature and science. Nature, which he sees, is a representation, the reverse side of which is a machine. Machines that he uses and with which he sometimes plays are the reduced models of a machinery which seizes him and which plays with him.

We find the same function of the reduced models, but on a different plane, in Fantasyland. This district is constituted by the real-realized images of the tales animated by Walt Disney. Fantasyland is the return of reality in a regressive and hallucinatory form. This imaginary *real* is a reproduction of the scenes the visitor has seen in the pirates' cave; but it is a regressive reproduction on a tiny and childish scale. We find the same fantasies of death, superpower, violence, destruction, and annihilation, but as reduced models of the attractions of the left side. Reduced models like those of Tomorrowland, but reduced models of death, strangeness, exoticism in the imaginary; they are the opposite of the reduced models of the right side, which show life, consumption, and techniques in their images. The realm of the Living in life-size is the realm of natural appearance in its historical past or geographical, anthropological remoteness. The realm of the Machine as a reduced model is the cultural truth of the American way of life, here and now, looking at itself as a universal way of living.

The function of Disney's utopia is to represent the exchange of the first and second realms of Natural Life and Scientific Technique and to express the ideology of this exchange on the stage and in the decor of utopia. Disneyland's ideological exchange can be illustrated by an elaboration of the semantic structure of the map (see figure 3.3).

Five years ago, I concluded my first visit to Disneyland by making the following statements:

Axioms: 1. An ideology is a system of representations of the imaginary relationships which individuals have with their real living conditions.

2. Utopia is an ideological locus: it belongs to the ideological discourse.

3. Utopia is an ideological locus where ideology is put into play and called into question. Utopia is the stage where an ideology is performed or represented.

4. A myth is a narration which fantastically "resolves" a fundamental contradiction in a given society.

Theorem: A degenerate utopia is a fragment of the ideological discourse realized in the form of a myth or a collective fantasy.

Louis Marin

It seems to me, today, that these statements articulate only one side of the utopian problem, a side that relies on some questionable philosophical presuppositions, as I attempted to show at the beginning of this essay. Perhaps I was not aware five years ago that my own discourse in the past and, in a sense, the paper I publish today are also degenerate utopias, critical myths, theoretical fantasies. Perhaps I was not fully aware that science, theory have to get out of their Disneylands to discover their utopias.

NOTES

1. *Utopiques, jeux d'espaces* (Paris: Editions de Minuit, Collection Critique, 1973).
2. See Jean-François Lyotard, *Discours, Figure* (Paris: Klincksieck, 1971).
3. However, today I would be more careful: these statements are perhaps like the statements of an anthropologist visiting his research field for the first time. They may be characteristic of a foreigner reading the "Other" by superimposing upon it his own set of values and notions.

FOUR
PRAMOEDYA'S "THINGS VANISHED"
with a Commentary by James Siegel

"THINGS VANISHED" is the first of a collection called *Stories from Blora* by the Indonesian writer Pramoedya Ananta Toer. Most of these were written just after the Indonesian revolution and were first published in 1952. The stories focus partly on the author's childhood and partly on events during the Japanese occupation and the revolution, all of them taking place in Blora, a town in north-central Java. Professor A. Teeuw has called Pramoedya "the most important prose-writer of the [revolutionary] period" and few would deny it. Pramoedya has been a political prisoner in Indonesia since 1965.

The present translation was made from the text published by P. N. Balai Pustaka (Djakarta, 1963). Portions of it were made by James Castle, Elizabeth Morris, and Susan Rodgers during a seminar on Pramoedya given by Ben Anderson and myself at Cornell. I have also consulted an earlier translation of the story by Harry Benda in John Echols (ed.), *Indonesian Literature in Translation* (Ithaca: Cornell Modern Indonesian Project, 1956) and received some helpful advice from Ben Anderson.

J. S.

James Siegel

THINGS VANISHED[1]
Pramoedya Ananta Toer

The Lusi River encircles the southern section of Blora.[2] During the dry season, its[3] bed of rocks, pebbles, mud, and sand churns up and strains toward the sky. The water is just a few inches deep in its shallow places. But when the rains start to come down and the mountains in the jungle are covered with clouds and the sun stays hidden for forty or fifty hours, the brackish water seems to change—yellow, thick, filled with mud. Its depths surge out of control. Sometimes twenty meters. Sometimes more. And the water which had flowed peacefully, suddenly churns madly. Clumps of bamboo along the banks are carried away like grass pulled up by little children. Banks are destroyed by it and the fields of the local people are swept away.

The Lusi: It destroys its own banks.

And in this life sometimes a rapid current carries away a man's body and fate. And without knowing it, he loses a part of his own life—

From the front of our house we could see the dark green tops of bamboo. When the wind blew, they bent seductively [or mournfully]. Sometimes they whistled quietly in the rustling of the wind. And when I was little all this seeing and hearing often frightened me. I would run quickly to the lap of my mother—crying.

Even now I still hear my mother asking, "Why are you crying?"

And her hand, which no longer had its girlish softness, stroked my thin cheeks. And my childish voice, still uncertain, answered between sobs, "Mama, the bamboo is crying."

And at this, mother took me and sat me on her lap. And, speaking, she gave me courage. "It isn't crying. No, it's singing."

Then she sang. Her soft voice never failed to still my fear, sadness, or aversion to something. They were Javanese songs. Often her voice was softly plaintive, inviting me to fall asleep. Sometimes during the singing I caressed her hair which had been blown by the wind. I played with her ear which was decorated with a diamond earring. Later—later I heard the voice, its song finished.

"You're sleepy," it said. "Come, let me put you to bed."

And I opened my eyes wide so I could enjoy mother's song some more. But I couldn't keep my eyelids open any longer——

But now, all of this has vanished. Vanished like the riverbanks and the bamboo clusters, swept away by the high water of the Lusi River. And I am powerless to stem the great current which nature spouts in each human being. I am touched by how easily man is set aground by the waves of time, from place to place, from feeling to feeling.

One time—I still remember—I dreamed I found a penny. And when I opened my eyes, my hand was still tightly clenched, frightened that the money which I had found in my dream would fall and be lost. At once I got up and found mother. I shouted gaily:

"Mama! Mama! I found a penny."

And I saw her smile, sharing my happiness. Her asking showed her interest:

"Where did you find it? Where is it?"

I held up my clenched fist to her and shouted happily:

"Here! Here!"

Then I opened out my fist. But the hand was empty. And mother continued in her sweet voice:

"Where?"

I was stunned by surprise and disappointment—the penny I'd found in my dream was not in my fist. And I cried. A great emptiness swept through me. I heard mother laugh and she cajoled me:

"You just got up. You were only dreaming. Don't cry."

But a disappointment which closed in on that emptiness still wound its way through my breast. Mother wiped away my tears with the hem of her blouse.

"Hush. Hush." she said again.

She took out a half-cent piece from the fold of her waist band and handed it to me. And although I was quiet while playing with that half-cent, I was still disappointed.

"It's already afternoon," mother said. "Go bathe. Ask Nji Kin to bathe you."

And I got up from her lap. But I didn't go ask for a bath right away. I saw mother's face suddenly darken. And I heard her voice, no longer gentle, but filled with firmness,

"Go!"

Her firmness prompted me to get up and trot slowly to look for Nji Kin in the kitchen. And from behind me, I heard a voice scolding:

"Hurry up! It's already afternoon."

Her tone of authority made me afraid to whine. Slowly I went to the kitchen to find Nji Kin and ask for a bath.

Even now I can still visualize Nji Kin. She was a girl like many in the world who are married to someone they have never seen before. And from her marriage she got syphilis: a disease which ultimately made her disgusting to the husband. It was syphilis which caused them to separate and seek their own livelihoods. It also seized one of her ankles. It ate away one of her eyes. It had completely destroyed her beauty. One of her feet had to be dragged along when she walked.

During the day, she didn't have time to regret her fate. Daily life consumed most of her attention. Only when night arrived and she was too tired to sleep did she regret everything that had slipped from her possession.

She was already in this state when she became our maid.

She had no children. The syphilis had also consumed her womb. And because she had no children of her own, she always loved me. And I still feel this affection whenever I think of her. Nji Kin, who was beautiful before, had become the victim of her own beauty.

Sometimes she caressed my cheek as though she were caressing her own child who was never to be born. And still I remember when she carried me on her hip and hid her face behind her shawl. Suddenly the shawl would be quickly drawn away and she would say:

"BOO!"

She did this over and over. I was thrilled at being treated like this and laughed happily. She also laughed happily. But often the shawl would cover her eyes for a long time and not be drawn back. And when I yanked it away, I could see her pale face with its attention focused on the precariousness of the world. Her eyes were red. Then quickly her cheek would be placed next to mine for a long while; she longed for her children who were never to be born into the world.

From her wages, Nji Kin managed to save a bit. And almost half of those savings were used to buy food. And that food was for me. Later I learned that she received eighty cents a month from mother.

Like mother, Nji Kin liked to tell me stories. The difference was that mother always told stories about heroes of wars which occurred in the Near East, while Nji Kin's were about the life of the ancient animals who were able to talk and to build kingdoms in the jungle.

I don't really know whether all of them were told to me when I was two or a few years later.

Nji Kin often explained to me in her stories how men used to be so pure they could understand the languages of animals. But people today, she said, are mostly sinners. Nowadays they like to humiliate their fellow men.

She also used to tell me about her childhood—when she was a few years older than I was at the time. I was always asking for the story to be repeated and she never denied me. I listened with astonishment and admiration. It went like this:

She was still small at the time. The regent in charge of Blora Regency was Ndoro Kandjeng Said. Once our town got a doubly heavy rain. The Lusi River overflowed its banks. And kept overflowing. And our still, peaceful small town was inundated by muddy yellow flood waters. And because our town square was on top of a hill, its clods of earth finally formed an island in the midst of a vast sea. The water drove the inhabitants there. They brought their children, their carabao, their cattle, and their own selves. The water would sweep away anyone who wasn't quick about it and carry them to the river mouth.

The heavy rain continued to fall. The house of the Regent was crammed with people.

Later she saw the Regent emerge from his house carrying a whip. He whipped the water which licked at the edges of the town square as he chanted a spell. And slowly but certainly the water began to ebb back into the indentation[4] which is the Lusi River.

Even today I remember exactly how it went. Twenty times that story was repeated. And I listened, fully attentive. And she told about the crying of babies in the rain. She told of the proud bearing of the Regent and how the people submitted to him. And how readily the people squatted before him, asking for his blessing.

This tale filled me with admiration for the Regent. But by the time I was born he was already in the grave. Nevertheless his fame was firmly fixed in the memories of our town's older generation.

Nji Kin had other stories, no less interesting, about beings half animals, half spirits which loitered about day and night, whenever human beings were inattentive. She could also tell stories about moving clouds—she was telling an excerpt from the Ramajana—and behind these clouds were Dasamuka, the abductor of Sita, fighting with Djataju who tried to prevent the abduction. And as she spoke she gazed at white clouds in the sky.

She would often tell of the heroes of the Mahabarata. All of her stories were simple and beautiful. And I even understood a bit of them too. And my thoughts turned to admiration for the wondrousness of the people of ancient times. I was the same at that time as people nowadys whose own era has vanished and who admire times long since passed.

And when I could not sleep at night and cried and raged, mother would rub my thighs. Usually she enunciated beautiful words. Sometimes she even sang Javanese songs—or Dutch or Arab ones. But her clear voice was not always beautiful to my feelings; not when those feelings were spiteful. Yes, even a little child can feel spite.[5]

It's always difficult for important moments to simply vanish from memory. So too with the memory of children. They will surely stay in one's head for life.

I still remember a time when I cried and cried. Because our house was far from any electric lines, when night came things got gloomy. Mother brought me outside. The mist cooled and relaxed my body. Its chill cooled the flush of spite in my heart. Apparently I had been affected by the mugginess earlier. And in the front yard, mother kissed me and whispered in a soft, gentle language:

"Do you love me? Why do you cry so? Don't you know your mother is tired from working all day? Sleep, love. Tomorrow will be a new day with new sky and new sun and with new air. And you can play again to your heart's content."

The caress of that voice soothed my feelings then. I hugged mother and sent my sobs into her bosom. And she pressed her bosom into my face. And I heard the beating within her breast. The cool evening mist sweetened mother's song. Finally I lost track of things. And when I opened my eyes, the sun was already high. The new day which mother promised last night. A new day, with a new sky, new air and new songs as well.

And now all this has vanished. Vanished from the realm of the five senses to be eternally enthroned in memory.

I still remember the time that Nji Kin fell ill. Yes, she's sick, the children said. She left without saying anything about it to me. I looked for her everywhere. But she wasn't to be found. And I cried on and on. For two hours. Mother consoled me with bananas and milk, but I could not hold back my weeping. A great emptiness made itself felt in my heart. And mother said over and over:

"Nji Kin has gone home, love. Nji Kin is sick. When she is sick you must not go near her or you will get sick too."

But these persuasive words could not fill the emptiness in my heart. I wept on. It was only exhaustion which sent my body to sleep. When I woke again, the emptiness was still there. And I wept on. The tears trickled out like the eye of Nji Kin which no longer had an eyeball and always leaked water which she wiped with the corner of her shawl.

The emptiness gradually lessened with the passing of time. I got new interests. I only occasionally thought of Nji Kin and asked mother, "Why hasn't she come back yet?"

"She is still sick."

At that time, I did not yet know that Nji Kin's house was not far from ours—only seven houses away. But I was satisfied with this answer. Later I heard from my mother's own mouth why Nji Kin left our house: she stole some spices. And mother did not allow such things in her house.

Nji Kin was replaced by a rather young woman. At that time I was three years old and already had a year old brother.[6] I usually got up at five in the morning. For that reason, mother slept with my little brother and I slept with the maid. She had to get up at five to take care of the kitchen. First of all she had to fry rice for the children going off to school; these were children who lived with our family or who father had adopted.

The two of us stood in front of the hearth while the rice was frying. And each time there was a crust of fried rice I asked the maid for it to eat.

I don't remember the name of the maid any longer. But, like Nji Kin, she was fond of me. She was the daughter of a farmer from outside town and a young farmer herself. Because of crop failure they had separated, each to find his or her own way.

A strange experience I had with that nurse when I was about three or four is still bright in my memory.

Our kitchen was not attached to the house. Its roof was nothing more than a sheet of zinc bent a bit and set on the legs of the kitchen frame. This kind of roof is called *bekuk lulang*, which means 'a fold of skin.' Two gaping triangular shaped holes, one at either end of the roof, were visible from inside the kitchen. I saw many astonishing events at one of these when I was small. But as time went on and I got older, these astonishing occurrences became fewer and finally no longer appeared at all.

From inside the kitchen at five in the morning the world outside seemed black. And blacker still since we stood in front of the hearth fire.

At that triangular opening I saw a huge head thrust itself in. And the hole was two meters high. I saw the beard, eyebrows, and mustache were white while the entire rest of the face was black—blacker even than the world outside. I quietly watched the huge face as I nibbled crusts of fried rice.

And that head thrust itself in every morning.

I pointed him out once, saying to the maid: "Look! Look! That huge head is thrusting itself at us again."

The maid raised her head and looked at the hole in the roof. And as usual she only laughed and said in a cool voice, "I don't see anything. What is it you see?"

"A head—a gigantic head."

"I didn't see it. What was it like?"

"Black. I saw black."

"You are fibbing. I didn't see a thing."

And usually I didn't insist that she believe me. Those sort of conversations always stopped dead. The maid went on washing dishes and I stirred the fried rice with a metal spoon that clinked [against the pan]. That is a beautiful sound to my ears. And the smell of the rice pressed into crusts wafted up to please my sense of smell.

I once told mother what I had seen. She did not want to take me seriously. Indeed she once insisted, "Who has been telling you stories about evil spirits?"

It was at that time that I learned the word 'evil-spirit.' I asked, "So that was an 'evil-spirit?' "

"Who told you about it?"

"I saw it myself. I saw it myself." And then I told her what I had often seen at the triangular opening. Mother listened attentively. And I went on telling[7] her what I had seen. There were some things I did not mention. And there were parts that I added from my childish imagination.

Finally, "You are still small. You must not lie."

"I am not lying," I said.

"Who taught you to lie?"

I looked at my mother's eyes. But the seriousness that shone from them made me dumb.

"Who?" mother insisted. "Nji Kin? The new maid? Who?"

"I saw it myself."

Later mother questioned the maid. And the maid said, "Practically every day he tells me he sees an evil-spirit in the opening in the roof. I myself don't believe it. I did not see anything."

"You must not lie to him."

"Never, m'am."

"Don't tell him fantastic tales."

"No, m'am. I have never told him stories."

"Be careful. Don't frighten him."

"Never, m'am. Never."

And from then on I never again told anyone about what I had seen at the opening in the roof. But:

Once something more sensational than anything I had ever seen happened. That morning we—myself and the new maid—were in front of the hearth early as usual. The huge head returned and thrust itself at us. I quietly watched it. But suddenly that head vanished and a monkey, as big as me, leapt down from the opening. The monkey quickly chased our maid. And the maid ran round and round the octagonal hearth. By the dim light of the fire I saw the waves of fear pass over the maid's face. But she did not scream or ask for help. She ran and ran, the monkey chasing her round and round. And I did not understand why she did not scream for help. Again and again the animal brushed against my body. But he did not disturb me. He only wanted to catch the maid.

The two creatures ran and ran and ran in circles. One the hunter, the other the hunted. But then I saw that the monkey had disappeared just like that. I do not know where he went. And I saw the maid squatting, exhausted and panting. The fear was still passing over her face. I watched her silently. And when she got up again, the earth under her was soiled with liquid.

"You urinated there," I said.

The maid looked at the liquid shining in the light of the kitchen fire. Then she took some ashes and sprinkled them on the urine, and it vanished from sight.

This experience tortured me. I felt that I had to tell it to someone. And I was nervous so long as people did not yet know about it. When the other children got up, I hurried to them. But when I saw that mother had also awakened, my desire to tell about the event was extinguished altogether. My courage vanished. I knew that mother would say I was lying.

The house was quiet. The children were in school. So was father. The new maid said to mother, "M'am, I would like your permission to leave today."

"Why? Aren't you happy here?"

"Well, happy enough, m'am, but . . ." She did not go on.

Mother did not insist on having her way. And that day the maid left our house—forever. I wanted to tell why, but I hadn't the courage. So the leaving of the maid left no trace whatever on us in the house.

Only several years later was I brave enough to tell the story to mother. And mother quickly said, "That was the monkey from next door which was free at dawn."

And in fact the neighbors back of us had a male monkey. But that was several years after the event of the morning had occurred. Once there was the noise of some excitement; Pa' Suro's monkey had attacked Si Inem. People gathered to watch the animal. Pa' Suro had put a dagger on the end of a stick of bamboo. Then he stabbed at the animal. The monkey avoided the thrusts, leaping about. But as he was tied up his stomach was finally pierced. And they went in a group to throw it in the river.

Now, the big monkey who chased the maid and the huge head with the white eyebrows, beard, and mustache have vanished. Vanished like the river bank and the clusters of bamboo carried off by the flooding of the River Lusi.

Father was a teacher in a private school. In the mornings when father wanted to leave for his teaching and I saw, I quickly asked to go along. And as usual father refused my request. And I cried.

What made me cry was the emptiness in life.

And mother and father said sweetly to me: "Later, when you are grown up you can go to school."

"Really, mother? Yes? Yes, father? Yes?"

"Certainly. You will go all through college. In Surabaja, Batavia, or Europe."

And when my interest had cooled a bit, father kissed me on both cheeks. Then he went peacefully off. But sometimes I ran to accompany him and mother hurried to catch me. And I cried again. But when mother spoke with absolute certainty, forbidding it, I did not have the courage to argue.

I still remember clearly when father was not there at home. I pulled a paint can which mother had given an axle and a string wherever I went. There was some large object hidden inside the can which turned and clanged, caressing my happiness. But this too has vanished just as the river bank and the clusters of bamboo which have been swept off by the Lusi River.

Father usually returned from school with a cheerful laugh. First he called my name and that of my younger brother, then a year old. After he kissed us, he went into his room to change clothes and then sat with mother at the dining table. And I stood beside mother, eating also. She fed me as she ate. And after I got a mouthful I ran about here and there till the rice was chewed and swallowed.

"Good? Good?" father usually asked me.

And usually I laughed and answered, "Good."

Father ate too little. He always ate just half a plate full. Only infrequently could he finish the rice which mother put on his plate. And before father left the table I was always sleepy from being full. And father disturbed my sleepiness, saying, "Ah, you're already sleepy. Go to sleep."

Only then was I aware that actually I was sleepy. Mother brought me to bed and patted my thighs till I slept. And in my sleep-blurred vision I could see her even rows of small teeth like cucumber seeds. And her rather narrow eyes shining with affection.

But all this has been swept away. What remains are only lovely memories which approximate the wonder of human life.

Mother was a pious woman. She was the daughter of a Muslim leader. But I can never remember how grandfather looked. When she was not pregnant, one could be sure mother would pray in a pure white prayer robe. Sometimes her hands held prayer beads. I never had the courage to come near her when she was doing that. I waited outside her room until she finished praying.

"Why do people pray, mother?" I once asked.

"So that they will be blessed by the Lord," she said. "So that those who have sinned can return to the right path. So that you will be always safe. Later when you are grown up you will understand the purpose of it yourself. You are still too small. Why not go and play."

And I never again asked about it.

If father had not yet come home by nightfall, I was often wakened by mother's voice chanting verses from the Koran, her voice clear and the rhythms touching—touching like a rather quiet night. Her voice was always good whether chanting or singing. And if father did not come home all night, mother went right on chanting.

Once I woke and went to her, asking, "It's so late and you are still chanting?"

Mother took me and sat me on her lap. But she did not say anything. She kissed me. And I can still feel how hot her breath was when she put her nose against my cheek.

Later mother went on chanting, but her voice was hoarse and faltering.

"Why do you keep on chanting?" I asked.

"So that your father will be safe. So that your father will keep away from sinful deeds. So that you will be safe. Aren't you going back to sleep?"

"Why hasn't father come home yet?"

Mother answered the questions with a kiss which pressed hard into my cheek. But she did not say anything.

"Where is father, mama?" I asked again.

"Working."

"So late at night?"

"Yes, he has a lot to do."

"When will father come, mama?"

"When you get up later on, father will have already come home. Now go back to sleep, child."

She brought me back to bed and for a moment I heard her singing a lullaby. And when I woke up again, I still heard mother chanting. Her voice was again clear. What I heard did not sound like a human voice, but like purity[8] itself. I wanted to ask if father had come home or not.

But I could not get up. I slept again. And I dreamt about father, about mother, and about my year old brother.

When I awoke in the morning I quickly called mother, shouting, "Where is father, mother?"

"He's already gone off to teach."

"Did father come home this morning?"

"Yes. Before he left he had a look at you. He kissed you and then left again to teach."

"Why doesn't father want to stay home and play with me, mother?"

"Father has to earn money for all of us to buy clothes and food for us and for your brother."

I did not ask further.

When father came home from school that afternoon I went to him quickly, asking, "Why didn't you come home last night? I woke up in the middle of the night but you still hadn't come. Why, papa?"

Father forced a laugh. I saw his face showed an affected cheerfulness. And mother, in the chair, bent forward.

"Mother prayed all night, papa. All night."

Again father laughed. But this time it wasn't forced. He still did not want to answer my question. Later we faced each other at the dining table and as we ate I again asked him, "Can I go out with you at night, father?"

Father laughed again. Then: "You are still too young, son. When you are grown up you won't need to go along with anyone. You can go wherever you like."

I suddenly felt that being young was a disgrace. But I lept up with happiness at getting that promise. "Could I go to grandma's house by myself, papa?"

"Of course. But not yet. You are still too young."

"Enough questions," mother said. "Father is worn out and wants to sleep. And you should sleep too."

And all of that—all of that has been swept away and can never possibly return.

Even now I clearly remember how one day I was frightened to be with mother. It was a Sunday morning. My parents' adopted children— actually not truly adopted, but rather children put in the care of my parents—had gone out to a favorite spot of our town's youth. The house was quiet. There were only mother, my small brother, and the maid. Father wasn't at home at the time.

I felt lonely and went looking for mother. I found her lying next to my little brother on the bed. My brother was sound asleep. And mother was staring at the top of the mosquito net.

"Mother, mother," I called.

Mother did not answer. And she did not move from her spot. With some difficulty I pulled myself onto the bed. And I saw that mother's eyes were red. Every once in a while she would wipe them with my brother's wool blanket. I was suddenly silent. For a long time. Quieted by fear. Then, in a whining voice, "Why are you crying, mama?" I asked.

Only then did mother look at me. She lifted me up and laid me down beside her.

"Why, mama?" I asked again.

"It's nothing, dear."

I thought about a very pleasant time at that moment—a trip by train to Rembang—to see the never quiet sea, with its waves hurrying to beat on the shore. And a dark blue, almost black horizon. Closer to shore the sea lost its darkness. And just at the shore, where ripples lapped at it, the sea was yellow from mixing with the rolling sand.

I asked again, "When are we going to take the train again, mama? To Rembang? And see the blue sea?"

She was quiet as she sensed the wind whistling through the tops of the casuarina trees along the sea shore at Rembang.

Mother's father and mother—my grandparents—lived at Rembang. And hearing the word 'Rembang' I suddenly heard her sob. I did not know why and asked, "Why are you crying, mother?"

She got up and kissed me over and over again. I felt her tears cooling on my cheek. She said slowly between her sobs, "Later we will leave Blora, my darling, and live in Rembang for good."

"Why for good, mother?"

"Wouldn't you be happy to see the sea, dear?"

"Very happy. Of course I would be happy to live by the sea. When will we leave, mama?" I asked happily.

But my happiness only made mother cry harder. Then she said, "Soon."

"How soon, mama?"

"I don't know. I don't know. But would you be happy living in Rembang, dear?" And mother wiped her tears away with my little brother's blanket.

"Of course, mama, of course. And father?"

Mother was startled to hear this. I saw that her eyes had stopped moving about and she threw me a glance. I did not know why. But that look suddenly frightened me. I screamed suddenly. Mother kissed me again and said softly, "Don't cry dear."

Before I had cried myself out, my little brother screamed, startled by my screaming. Mother quieted him with her breast.

She said, "Do you love father?"

I answered "yes" in the midst of my sobs.

She quickly said, "Father will go along and see the sea with you."

She was silent as she continued to nurse. She did not say anything more. Her eyes were nervous. Her glance moved from spot to spot. She was weighing something. I was silent. I was imagining the blue sea with the brick pier that stabbed into the ocean, the dark blue horizon and the ripples lapping at the shore. —We were quiet for a long time. Suddenly, "Why did you scream?"

"If father doesn't come I don't want to go to Rembang. I am happy here with you and father and brother. Where is father, mama?"

"Father has gone to work."

And I repeated the question I had asked her before. "Why doesn't father like to stay home and play with me?"

"Father has a lot to do."

"Does father always work, mama?"

"Yes," she said. And in the pronunciation of that word I felt something. But I did not know exactly what.

I stopped crying entirely; there wasn't a sob left, and asked again, "Why were you crying before?"

Mother did not answer. She only asked another question in a tone of resignation, "Have you eaten?"

"Yes. Later if father comes I will eat with him again. I like to eat with you and father and brother. But it's been so long and father still hasn't come. Perhaps he will come later tonight. Will he come, mother?"

"Perhaps. Just perhaps."

"Was father home last night, mother?" I asked again.

"Yes, but you were asleep. You didn't know it, but father came to your bed and kissed you four times."

I laughed happily.

"Did you pray last night?" And while asking I remembered that I did not hear mother pray last night.

"No. I crocheted. And you were already asleep. Father read a book. And the other children were already asleep. Now go to sleep."

"If father comes, wake me, will you, mama? Please?"

"Uhm hm."

After that I was silent and asked no more questions. I saw mother finish nursing. Then she lay back quietly. Her eyes stared at the top of the mosquito net which was spotted where it had been leaked on.

I didn't say anything. Mother was silent. I saw her eyes redden again for a moment. But I didn't say anything. Nor did mother. Then I fell asleep.

When I woke up mother was still beside me, quietly watching the top of the mosquito net. But her eyes were no longer red. And before I was fully awake I asked quickly, "Did father come yet, mama?"

I saw mother start. She turned on her side and looked at me. My little brother was still asleep beside her. "Not yet, dear. You slept a long time. You have a healthy body. Go now and ask the maid to give you a bath, alright?"

But I could no longer restrain my desire to be with father. I argued with mother. I said, half whining, "Father. Father. Where is father, mother?"

"Father will come later, dear. Bathe first. When you are clean, later, father will come."

But I still did not get up. Suddenly mother's voice was as firm as usual. "Go. Ask the maid to give you a bath."

This time I paid no attention to the firm tone of the utterance. "Father. Where is father?" I whined.

"Father is at work," mother said, keeping her firm tone. "Bathe!"

I paid no more attention to mother's voice. Suddenly mother's firmness disappeared. She kissed me fondly. She got off the bed and took me off. She set me on the floor and said, full of affection, while kissing me, "Father will come later. Bathe first, child. If you are bathed, father will want to play and kiss you. Bathe now, it's already late. When father comes I will call you. Quickly now, bathe."

The affection in this tone put down my rebelliousness. Slowly I went to the maid to ask for a bath.

After the bath father still had not come. I began to cry. (It was the emptiness of life that made me cry.) I refused all promises and food. I drew back from all endearments and seductions. I threw away the food put under my nose. And that night father still did not come.

I cried and cried. The emptiness seemed to hollow me out as time went on. I screamed tirelessly. In the evening, mother brought me outside. But the cool night had no effect whatsoever on the emptiness that was hollowing me out. I knew that mother had had enough of my weeping. The pity she poured out for me had no effect. For a moment mother's voice became stiff with annoyance. But I wept on. She again spoke gently. I screamed and screamed for father. It was very late.

Several times in the midst of crying I heard mother mention the Lord's name and ask forgiveness. But I went on crying—crying and saying "father" over and over. Mother never frightened me. When I cried she was either firm or showed me all the love she could. But this time, nothing worked.

Then I heard mother call one of the children. "Dipo! Dipo!"

And she called him, she said, "Look for father."

"Where?"

"Look for him, I said. Tell him his child is in a state.[9] I don't know where. You will have to look until you find him."

Dipo went, vanishing in the darkness of the night.

Mother carried me back into the house and my crying slackened. But when father did not come for some time I screamed again. I still vaguely remember that it was three in the morning. I know that mother brought me into the front room. She brought along a lamp and it illuminated the clock fastened to the front room wall. She said bitterly, "Three o'clock."

Mother went to the back room bringing the lamp along.

"Father! Father!" I cried.

"Father will be here soon, love. Sleep now, sleep."

But father still did not come. And I cried on and on. Sometimes slowly, sometimes screaming and yelling.

Finally father came accompanied by Dipo.

"Father!" I screamed. And screamed again. And again. I don't know how many times I screamed "Father!" over and over.

Mother went up to father. She did not say anything, but handed me over to him. Then she went silently to the bedroom.

"Father!" I screamed again.

Father held me next to his breast. His clothes felt wet—moistened by the evening mist. And slowly but steadily my screams abated. And finally ceased, leaving only sobs filling my chest. Slowly, while holding me, he said, "My dearest, dearest boy. Don't cry. Father's here now. Sleep now, sleep. It's nighttime. Listen—do you hear the rooster crow?"

I listened quietly. And it was true, I did catch the crowing of a rooster.

"It's dawn now," he said even more slowly.

There was a deep quiet that dawn. Only my sobs trailed on to finally vanish as well. And I heard mother sobbing. She hid her face in the pillow. I saw too that father was stroking her hair. But mother kept on sobbing almost inaudibly. Father said nothing to mother. Between the three of us there were only the barely audible sobs to be heard—sobs which wracked our hearts. Then, father quietly left the room. He took me outside into the cool, black, peaceful and lonely and total night.

"Why were you crying?"

"I waited and waited and you did not come," I said, complaining. "Mother said, later tonight father will come, but father did not come."

"But now I am here, right?" he said affectionately. "Now, sleep. Go to sleep."

Father sang slowly. His voice was deep, soft and rhythmical. I do not remember what else happened. Only that when I woke up father was sleeping beside me. His powerful arm held my body and I felt warm and happy. Off and on I could catch the crowing of roosters and hens as they answered one another. Finally sleep came over me. It was still dark out. The pane of glass above was still dark blue, almost black.

That morning was free. Father did not have to go to work. It was light out when I woke. I found father and mother sitting in the living room. After the maid bathed me I went to them, calling, "Father, you won't leave again, will you?"

I saw mother look at father. Father laughed as he looked at me. He said, "No. Today I won't go to work. Don't cry again, all right?"

I nodded. Father laughed. Mother's eyes were shining lively.

"Father, father! Mother cried yesterday too."

I saw father look at mother. But mother said nothing. And father did not say anything either. Then I said exuberantly, as though nothing had occurred between the two of them, "Mother said we will go to Rembang."

Again father looked at mother. But he did not say anything.

"And I will go too. And brother. And we will see the ocean. Will you come too, father? Please? Come too, please?"

Again father looked at mother. Then he said to me, "Of course, father will come too. When should we go?"

I faced mother. And in a childish voice said, "When can we leave, mama?"

I saw that mother was silent. She looked as though she weren't capable of replying. And I saw too that her rather narrow eyes were inflamed and glittering. And that then they were distorted with tears. She quickly wiped away the drops as they began to fall. When I saw that I screamed and yelled and cried. Something happened inside me so that when mother got up from her chair and left us, I continued to scream. I ran and pulled at her clothes, yelling, "Why, mama? Why, mama?"

Mother lifted me up, rocked me and held me, but she stayed speechless. She held my head in her breast until we reached the bed. Father did not come to the bed.

Yes, that is still clear in my memory. And like everything else it too has now vanished—like the river banks and the clusters of bamboo which were swept away by the Lusi River.

It is a wonder to me that things that have happened do not keep on happening. Each of these continuously shifting changes does not or cannot be fully perceived by humans and thus so many people are tossed back and forth in this world.

Every Lebaran,[10] father bought a cart full of fireworks for us at the house. My brother and I and mother and our parents' adopted children got new clothes and money from father. The fireworks were set off, the remnants strewn over the front yard. The neighbor's children were all over the unlit fireworks. I was extremely happy on Lebaran holidays like those. Nonetheless, all of this did not make my mother happy in the least; on the contrary, it made her weep. I saw mother was always gloomy and that father frequently left the house.

Eventually I was used to being separated from father and no longer made trouble. It wasn't necessary to summon father home again. I never knew where father went to when he wasn't working until I was grown up. Even mother never asked him where he was coming from or where he was going. She was silent when he left and did not ask him where he was coming from when he came back. And I did the same. Usually he left when mother was in the back room, the kitchen or the garden. I once asked him, "Where are you going, papa?"

"To work," he always answered.

"Can I come with you?"

And tersely and hurriedly, without even a glance, he answered, "No. Later when you are grown up you can go by yourself. Play with your brothers and sisters."

And I was satisfied with that answer.

On Lebaran she watched the children who set off fireworks from a chair in the front room. She said nothing. But her lips kept moving, mouthing *"Allahu Akbar."*[11] And once when I came up to her she said, "Those fireworks should not be set off on Lebaran. It is forbidden in Islam," she said. "Those fireworks are for Chinese ceremonies and have absolutely no place in the ceremonies of Muslims."

But every Lebaran, father would simply buy a cart full of fireworks till once one of the adopted children was injured. And after that father bought no more.

Something important happened after that. Mother's father—my grandfather—who lived at Rembang died after twice going to Mecca. Father immediately rented a car and we all set off. I don't remember what happened after that. Only that when mother returned to Blora, she seemed to wilt, to loose strength—like someone who has lost the last sanctuary in this world. For a week after the visit mother constantly cried. But she still had one final refuge: religion, so rich in its promises.

"Death is the price all men must pay," I heard father console her once.

But mother did not want to listen to that advice. I saw mother cry more and more. Had I been able to say so at the time, I certainly would have said that, except for religion with its many promises, mother had lost a sanctuary that she at times longed for when she wanted a place of escape. In later days I too would suffer a certain loss in my life—the vanishing of something that could not possibly return and for which there is no substitute in this world. I think every person at some time experiences a loss such as that.

A week passed. And had I been able to control the pouring out of my feelings at the time, I would surely have said that mother seemed to surrender herself to *time*[12] after that. And though she would see father go off nights before her very eyes, she would not say a single word, as if nothing had happened within her own sphere. This made mother closer to us, her children. We finally became a sanctuary too.

In solitary moments—not the solitude of the world, but the solitude of the heart—she would take us walking as much as two and a half kilometers from the house and tell us tales about things in the natural world. She was also happy telling us about the birds and their cleverness and their daily food; about the water of the Lusi River while we were crossing the Lusi River bridge; about the rice fields and crops and the pests that often ruined the harvest and hopes of the farmers; about the wind and storm clouds; about the sun and the stars and especially about the lot of the common people. My child's store of knowledge increased for it. When late afternoon had come, she would sit us down on benches in the yard and tell about plants, about bamboo clusters bent in the wind, about ships, trains, cars, and bicycles. Mother was good at telling stories. Sometimes she would tell us tales about cities she had seen; about her brothers and sisters and her family in the old days; about her lessons at school; about her teachers. And, never forgotten by us small children, mother would tell about the results of colonialism. I still remember clearly mother telling me about how men who were in the political movement were exiled and imprisoned. And I remember mother telling about Ki Hadjar Dewantara[13] who was exiled to Holland.

And like all the rest this too has been swept away and has vanished beyond the reach of the senses.

Mother's real mother—my grandmother—lived on the outskirts of our town, Blora, after marrying someone from there. Occasionally grandmother would come to our place bringing along different sorts of fruits. Grandmother's livelihood was selling vegetables. She got up very early in the morning and waylaid farmers carrying vegetables from their gardens to sell at market. She bought wares from them and then hawked from door to door at the houses of the officials—or, I should say, those who called themselves officials.

The grandfather who lived on the edge of town with grandma made his living selling roasted chicken at the market. Grandfather himself seldom came to the house unless he had to borrow money. He had been a farmer but his crops always failed. The people of our small town had a queer belief. And this I only found when I was an adult. Bad luck—for the rest of their lives—would befall those who had a child which people called illegitimate. So it was with grandfather. But as to the truth of this belief I myself wouldn't dare say.

I sometimes saw mother look annoyed when her stepfather came. Once I asked her indirectly, "You must not do anything that is against God's law. Just look at your grandfather. That's what happens. Everything he tries fails. Resentful and futile. It's not possible that his prayers and hopes could be realized."

But with my child's mind I could not understand what she meant by that. And once I asked, "Why are things like that with grandfather, mama?"

"When you are grown up you will know yourself."

And I did not ask again.

Mother usually hoed in the garden. At such times when I wasn't happy playing, I was sure to join her. At times like that stories which contained a moral issued from mother's mouth—a moral to ensure that her children love nature, love a certain occupation, and work at it earnestly. But my child's mind could not grasp the complexity of the meaning in her remarks. Only years later would I understand it.

"Man lives by his own sweat, child. When you are an adult it will be the same with you. Everything you get by anything other than your own efforts is not valid, yes, even though it be the gift of a charitable person."

And as is the case with other things, all of this has vanished. Vanished not to return again—vanished to be retained in memory. Forever.

The River Lusi experiences floods and drought, rise and fall, shallowness and depth. That too is the way with everything which happened during my childhood.

"And you may do whatever you like with those things that you have gotten properly—including your own life and body. But everything, everything that you get properly, my child," my father once said to me, though it was intended more for himself.

That voice is only heard for a few seconds in life. The vibrations resound, not to be repeated again. But as with the River Lusi which eternally marks the outline of the town of Blora, and like the river, the preserved voice that marks out thoughts and memories flows on too— flows out to the estuary, to the endless sea. And no one knows when the sea will dry up and stop its beating.

Vanished.

All of that has vanished from the reach of the senses.

NOTES

1. The title could be translated in a number of ways. An awkward but closer approximation would be, "That Which Has Vanished."
2. Blora is a town in north-central Java where Pramoedya was born.
3. As Indonesian pronouns do not specify sex, "its" could as well be rendered "her."
4. The actual word used is an idiosyncratic inflection of a root word which means 'hollow,' 'indented,' 'creased' and is used in other compounds to mean 'to be hollow' or 'to be indented' and 'to be devious' as well as 'hollow of the knee' and 'eye socket.'
5. The word for 'spite' is actually better thought of as a mixture of regret and annoyance or vexation.
6. It is not possible to tell from the text if it is actually a brother or a sister that is indicated here.
7. The root of this word for telling and the one that occurs two sentences earlier also designates 'story telling.'
8. Or clarity. The root is the same as that used for 'clear' in the previous sentence.
9. The word used here is Javanese.
10. Lebaran is the holiday of the end of the Muslim fasting month.
11. "God is the most great."
12. Italicized in the original.
13. The founder of an educational movement which synthesized Western and Indonesian cultures. The movement began in 1921 in Jogjakarta.

"THING(S)[1] VANISHED" REDISCOVERED
James Siegel

We are told by Pramoedya that this is an autobiographical story.[2] The story does not turn on the difference of view of the boy and the narrator, however. We never learn, for instance, why the father does not return home, where he goes when he leaves the house or what difference it would make to the narrator if he had learned these things. Similarly, nothing is made of the revelation of the true reason for Nji Kin's leaving —that she stole a few pennies worth of spices. How this revises his view of her and of his mother never comes up. Like most of the other incidents in the story, these are left unresolved, open-ended, for what seems to be no purpose at all.

Pramoedya's attention is instead focused on the fact that "all this has vanished. Vanished from the realm of the five senses to be eternally enthroned in memory." His concern is not with what is accessible to memory, with what happened, but with the question that memory of events raises: "It is a wonder to me that things that have happened do not keep on happening. Each of these continuously shifting changes does not or cannot be fully perceived. . . ."

The implications of the vanishing of memories from the grasp of the senses are not immediately apparent to us. And though the subject Pramoedya seems to be dealing with is not the loss of particular objects but the effect of loss or vanishing in general, we might be able to see the place of the second by looking at the first. Indeed, there are a great number of things that have vanished—or are lost, or missing or simply gone—the Indonesian (*hilang*) means all of this. One could think of the bamboo clusters swept away by the Lusi, the dream penny, Nji Kin's beauty, Nji Kin's nonexistent children, Nji Kin herself, the new maid, the huge head, the monkey, the father, of course, the mother's father, and the idea of Rembang as a sanctuary. It would be oversimple to speak of all of these at once. Nonetheless, that there are so many things that do vanish in the story surely is significant. We can get an approximate understanding of the implication of things vanishing by looking at a couple of instances.

Perhaps the two moments in the story when we are most drawn into it, when we see what is portrayed most vividly, are the incidents of the head that the boy sees in the kitchen and the description of Rembang as it passes between son and mother. Here we are least bothered by alien metaphysics as Pramoedya simply and vividly describes two different but equally engrossing scenes in terms of their actual objects. In these scenes, unlike others that I will speak of later, we have the least sense of the difference between language and what it describes. The translation itself seems least apparent here, as the task of language is to name objects rather than to convey ideas or sensations. For example, the head is described in such a way that it looms at us, seeming thus to duplicate the way certain memories of the past loom. When we read of the white eyebrows, mustache, and beard against the black face and this set above in the black opening of the roof, we feel the way that memory seems sometimes to be nearly fully present, yet still beyond our reach. After this description, however, there are incidents which not only distance us from the sensation of vision, but do so in such a way that we are left sensing the emptiness of the terms in which we actually thought of the head. For example, we are told that just before the monkey enters the kitchen, "the head vanished and a monkey, as big as me, leapt down from the opening." Thus, the monkey that chases the maid cannot be taken as the same creature whose head the boy saw. We learn that later Pramoedya told his mother about the creature. She identified it as the neighbor's monkey which was set loose in the mornings. But, we are told, "that was several years after the incident of the morning." Nothing is made of these identifications. Pramoedya does not challenge his mother on the point and we go on to learn of the killing of the neighbor's elusive monkey and the procession that throws it into the Lusi River. Thus, the mother identifies three separate creatures by the same word as the same object—the head, the monkey that chased the maid, and the neighbor's monkey. The text forces us to resist these identifications. In doing so, we resist applying the same word to three different objects—was the first creature a monkey at all, or the boy's hallucination? The second and third creatures are different monkeys and we want to so qualify the word. What has happened is that the bond of object and word, a bond so tight that in the description of the head we did not notice it at all, has been loosened to the point where word and object seem entirely different. Put another way, the word has been emptied of its content. The scene of the killing of the monkey and the procession that throws its corpse into the River Lusi which will carry it away, images and completes this process. "Monkey" no longer means all that we have been told about—it is simply a word.

The incident of Rembang is similar. While the father is away, the boy thinks of Rembang for no apparent reason, and we are given a description of his thought that makes it, again, seem like a vision. Rembang is described beginning in the far distance and continuing to shore. "I thought about a very pleasant time at that moment—a trip by train to Rembang—to see the never quiet sea, with its waves hurrying to beat on the shore. And a dark blue, almost black horizon. Closer to shore the sea lost its darkness. And just at the shore, where ripples lapped at it, the sea was yellow from mixing with the rolling sand." That Rembang "means" this scene is indicated by the peculiar way in which the word alone leads the mother to pick up the description at the same point where the boy had left off—at the shore. "I asked again, 'When are we going to take the train again, mama? To Rembang? And see the blue sea?' She was quiet as she sensed the wind whistling through the tops of the casuarina trees along the sea shore at Rembang."

Pramoedya has lifted this scene out of its setting by having it occur as a pleasant thought in the midst of a distressing incident and by having the idea be completed by the mother as though the strength of the word "Rembang" was such that no individual consciousness could think anything other than the sea and shore. It is again a meaning that in its visionary quality seems so closely bound to the word as to make the difference between the word and its referent invisible. After the grandfather's death, however, the family goes to Rembang and there is no mention at all of any incident there, much less any reference back to the details of the vision. The sanctuary of Rembang has been lost and it is clear that "Rembang" has been emptied of its meaning just as "monkey" was emptied of its.

The disjunction of language and meaning is a constant theme of the story. We are given the tales Nji Kin related to the boy and then told, "I even understood a bit of them." Incidents like this recur till the very end, where it is said that the boy did not understand the advice of his mother when she gave it. What is conjured up is an environment of puzzling, empty words; words that fill one's mind, but have no significance to them. Such words can only be described in terms of sensation—they are the sight of the written word or the sound of the spoken word (it is the latter that concerns Pramoedya). We can ask what the relation of these sensations of words of vanished objects is to those sensations that Pramoedya has said have "vanished forever, beyond the reach of the senses." Is the emptying of words, the conversion of them into sensation, an attempt to retrieve what has been lost by bringing sensation again to our attention? If not, what is the point of showing us "loss" as a function of language?

If we look carefully at the way the narrative is put together, the same question is raised. Let us first take a short episode, the early one of the crying of the bamboo.

From the front of our house we could see the dark green tops of bamboo. When the wind blew, they bent seductively [or mournfully]. Sometimes they whistled quietly in the rustling of the wind. And when I was little all this seeing and hearing often frightened me. I would run quickly to the lap of my mother—crying.

Even now I hear my mother asking, "Why are you crying?" And her hand, which no longer had its girlish softness, stroked my thin cheeks. And my childish voice, still uncertain, answered between sobs, "Mama, the bamboo is crying."

And at this, mother took me and sat me on her lap. And speaking, she gave me courage. "It isn't crying. No, it's singing."

Then she sang. Her soft voice never failed to still my fear, sadness, or aversion to something. They were Javanese songs. Often her voice was softly plaintive, inviting me to fall asleep. Sometimes during the singing I caressed her hair which had been blown by the wind. I played with her ear which was decorated with a diamond earring.

The interesting feature of this episode is the duplication of singing and crying. First the boy cries, then he says the bamboos are crying. The mother then says, no the bamboos are not crying, they are singing; and then she sings. In this way an opposition is established between the bamboos and crying on the one hand and the mother and singing on the other. This opposition, or pairing of four elements, is reinforced by drawing an identity between them. Thus, the bamboos are said to sing because of the blowing of the wind, while the mother's hair is also described as being blown by the wind as she sings. Furthermore, the bamboo is said to be seductive or mournful—the word means both—while the mother's song is described as "plaintive." A more literal gloss here would be "a low moaning." In addition to the similarity of meaning the words themselves are similar in sound. The first word—seductive or mournful—is *"meraju-raju"* while the second—"plaintive"—is *"mendaju-daju."* In both cases the duplication is optional, so that its use heightens the identification.

By making the distinctions and identifications between these pairs, we break up the sense of looking on a scene which proceeds simply as it might have in life. The contrast of narrative and linguistic movement picks up the boy's understanding of his mother's words as she furnishes signifiers which fail to fix meanings. One is aware of the contrasts and identities between the pair and thus of slipping from one to the other. This movement marks out a trail which is important not for what we know of the scene portrayed, nor for the importance of the identities and contrasts of mother/singing and bamboo/crying as such.[3] Rather the identities and differences are drawn so that we will sense that we are moving between the two. And, I would suggest, a good deal of the emotional impact of the story, which, in Indonesian, at least, is considerable, comes from this sense of slippage—of being borne away from one's moorings by following the markers of association despite the sense that is represented. The sense of "loss" (*hilang*) here is not personal loss but loss of balance.

One can find similar kinds of devices used in most passages of the story though the same device is seldom used twice. In one case, for example, the structure of two incidents is sufficiently parallel that one is diverted by the similarities. I have in mind the incident where the boy dreams of having a penny only to open his hand and discover it never existed except in his desire for it. Nji Kin, in the following episode, plays with him, treating him, we are told, like "her own child who was never to be born."[4] As they play peek-a-boo, she hides her face and he discovers that she is "long[ing] for her children who were never to be born into the world."[5] The repetition of incidents centering around the loss of something one never had is striking enough. But our attention is drawn to the similarity by other resemblances. Both Nji Kin and the boy have a substitute for what they desire but cannot have and that substitute is furnished by the mother. In each incident, the boy and the female figure are engaged in mutual happiness—the mother said to "smile, sharing my happiness" when he tells her he has a penny just as we are told that he and Nji Kin both laugh as they play their game. And of course this mutual happiness is disrupted in both incidents by the realization of loss. That these similarities are not fortuitous is shown by the passage where we learn that Nji Kin has given half her wages to the boy in the form of food. One must ask why this incident is included, and if it is to be included, why it is put in just after their game turns sour, if not to recall to us that the mother gave the boy a half penny to replace the dream cent just after their mutual happiness is disrupted.

The temptation is to take the similarities as rhetorical devices which emphasize loss as a theme or idea. We would like to say that the role that the mother plays in one incident, the boy plays in the next, for instance. We would then be able to say that Pramoedya is telling us something about loss as a common event in human life (he in fact says so much later on). But we cannot draw the parallel. If we try to identify Nji Kin and the mother on the basis of the sharing of happiness with the boy we are confused because it is of course Nji Kin who is bereft. In a similar way, if we identify Nji Kin and the boy because each is a figure who loses something they never had but only desire, we have to explain why it is Nji Kin who plays the mother's role in giving the boy half her wages, thus disrupting the identification. The point lies in the way that we are teased to make the identifications and then are prevented from doing so. We would like to say "Yes, it is all about loss," but when we see similarities and try to draw them out to conclusions, we are prevented from doing so. What is held out to us slips away and we are left with a sense of motion again, this time, of recession.

The contrary motions of narrative and linguistic patterns create the effect we spoke of earlier. What we read becomes important for its patterning; we attend to language as we would to music, for the internal relationships of its elements rather than for its reference outside the text. Language is thus emptied of reference to become simply marker and, as marker, primarily sound and pattern. One of the failures of the translation is that it does not communicate an important device by which this is done. Pramoedya's sentences are brief, frequently only a word long.[6] His paragraphs as well are shorter than we are accustomed to, often two paragraphs serving for a single topic. The result in Indonesian is to break up the message. This cannot be adequately duplicated in English, as short English sentences conveying messages similar to the Indonesian indicate unspoken meanings. As a consequence, the sentences of the translation often seem to be mysterious while the Indonesian lacks that effect. In the latter language a fragment remains a fragment. The result in Indonesian is merely to break up the surface and thus to disjoin sense and signifiers rather than to point to unsaid sense.

I want to give one more example of the way in which this story is structured. After the long scene in which the father does not return and the boy cannot stop screaming, there seems to be a transition. I am referring to the section which begins by telling us about the fireworks the father purchases each Lebaran, which continues by telling us about the death of the mother's father, and which concludes with the mother telling her children about the world. This section seems to make explicit what we have been speaking about. The disjunction of sound and sense and the feeling of movement or recession from one to the other seems practically drawn for us by the juxtaposition of the mother with her "sanctuaries," her own area in which she can try to remain untouched, and the images of loss and extrusion. The fireworks, which are mentioned in the very first sentence of the section, are practically an emblem of "things that vanish." They are objects that are converted into sound and leave, finally, only tatters, small remnants of themselves that give a hint of their outline, but contain nothing of the sound and light which have been forever lost. Furthermore, the conversion of object into sound is by explosion, an outward movement, and as we have seen, extrusion, throwing out, is one of the principal means of things vanishing. The rest of the section is full of the imagery of going-out, of exiting. The father, we are told more than once, leaves. And we are not only told that he leaves, we are given a vignette of him as the boy asks to go along. What is more, the action of the story itself for the first time moves out from the house further than the neighbor's yard. Not only does the mother take her children on walks as long as two and one-half kilometers, but the whole family drives over the mountains to Rembang. In the space of three pages we are told not only all that, but also exile or banishment is twice spoken of, and we hear the mother tell her children of everything in the outside world from nature to politics.

Against this profusion of the imagery of exiting, we are told that the mother has sanctuaries which she replaces one after another. Rembang, her original home, has been lost to her, but she has in its place "religion with its many promises." Yet this too is impermanent. For no sooner are we told of her reliance on religion than we are shown her refusing the traditional Muslim consolation for death—that it is the "duty," literally, of everyone, or, as it is translated in the text, "the price all men must pay." Nonetheless, she still has another "sanctuary," or sense of her own space that, at least for the moment, makes her invulnerable to the losses around her. Her final sanctuary, we are told, is her children. Because of them, "though she would see father go off nights before her very eyes, she would not say a single word, as if nothing had happened within her own sphere."

Yet there is a paradox in this notion of sanctuary. It exists finally, we are told, because the mother has "surrendered to time." Whatever other metaphysical meaning "time" has in Indonesian, it implies here both an acceptance of the loss of things, including loss of the mother's specific sanctuaries and particularly the loss of her children as sanctuary, and thus her own movement from sanctuary to sanctuary. The mother is the one figure in the story about whom one feels that loss means personal loss, loss of something that was "hers," as she is swept away from sanctuary to sanctuary.

It is useful here to think about the mother for a moment in the terms we have been using. From the opening episodes on, the mother is the instrument of sense. It is in part through her that we are brought to see the disjunction of sense and sound. We can recall the episode of the bamboos. When the boy is overwhelmed by "all this seeing and hearing," the mother says, the bamboos are really "singing"; she is also the one who insists on reality against dream and the person who insists again that he not lie nor be told lies. On the other hand, we have also seen that exiting, extrusion, is one of the chief ways by which sense is devalued and reduced, as far as possible, to sensation. This section, then, gives us almost a diagram of the continuous and widening gap between the two.[7]

Yet once again we are not allowed to consolidate what we read, this time for two reasons. In the first place, the neat diagram we have outlined here is actually broken up in the text by the use of repetition. Not only are we told about events twice—such as the setting off of the fireworks, or the acceptance of the father's leaving, but the language itself is almost awkward in those places where repetitions occur. For instance, first we are told that the fireworks are set off and then we are told that the "neighbor's children were all over the unlit fireworks." As another example, we are told twice not only that the father buys fireworks, but that he buys "a cart-full of fireworks." The awkward repetition of the use of the same word is unlike the ordinary clarity of Pramoedya's prose. Furthermore, certain phrases are repeated in a way that can only draw attention to the language. Thus, we are told that, "Had I been able to control the pouring out of my feelings at the time, I would surely have said that . . ." [the Indonesian is more succinct] and, in the preceding paragraph, "Had I been able to say so at the time, I would certainly have said." The result of these repetitions and awkwardnesses is that the surface is broken up, and the diagram that seems to have brought understanding into focus slips back into a slight blur as one's attention is drawn to the presence of the words as well as their referents.

The other unsettling part of this section is the final two paragraphs where the mother tells her children about the world, beginning with the birds and ending with the Dutch. We are given what seems to be an absolute miscellany, devoid of any order. We might take it as simply the jumble produced by memory as it registers events without systematizing them. But the catalogue is so very long that we lose sight of the narrative; we have to block out the specific meanings of each category in order to keep in mind the narratively more significant fact that this is what the mother taught the children about if we are not to be diverted into thinking of each subject as it comes up and so forget the general context. The tension between these two readings, of course, is similar to the point we have been making all along. But these paragraphs are so heavily weighted against narrative context and in favor of simple movement that it produces a change in tone.

Furthermore there is an underlying pattern of association between the items of the catalogue that helps one to move along. Here is a list of the subjects:

1. Birds, their skills and their everyday food
2. The River Lusi, told about when they walk over the bridge
3. Ricefields, rice, pests, the dashed hopes of farmers
4. Wind and storms
5. Sun and animals

There is a break and the list continues:

1. Plants, bamboo clusters bending in the wind, fruit
2. Ships, trains, cars and bicycles
3. Cities seen by the mother
4. Her relatives and family
5. School teachers
6. Colonial policy of the Dutch
7. Exile

Let us start with number two—the river which is told about as they walk over it. This leads to rice fields because of irrigation and to pests because birds are one of the chief pests and this, of course, to dashed hopes of the farmers. Wind and storm stem both from the description of things having to do with rice and with dashed hopes while storm leads to sun.

In the next series, bamboos are, of course, a kind of plant, but to say "bamboo clusters bent in the wind" recalls those of the opening section and those swept away by the waters of the Lusi. Wind and water lead to ships and ships to the series of vehicles which emblematize the city. That it is the city the mother has seen leads to her relatives and family who lived there and thus to her past, including school and teachers. The connection to the Dutch is via the father, who is both a teacher and a nationalist, and we end with exile.

The point here is only that one item leads to another; the associations are important not for anything they build up to or anything substantive they evoke; the pattern remains as miscellaneous after we trace the associations as before. Rather they trace a path that is independent of the narrative, leading one along new lines. The subjects are in themselves not important. That they end in exile is significant, however, because it shows that the empty words, the series of signifiers, lead out and away from the domestic scene of mother and children.

These paragraphs are set in "times of solitude," but their tone is not that of loneliness or sadness. In contrast to the tone of loss that we get in memories of childhood, and that is explicitly evoked in the beginning, the sense of movement is light, quick, and practically lyrical.

The key to understanding this change of tone comes in the next and final section. Here the boy is told by his father that with what he has gotten "validly," "legitimately," (the Indonesian means both) he can do whatever he wishes. This amplifies the final words of the mother—that "man lives by his own sweat. . . . Everything you get by anything other than your own efforts is not valid, yes, even though it be the gift of a charitable person."

These words are spoken about the boy's step-grandfather but they are intended as advice for the boy as well. As such they refer to everything we have read, to the story of the narrator's past; a past not of his own creation, but one that, as with all children, was only one that happened to him, that, in a broader sense, was given to him and is therefore a legacy, a gift, and thus not something gotten by "his own efforts."

In these narratives of things that have vanished there are three movements—there is the "original" sensation said to have vanished before the story is told, there is the remaining sense of the story—the outline of events—and finally, there is the third movement, the conversion of this sense into signifiers, into words emptied of their meaning. The medium, obviously, is language. It is through language that sensation as Pramoedya speaks of it is turned into meaning and preserved. As the last paragraph of the text indicates, the primary sensations are the sounds of voices. We can now answer the question of the relation between things in general that have vanished and the sensations pictured through the disappearance of specific objects. The latter is not a means to recover the former. Extrusion, expulsion, effects not the coming to life of the original sensation, but rather continues the process that begins with the vanishing of the original moments by reducing the residue of that moment, sense, to signifiers. In this way the past is emptied of its significance and of its resonance. One is released from it. As one moves out from the domestic scene, the scene itself is eradicated.

The change of tone in the scene of the mother and children is thus due to the feeling of completion of this process, of release from the meanings of the past. Language and self become identical when one is freed from the language of others. Language thus becomes one's own. The sense of "ownness" is here anomalous, however, as the only self that can be identified with language is that which is not the self of the past, which is in fact defined by not being that "past" self, at the same time that that self is erased.

The erasure or emptying of the past has two dimensions. It is a process of active neglect or turning away from it, and it is one of being rid of it for purposes of one's own. In this sense, it spells out two meanings of the Javanese word for "vanish." This word, practically the same as the Indonesian (*ilang* versus *hilang*), has two compounds that the Indonesian lacks.[8] One of these is "to be remiss." The example given by Horne in her dictionary is "The boy completely disregards the fact that his father is a teacher." The other is "to cause to vanish" as in to make an illness vanish, thus "to cure." "Thing(s) vanished" spells out the Javanese senses of this word. For if the emptying of sense from language makes one's heritage vanish, it is also being remiss toward those vanished, of voices about whom one speaks, (including, of course, one's own former voice). Only by turning his back on those voices, regardless of whose they are, can Pramoedya be cured of them.

There is more to this active neglect, however. One notices that many of the things that have vanished are still to be found, albeit somewhere else. Nji Kin, we learn, lives only a few houses away. The monkey is in the river if not in the sea while the father, though he is not at home, is always somewhere else and reappears at the end. What has vanished still exists, on the whole. The significance of its existence is not that the missing signified will be rejoined with the signifier at some later point. It is rather to show the ease of displacement of signifier and signified through speech. One sees this through the figure of the mother. She not only exemplifies sense, she also figures the suppression of speech. From the time the boy begins to speak, in the section where he claims the bamboos are crying, the mother refutes him and from then on, consistently stops attempts at expression. For instance, after the monkey has chased the maid, the boy "felt that I had to tell it to someone. . . . I was nervous so long as people did not yet know about it. When the other children got up, I hurried to them. But when I saw that mother had also awakened, my desire to tell about the event was extinguished altogether." He tells us it was the fear of being called a liar that stops him, which here means being told that what he saw did not exist. It is speech itself that displaces meanings. By not telling his mother what he saw he can hang on to it. Telling itself thus opens up the possibility of a difference between language and referent. The long incident of the absence of the father turns on this. He asks "where is father," and his mother attempts to stifle the question, because to ask it is to ascertain that the father is somewhere else. It is in this way that we can understand that what is important about the father's absence is not where he is, but that he is not there, that he is anywhere else; that to ask where he is is to create his absence. The mother, for her part, never asks the father where he has been or where he is going, consistent with her role as the guardian of a sense. To speak is to reveal the existence of lost objects in another place.

The result of the stifling of questions is noise—the weeping of the boy and of his mother. This noise dominates the text in places, seeming to drown out the voices of the characters. It is not, however, another example of the reduction of sign to signifier but its opposite—the attempt to keep sense in place by suppressing the act of speech which would indicate the displacement.

The vanishing of the voices of the parents has marked out thoughts and memories. This is the emptiness we read of and it is equivalent to the hollowness, the furrow (*kelekukan*) of the River Lusi, which marks out Blora, the scene of childhood. To reply is to remove these marks by a rising tide of sound. To speak, to reply in particular, is to displace. This means, of course, to speak one's own words rather than to repeat the stories of the past that one has heard from others. One must not market other people's goods, as does the grandfather. To speak one's own words is to continue on the path away from the domestic scene rather than, like the grandfather again, to continue to return to it in order to borrow. Thus, the ability to tell the story, the "courage to speak" is the movement away from the past, the continuous eradication of past selves. The telling of the story places the narrator "somewhere else."

Presumably, then, there should be only a continuous decentering of both others' words and one's own. However, the final scene, by making decentering the subject of the tale, has recentered it. One sees the message of decentering told in three ways—through the story of the grandfather, through the words of the mother as she hoes in her garden with the boy, and through the words of the father. These three scenes are quite different from one another, but they all contain the same message. The insistence of this message despite the various means of signification is the reverse of the previous sections of the story. Here, regardless of formal elements, despite the means by which the moral is conveyed, the message remains unequivocal. A refuge of sense, both necessary and unwanted, is thus created, resulting not in the elimination of the past but in the feeling of being carried away from it, of surrendering to time. It is in this way that we must read these sentences of Pramoedya's as being juxtaposed to one another: "I am powerless to stem the great current which nature spouts in each human being. I am touched by how easily man is set aground by the waves of time, from place to place, from feeling to feeling."9

NOTES

1. Indonesian does not ordinarily distinguish singular and plural.

2. In an autobiographical statement given to A. Teeuw and cited by him in Teeuw, *Modern Indonesian Literature* (The Hague: Martinus Nijhoff, 1967), pp. 164 and 174.

3. Though the opposition of singing and crying alone is significant, however, and is dealt with below.

4. The Indonesian standard phrase for not having children is "not yet!" This makes it possible to say here, "not yet ever to be born!"

5. The same use of "not yet" and "never" occurs here as in the sentence quoted above.

6. The temptation in translation, occasionally yielded to, is to combine two or more Indonesian sentences into a single English sentence. The gain in doing so is that the feeling of running-on of the Indonesian is better communicated. The shortness of the Indonesian sentences makes one move to the next while the same feature in English makes one pause.

7. The scene in which the mother silently mouths the Arabic formula, *Allahu Akbar*, God is the Most Great, as she hears the senseless noise of the fireworks is a compressed picture of this.

8. Ben Anderson has pointed out that the story feels as though it is a translation from Javanese. This recourse to a Javanese rather than an Indonesian meaning is duplicated several times in the text.

9. I am deeply indebted to Ben Anderson for pointing out the value of several of the scenes discussed as well as for much else. I would also like to thank Sandra Siegel for pointing out many unclarities in an earlier draft. I am particularly indebted to Piero Pucci for many acute observations.

THE ALL-EMBRACING METAPHOR: REFLECTIONS ON KAFKA'S "THE BURROW"
Henry Sussman

And the smaller rooms, each familiar to me, so familiar that in spite of their complete similarity I can clearly distinguish one from the other with my eyes shut by the mere feel of the wall: they enclose me more peacefully and warmly than a bird is enclosed in its nest.
"The Burrow"

I

THE EXTENDED narrative monologue, "The Burrow,"[1] represents an extreme for Kafka's fiction while at the same time functioning as a horizon toward which certain of its decisive tendencies gravitate. From the bureaucratic spaces which both engulf and exclude K. in *The Trial* and *The Castle*, from the deceptively open expanses of Karl Rossman's America, writing has now descended to a scene which is, in its every dimension, severe—an entirely self-contained subterranean enclosure whose reference to the outside is every bit as incidental and deceptive as it is inescapable. Darkness is the only raw material available for metonymic annexation. The earthen passageways and walls of the burrow describe a barren narcissism. The absence of things to which the narrative voice may refer is matched by a dearth of actions which the text may pretend to dramatize. Early generalizations as to the nature of the burrow and its hollowing (pp. 325–33) provide a scenario for the specific movements taking up the remainder of the text, where the voice presumably furnishes a direct transcription of the action. Such events are, however, like their setting, limited. The still silence of the burrow is articulated only by a brief visit to the outside, by abortive attempts to revise the structure, noises construed as issuing from an invisible adversary also inhabiting the depths, and, repeatedly, by sleep.

Kafka's term for the burrow is "the construction," *der Bau*. This terminology is inherently ironic, as the construction consists in hollowing, not protrusion, in the addition of complication, not assertion, in the expansion of darkness, not illumination. The construction is already deconstruction to the same extent that it has been constructed. This concept of a deconstruction equiprimordial to a constructive assertion preempts the fictive temporalizing underlying the history that traces the breakdown of the refined orders of civilization into their animal components. Here, the classical hierarchies are viewed a priori in the condition of reversal. Deconstruction has, from the outset, demanded and received the same ontological priority reserved for *arché* and production. In its anticipatory imaging of hierarchical implosion the text preempts any orientation toward deconstruction as finality or end.

Kafka has placed the monologue in the mouth of an unidentified burrowing animal, perhaps a mole. This animal is itself absurd. Although its behavior corresponds to what we would roughly expect from a carnivorous burrowing rodent, at several points (Fischer, pp. 416, 436) it describes itself as "galloping" (*gallopieren*) through the tunnels. The discourse uttered by its voice is human discourse. The humanity of the discourse is, however, stripped away as its concerns increasingly reveal it to be human. Animalism is thus not merely an anticipation of humanity, a precursor on an evolutionary ladder, but is reached only after humanity has been lived, penetrated, and disqualified.[2] Just as the animal's incessant ruminations attain self-consciousness from which only the self has been evaporated in the intensity of introspection, the concept of the animal in this text is merely a rendition of humanity from which the self has been excluded, a humanity whose concerns have been allowed to rise to their highest and starkest abstraction. It is in this sense that the primitively deconstructive setting implies its own elaboration in an evolution toward a more abstract statement of the conditions of fiction.

Absurd as it may seem, given the complexity of the novels, to insist upon an evolution in Kafka's writing toward the circumscription in a here and now characteristic of the sense-certainty where the Hegelian *Phenomenology* takes off, not ends, the containment of "The Burrow" serves indeed as an end to Kafka's writing, an ending worthy of the body, a culmination of its exploration into the limit disclosed in the process of metaphor, of which the burrow is both an extreme and a paradigmatic example. Containment in the construction bespeaks the same duplicity reaching its most elaborate expression in *The Trial* and *The Castle*. Although the transposition of the limit to the stark setting of a hole may entail a certain simplification, this does not imply simple reduction. Kafka's fortitude, in this case, consists in the intricacy and ambiguity that he is willing to implant in a hole. If this descent in any way entails a devolution or regression, the reduction is inseparable from elaboration. The metaphor stands at the fissure where development and reversion take off from one another. Orientation loses the naiveté ascribable to a simple progression, a thrust toward a yet-unrealized telos, for it has been marked by the stigma of infantility, regression, unadulterated yearning for the Earth-womb.

"I have completed the construction of my burrow and it seems to be successful" (p. 325). Stepping into a human guise, the animal author of the construction begins its monologue, retrospectively evaluating the product of a life's work, conceding its strengths and weaknesses. Unified by plazas and tunnels, the opus finds the fictive totality underlying the consideration of the work as a whole. Whether we regard the voice of self-critique as emanating from the animal, Kafka, or from Kafka's opus, from the outset we are apprised that the work under construction is a literary as well as an architectural object, bespeaking the same duplicity, illusoriness, impenetrability, and limit characteristic of the literary text. "All that can be seen from outside is a big hole; that, however, really leads nowhere; if you take a few steps you strike against natural firm rock" (p. 325). The construction begins as a false start and a deception. It incorporates both a stratum of apparently solid and "natural" reality and the convolutions of its internal logic, calculated to befuddle possible intruders. The construction resists penetration. One of its doubled openings is self-evident. This is the one, however, leading nowhere. The only available access is by way of fiction, through the moss camouflage which is the entrance's only protection. And yet, from the beginning the voice demonstrates its awareness that the construction is not necessarily in control of its own ruses, that its in-built controls may be transformed at any moment into subjection. "True, some ruses are so subtle that they defeat themselves" (p. 325).

In its very opening, then, the construction sets into play the uncontrollable oppositions between appearance and reality, transparency and obscurity, and mastery and subjection. To these must be added two other oppositions, joined by mutual implication, which are crucial for the text as a whole. In its deceptions and strategies, the construction is calculated, from the outset, to be contemplated and interpreted by an autonomous and possibly malevolent Other. This adversative relation is presupposed by an even more fundamental tension between the interior and the exterior of the construction. "I live in peace in the inmost chamber of my house, and meanwhile the enemy may be burrowing his way slowly and stealthily straight toward me" (p. 326). This sentence is suspended between the interior tranquillity of the burrow and the immanent threat posed by the malevolent Other, contrary assertions which do, however, coexist. The certainty of the belief in the adversary does not disqualify the imputed tranquillity of the interior. The existence of the adversary is certain, only nothing about this entity, by definition, can be known. Such incongruities are characteristic of all of the oppositions woven into the opening both of the construction and the narrative. These oppositions both account for an indeterminable opponent (an exterior element, whether regarded as ruse or an adversary) and are themselves indeterminable, resist any terminal resolution.

It is, then, in the sense of the construction as a literary work, a cumulative opus, that its flaws are, according to the animal, inevitable: ". . . it is always a fault to have only one piece (*ein Exemplar*) of anything" (p. 330). Such a life's work is, necessarily, a limited edition of one. Revising the construction likewise takes the form of proofreading. "I begin with the second passage, but break off (*die Revision*) in the middle and turn into the third passage and let it take me back again to the Castle Keep, and now of course I have to begin at the second passage once more . . ." (p. 342). When the monologue turns to the noise metamorphosed by the creature into a verification of the existence of the malevolent Other—whose scheme is to bracket or circumscribe the burrow (pp. 354–55), the noise is described as an entry in an etymological dictionary, whose derivation (*Herkunft*, Fischer, p. 429) must be determined. There is no more prevalent hint of the textuality of the construction than the repeated use of the verb *graben* and its substantive forms to predicate the activity of digging. As will be elaborated below, this verb, in evidence both in the English *grave* and *engrave*, marks the coincidence of the text and interment.[3] The opposition between life and death must be added to the other duplicities in the text, duplicities whose discomposing facets are rendered more, not less immanent by virtue of their indeterminacy.

The factor of uncertainty in the text's decisive oppositions does not, however, prevent the construction from functioning as an epistemological instrument, a scientific enterprise conducted on the basis of research and experimentation. ". . . it is certainly a risk to draw attention by this hole to the fact that there may be something in the vicinity worth inquiring into (*etwas Nachforschungswertes*)" (p. 325). "I dig an experimental burrow, naturally at a good distance from the real entrance, a burrow just as long as myself, and seal it also with a covering of moss" (p. 336). Although the creature's attitude toward the efficacy of the science varies from confidence ("That truth will bring me . . . peace . . ." [p. 348]) to skepticism ("This trench will bring me certainty, you say?" [p. 358]), such a process of verification naturally carries with it a technology: "In such cases as the present it is usually the technical problem that attracts me . . ." (p. 341). Such pretensions, however absurd, to scientific rigor, join the textual duplicities staged by the narrative, its retrospective (critical) stance toward a whole opus, and its functioning as an engraving, to suggest the close affinities linking the passages of the narrative to the passageways of the labyrinth. The commentary generated by "The Burrow" applies synechdocally to the totality of Kafka's opus as much as to the strengths and weaknesses of the burrow.

If the passages of the construction are the passages of the text, the construction is no less identified with the voice uttering it, with the animal self of which the text is presumably a transcribed expression. In an apostrophe directed at the passageways and the widened alcoves occasionally interspersing their path, the creature exalts: "What do I care for danger now that I am with you? You belong to me, I to you, we are united; what can harm us?" (p. 342). Animal and burrow not only belong together but have, given the setting's sparseness and its removal from the external world, only each other, are united in a symbiotic relation. Identified, through the voice, with the animal self, the construction has only itself to refer to. The voice of the animal is therefore also the voice of construction, the voice of the rhetorical constructs employed in this particular production. Since this construction is defined by physical as well as referential circumscription, the voice of the animal becomes, in terms of this text, the voice of language in general. This perhaps explains why the occasional "autobiographical" references to the animal's life are hastily shunted aside as the narrative reverts to the temporal present and the physical setting of the construction.[4] The single sustained recollection of the past revealing something of the animal subject occurs at the very end of the text and serves only as a retrospective confirmation of the inevitability of that life's movements, registered corporeally in the subterranean engraving. In having recourse only to the here circumscribed by the construction and the now in which the work of construction goes on, or at least is contemplated, the voice of the text abolishes the "subject" which is presumably its source and master. Although the ruminations of the animal are always in "self-"interest, in the absence of any subject, the self becomes the self of language, whose existence, like the concept of the animal, defines the negation of the (human) self.

It is, then, with some skepticism that we must observe the animal "embrace" its work. The creature issues a voice to publicize the construction and preserve it for posterity. But the voice is already the house organ of the construction. The animal "self" which is the master of the voice is likewise already in the employ of this work. The creator finds itself circumscribed by its own creation, by the reality for which the construction serves as limit. The author embraces its work, but the labor, as is evident in the epigraph of this essay, hugs back, its grasp not constrained and certainly not so loving. The author may suffocate, loved to death by its own work. It is perhaps for this reason that air was for Kafka a genuine literary problem.

II

The literary potential of the cartoon has yet to be fully explored. Within the stark two-dimensional plane framed by the cartoon, writing represents itself to the fullest degree of literality. What is revealed in the play between this depthless space and the line is the law of the line. In a bizarre sense, then, a logos capable of representing nothing less grandiose than the universe reaches its highest distillation in the cartoon, where the line is suspended squarely between its representational function and absolute meaninglessness, line acting as line. The animated cartoon opens the dimension of time within the plane of the line, abolishing the need for the separate and successive panels which constitute, in the printed media, the fictive basis for the cartoon's temporalizing. We have already observed how "The Burrow" is, in more senses than one, animated. Like the cartoon, Kafka accommodates a certain level of blunt literality within the action of his (narrative) line. The preoccupation with Charlie Chaplin most evident in *Amerika* also attests to the fact that Kafka's interest extended from the most enigmatic cloudy spots of fiction to the most mechanistic of events.[5] The literality which we observe pervading the work of construction in "The Burrow" makes the story a cartoon (in the highest sense) of movements characteristic of Kafka's entire fictive corpus.

To the strategy, ruse, and dissimulation making the construction metaphoric for the calculated schemes of fiction, Kafka adds a dimension of explicitness exhibiting the head-work in its most concrete form:

My labors on the Castle Keep were also made harder, and unnecessarily so (unnecessary in that the burrow derived no real benefit from those labors) (*Leerarbeit*) by the fact that just at the place where, according to my calculations, the Castle Keep should be, the soil was very loose and sandy and had literally to be pounded into a firm state to serve as a wall for the beautifully vaulted chamber. But for such tasks the only tool I possess is my forehead. So I had to run with my forehead thousands and thousands of times, for whole days and nights, against the ground, and I was glad when the blood came, for that was a proof that the walls were beginning to harden; and in that way, as everybody must admit, I richly paid for my Castle Keep. (P. 328)

Here, images of construction as originality or inspiration are bypassed in favor of the most literal, animal representation. The construction is the product of a head-banging concretized most fully when the hardened walls draw blood. In view of the demystified picture of the head's creation of the burrow, the description of the work as *Leerarbeit*, emptying, is ironic. What the creature describes as "a beautifully vaulted chamber" cannot be visualized by the reader as anything other than a void. If the construction represents a life's work, a complete opus, the *Leerarbeit* implemented by the head proceeds by an ongoing emptying of significance.

The element of literality in the description of the burrow's production extends to the implicit posture of the narrator, the animal, toward the narrative. The reader is asked to believe in the concurrence of the text with the actions which the animal claims it is performing at the moment. If for no other reason than because these actions are mediated by a written text subject to time in different ways than the unidirectional thrust of experience, this presumption is absurd. The narrative confines itself, nevertheless, on the basis of this fictive temporal immediacy, to a now which is remarkably resistant to reversions to the past or projections into the future. The animal thus becomes the agent of a temporal paradox, that the now, capable of feeding upon itself endlessly, is wider-reaching both than the past, which is ended, and the future, which may be projected only so far as its underpinnings in the present can sustain it. Enclosure in the construction is complete because its lateral expanse is potentially endless. The narrative's containment in the now is every bit as complete, and likewise derives from an inexhaustible potential, the limitless capacity of immediacy to generate itself. Spatial enclosure and temporal immediacy arise within a context where the literal is allowed the same full play as the figurative, therefore attaining the same status.

As a figure, then, the construction widens to embrace a certain ground of literality, utter explicitness, within its perimeters. There are varying degrees of figurativeness and literality within the metaphor, yet the entire text remains within the metaphoric sphere. The metaphor is, in this sense, both absolutely open-ended and absolutely closed.

It is as a result of the bifurcations already within the figurativeness of the metaphor that the creature has difficulty in resolving certain decisions. Although the construction is the product of hollowing, it does have some contents, rations (*Vorräte*), animal carcasses emptied of existence but stored for purposes of future consumption. There is an ample rhetoric of ownership in the text to suggest that the creature presides over the burrow like the petit-bourgeois shopkeeper over a small business, economy on a limited but controllable scale.[6] Even in the world delineated by the construction, the world whose existence is defined by its divorce from the presumably menacing exterior, a world entirely closed off, except to the "small fry" who are both its only links to the outside and its food supply, there is enough disquietude to make the choice between a centralized economy and a system of distribution frenetic:

Then it sometimes seems risky to make the Castle Keep the basis of defense; the ramifications of the burrow present me with manifold possibilities, and it seems more in accordance with prudence to divide up my stores somewhat, and put part of them in certain of the smaller rooms; thereupon I mark off every third room, let us say, as a reserve storeroom, or every fourth room as a main (*Haupt-*) and every second as an auxiliary storeroom (*Nebenvorratsplatz*), and so forth. Or I ignore certain passages altogether and store no food in them, so as to throw my enemy off the scent, or I choose quite at random a very few rooms according to their distance from the main exit. Each of these new plans involves of course heavy work. . . . (P. 329)

The vulnerability of the burrow's centralized economy is felt despite the separation from the outside world, despite the burrow's situation entirely within the sphere of the metaphoric. The disquieting element which has already penetrated the metaphor takes the form, in this particular case, of the multiplicity of plans presenting themselves as alternatives to the centralized economy. Satisfaction is bifurcated by the agonizing indecision between singleness and multiplicity in conceptualizing the burrow's economy. Already in the above passage it is evident that it is in the nature of the disquietude to extend, in the nature of the bifurcation to proliferate. The indecision between centralization and decentralization is indicative of related tensions between the head and the body and between the eye and the less critical senses. The substantive stem *Haupt* recurring in this passage derives from the Latin *caput*, head both as a bodily element and in a hierarchy, a derivation evident in the English *capital*.[7] The opposition in the passage between main and subsidiary repositories (*Haupt-* and *Nebenvorratsplatz*) extends to that between the head and the body, between the center of thought and the segmented body, articulated by organs limited in their specialization. In a similar fashion, the eye loses, throughout the text, its position at the head of the senses. The creature's relating to its rations through its nose (pp. 328, 30), as well as its complete preoccupation, in the latter third of the text, with the unidentifiable noise seeming to emanate from everywhere, suggest that the faculty of seeing has lost out to the less critical senses of smell and hearing. Thus, the problem posed by distribution is indicative of a variety of splits and limits already operative within the figurativeness of the metaphor. With a remarkable range, this fissure extends itself to tangential problematics.

The fissure within the metaphoric sphere asserts itself in spite of the attempt to segment the construction from the external world. The split's relentless penetration of the barriers erected to contain it occasions hysteria or frenzy on the part of that staid *Hausherr*, the animal. Having relented to a compulsive desire to see the inside from the outside, and having earned, upon its return, the "sweet" sleep of exhaustion, the creature will be (figuratively and literally) driven up a wall by the recommencement of the unidentifiable, sourceless noise. Kafka has not forgotten to provide us with a glimpse of the frenzy periodically breaking out as the bifurcation serves notice that it is free to penetrate the innermost thresholds of the construction: ". . . then I rush, then I fly, then I have no time for calculation; and although I was about to execute a perfectly new, perfectly exact plan, I now seize whatever my teeth hit upon and drag it or carry it away, sighing, groaning, stumbling, and even the most haphazard change can satisfy me" (p. 329). This explosive activity is in the implementation of plans which would not occur to the creature had not a fundamental disquietude already invaded the metaphoric sphere. But the plans for revision are forgotten as soon as they are taken up (p. 352). The onset and subsiding of frenzy comprise the model for repetition in the text, a decisive movement. Again and again, the facets of the metaphor regarded as absolute and inviolable (sleep, silence, security) will be disturbed by a frenzy-producing articulation (consciousness, noise, anxiety). The absolute belongs as much to the construction as do the factors of decomposition. While the temporality of frenzy is repetition, the bifurcating factors also move progressively, penetrating each successive barrier thrown in their path. It is not by accident that the final plan entertained by the creature is the encapsulation of the repository which is already the innermost sanctum by a new trench (p. 346). This plan calls for a partition to bracket the ultimate partition. This attempted blockage is, in conformity with the infinite regress at the heart of the logic of bifurcation, doomed like all of the other partitions.

By incorporating the literal within the metaphoric, the construction reveals the full range of fissures within its architecture. An a priori duplicity, whether between singleness and multiplicity, Self and Other, or the absolute and the articulated, proliferates itself algebraically within the enclosed domain of the metaphor. The repetitive cycle of disturbance and pacification merges with the progressive thrust by which bifurcation articulates each successive threshold, describing a movement akin to the Yeatsian gyre. Bound like a book, the construction opens itself at every stratum, inviting infinite penetration.

III

There is room for only one metaphor in the Kafkan text, yet this exclusiveness does not prevent the preeminent structure of the Kafkan metaphor from being duplicity. Singleness and duplicity are part and parcel of one another, in their play, mutually interdependent. Within the closed world of "The Burrow" the bifurcations proliferate uncontrollably, yet not even one bifurcation could be registered were it not for containment, the movement toward singleness. The singleness of the metaphor is the still plane where the unending outgrowth of bifurcations inscribes itself. The bifurcation extends, systematically, from one aspect of enclosure (silence, tranquillity, Self, security, sleep) to the next. In this sense the construction, in its limited set of conditions, is indeed a controlled environment, justifying the creature's pretensions to scientific rigor (although in no way nullifying their absurdity).

Throughout the text, the bifurcation, upon revealing itself to the creature, maintains the capacity to instigate a crisis, to create frenzy. Recurrence does not, however, disqualify the presence of a disquieting split *ab origine*, as is apparent in the very early sentence underlined above: "I live in peace in the inmost chamber of my house, and meanwhile the enemy may be burrowing his way slowly and stealthily straight toward me" (p. 326). If the threat is always already present, the fiction of reemergence requires a mechanism of temporalizing akin to repression. The recurrent oblivion of sleep is one factor allowing the discomposing threat both to be continuously present and to emerge, as if from nowhere, periodically.

The duplicity that has been staged by the text will receive its highest expression in the creature's postulation that the noise which has shattered its tranquility emanates from "two [noise] centers" (p. 345). At this moment the infinite regress establishes itself ultimately, for the bifurcation has passed from the realm of the interior/personal/Self to the discomposing sign that has articulated that realm. Not only has the creature presupposed the existence of a possibly malevolent opponent, but it has doubled the fundamentally unsignifying sign through which the adversary presumably made itself known.

On one hand, the movement toward this ultimate bifurcation is progressive. Oppositions staged since the beginning are developed and interconnected until the noise becomes their ultimate expression. There is, however, a sense in which this development is also a regression. The noise, as it will turn out, is the *only* basis for the oppositions elaborated so systematically and disinterestedly in the beginning. As we begin to grasp how the animal has fabricated ontological and teleological orders on the sole basis of the noise, itself merely an element of articulation, the system of oppositions with which we are confronted from the start becomes more and more subject to question. The bifurcation requires yet a further dimension of awesomeness as it moves on. Not only does it extend its range, but it takes on a life of its own, becomes animated, released from the system of oppositions upon which its initial comprehension depended.

The narrative divides itself into an introductory section (pp. 325–33), where the animal describes the construction from a detached point of view as a compendium of accomplished facts and predictable potentialities, an interlude (pp. 333–40) where, unable to contain itself, the animal ventures briefly outside, relenting to a desire to see the inside from the outside, and the final meditation upon the noise which interrupts the creature's sleep upon its return (pp. 340–59). As suggested above, the system of oppositions with which we are confronted in the beginning, and which therefore preconditions our understanding of the situation, will be undermined as the meditation upon the noise sheds new light upon the basis of the animal's knowledge. In the introductory segment of the narrative, an opposition between the tranquillity and silence considered to be the construction's natural state and the threats posed both by adversaries of the deep and congenital flaws in the architecture is systematically put into play. To that paragon of propriety, the creature, under optimal conditions, the construction could (and hence should) sustain uninterrupted placidity, unarticulated silence, and oblivion:

But the most beautiful thing about my burrow is the stillness. Of course, that is deceptive. At any moment it may be shattered and then all will be over. . . .
   Every hundred yards I have widened the passages into little round cells; there I can curl myself up in comfort and lie warm. There I sleep the sweet sleep of tranquillity, of satisfaction, of achieved ambition; for I possess a house. . . . but invariably every now and then I start up out of profound sleep and listen, listen into the stillness which reigns here unchanged day and night, smile contentedly and then sink with loosened limbs into still profounder sleep. . . . I lie here in a room secured on every side—there are more than fifty such rooms in my burrow—and pass as much time as I choose between dozing and unconscious sleep. (P. 327)

Here, silence and sleep join as figures for fragile non-articulation. As described by the creature, silence within the burrow occasionally reaches the plateau of the absolute, "reigns here unchanged, day and night." "The sweet sleep of tranquillity, of satisfaction," is the goal of housekeeping, the reward for attending to the variegated concerns of ownership. Sleep is tantamount to the absence of consciousness (*bewußtlosem Schlaf*), an oblivion enabling the hours to pass in pure continuity, with no breaks in inertia to draw their duration to attention. In its beneficent aspect, the construction is truly an Earth-womb. Though extreme, this romanticized image of tranquillity is regarded as normative and original by the animal.

It is one of the more bizarre aspects of this text that expressed generally, the opposition mounted against the series: interior/Self/tranquillity/sleep/oblivion/perfection takes the form of consciousness itself. Self, tranquillity, and sleep are disrupted, respectively, by adversaries (whether "real" or "imaginary" is not yet important), noise, and consciousness. Consciousness is, from the outset, tantamount to the articulation of hypothetically absolute conditions. It is both articulated and articulating, like the architecture of the burrow. Consciousness of a fundamental flaw in the architecture (p. 332, again, the actuality of the flaw is irrelevant) is what prompts the frenetic attempts at revision, redistribution, and reinterpretation taking up so much of the creature's waking activity. Though apparently operating according to the simple dichotomies Self/Other and security/danger, the beginning segment thus already describes the work of construction as an attempted blocking of consciousness, despite the fact that the construction is itself already a most conscious strategy. From the beginning, an internally split construction is opposed to an articulating consciousness whose effect is the same splitting.[8] Textual duplicity turns upon itself in an effort to supersede its inherent limits.

In the third section of the narrative it will, of course, become clear that the only positive basis for the creature's belief in the existence of adversaries and other dangers is the unarticulated noise. As critical readers we know that even this might be imaginary. The creature might be "hearing something." Remarkably, even though we know from the outset that the text issues from the mouth of an absurd galloping rodent, it dawns rather slowly on us that the factors opposed to the interior/ Self/tranquillity might be mere figments of the imagination, because in the gradualness of its unfolding, the narrative demands that we impute a greater literality to certain constructs of the construction than others, even though, as I have tried to demonstrate, the construction stands in its entirety within the sphere of the metaphoric. It is in this sense that the metaphor is, for Kafka, all-embracing. All of what it embraces is fictive, yet the fiction must also designate absolutes for purposes of legibility. These, like the creature, may briefly stand outside the construction, but they find themselves, as the text moves on, recycled within its fictionality. Other unsettling implications arise from the third segment of the narrative, when it becomes clear that the only possible source of the discomposing threats is the construction itself. If the threatening articulation takes the form of consciousness, and the revision of the construction proceeds by erecting further barriers against this penetration, then the textuality of the construction is barricaded against itself. In opposition to itself, the textuality of the text seeks a liberation from its own functioning.

But I anticipate the ending of my own story. At the beginning of the text (and we still find ourselves at the beginning) the threats posed to the construction's romantic tranquillity take the form of unknown adversaries and architectural flaws. Yet the existence of the enemies is already as dubious as absolute serenity is unlikely. This dubiousness should be apparent from the outset, because the first ontological proof of the existence of the predators takes the form of a literary footnote: "I have never seen them, but legend tells of them and I firmly believe in them. They are creatures of the inner earth; not even legend can describe them" (p. 326). The adversary, whose existence and evil intentions provide the rationale for so much of the creature's activity and determine such a large part of its world-order, finds its initial grounding in the para-literary corpus of legend, a not even very systematic product of the imagination. As the passage continues, there is even a foreshadowing of the realization that the ultimate origin of the adversary or adversaries is nothing more significative than plain noise. "Their very victims can scarcely have seen them; they come, you hear the scratching of their claws just under you in the ground, which is their element, and already you are lost" (p. 326). From the beginning, then, the threat to the creature's existence and security is identified as an at least possible figment of the imagination, that is, as consciousness itself, which announces itself in the noise effecting the literal termination of sleep and oblivion. It should not pass unnoticed that this noise is unarticulated sound, sign devoid of significance. The romanticized image of pure serenity, whole existence, has been discomposed by a sign as inarticulate and absolute as itself. The discomposing sound is not yet subject to the bifurcation of which it is both evidence and cause.

The fictive extreme of the construction's absolute tranquillity and inarticulateness is also spoiled by a congenital defect in the architecture, but this threat, like that of invaders, rests on dubious ground, in this case, the language of the narrative: ". . . my main entrance, I said in those days, ironically addressing my invisible enemies and seeing them all already caught and stifled in the outer labyrinth—is in reality a flimsy piece of jugglery (*eine viel zu dünnwandige Spielerei*) that would hardly withstand a serious attack or the struggles of an enemy fighting for his life" (p. 331). The ur-defect, here and in the two preceding pages of the narrative regarded as the potentiality for immanent disaster, turns out to be nothing more menacing than a "*zu dünnwandige Spielerei.*" No adversary has managed to penetrate the burrow in the course of a career which is now, as we are repeatedly told (pp. 331, 357), nearing its end. The primal vulnerability, then, is nothing more serious than a *jeu de mots*. The weakness of the defenses around the one entrance which *is* open (and given its openness, how impermeable could it be?) is transposed to the animal's characterization of the flaw, the "*zu dünnwandige Spielerei.*" The thinness of the walls at the opening of the construction is transformed, by punning, into the transparency of the deceptions presupposed to be essential to the defense. The derivation of the flaw spoiling the construction's inner perfection is suspect for the same reasons that the proof of the existence of the adversaries is questionable. The flaw is, in the end, a linguistic construction, a pun, a textual game, just as the initial substantiation of the threat rests on extratextual allusions.

The prevalence of the verb *beobachten*, to observe, in the second section of the text, treating the creature's brief exit from the construction, is indicative of a growing awareness on its part that its consciousness is by nature bifurcated. At the same time, the creature's rehashing the concerns and themes introduced in the initial segment of the text undermines the distinction between the interior and the exterior of the construction, a fundamental presupposition of the creature's ontology. As the old concerns redescend after a brief moment of ecstatic release, the distinction between the interior and the exterior is retracted, and it becomes evident that the two spheres are identical to one another. As opposed to representing the possibility of escape from one another, then, the two spheres only serve to reinforce the ineluctability of the bifurcated consciousness.

What the initial moment of joyous freedom offers is a perspectival supplement completing the only consciousness that can prevail within the construction, a necessarily bifurcated and limited one. It is insufficient that, "Then I usually enjoy periods of particular tranquillity" (p. 330), that brief interludes of tranquillity within the construction occasionally recur. The absolute serenity must not merely be experienced. It must be recorded by a second (double) consciousness in order to be absolutely confirmed: "I seek out a good hiding place and keep watch on the entrance of my house—this time from outside—for whole days and nights. Call it foolish if you like; it gives me infinite pleasure and reassures me. At such times it is as if I were not so much looking at my house as at myself sleeping, and had the joy of being in a profound slumber and simultaneously of keeping vigilant guard over myself" (p. 334). By realizing that the romanticized state of oblivion must be recorded by an active consciousness in order to be fully appreciated, the creature acknowledges the necessity of a fissure within consciousness itself. This realization supersedes the simple opposition between security and danger, oblivion and consciousness, established prior to it in the narrative. And yet, if the satisfaction of knowing that oblivion has been achieved is fuller than the unmediated experience of oblivion itself, the optimal happiness may consist in observation, not in enclosure and protection. The creature has considered this possibility:

> The burrow has probably protected me in more ways than I thought or dared think while I was inside it. This fancy used to have such a hold over me that sometimes I have been seized by a childish desire never to return to the burrow again, but to settle down somewhere close to the entrance, to pass my life watching the entrance, and gloat perpetually upon the reflection—and in that find my happiness—how steadfast a protection my burrow would be if I were inside it. (P. 335)

For an instant, the creature has considered redefining the optimal state from oblivion to residence at the entrance, that is, to placement at the foyer of exchange, at the point where the interior and the exterior, and hence the absolute and the articulated, merge. Consistent with its character, though, the animal has considered this shift from an ontology of containment to an ontology of duplicity and synchronic disjunction only for a moment. In the very next sentences of this passage, the animal compulsively retreats into a more substantial dichotomy, posing danger against the possibility of absolute security: "Well, one is soon roughly awakened from childish dreams. What does this protection which I am looking at here from the outside amount to after all? Dare I estimate the danger which I run inside the burrow from observations which I make when outside?" (p. 335).

It cannot be insignificant that in a matter of sentences following these questions, and only half way through the passage describing this ad-venture, the creature already debates returning to the "security" of the construction. "And I . . . find I have had enough of this outside life . . ." (p. 335). Ironically, the threat posed by an imaginary predator projected outside of the system of construction is preferable to the threat entailed in entertaining textual double-vision and synchrony. Aware of the threat implicit in the critical stance of observation, the creature steps back. Immediately, the image of the predator and the dangers of the master/slave dialectic assert themselves: "No, I do not watch over my own sleep, as I imagined; rather it is I who sleep, while the destroyer watches" (p. 335). The possible felicity of interchange between the interior and the exterior, between the unconscious and observing facets of consciousness, has been re-metamorphosed into the threat of subjection and violence.

At this moment, the exterior ceases to be a supplement of the interior and becomes identical to it, a setting in which the bifurcated consciousness and the anxiety prevailing within the construction may be exactly reproduced. The sudden shift from a relation of supplementarity to one of identity between inner and outer worlds is established when the creature returns to its experimental diggings (*Versuchsgraben*) on the outside of the construction, near the entrance (p. 335. Also see pp. 352, 357). From this point until the end of the second section (p. 340), the major concerns of the initial segment of the narrative will re-occupy the text, and in such a way as to indicate that they have not been significantly altered or elaborated. As usual, there is evidence of the danger ("And the danger is by no means a fanciful one," [p. 337]) posed by the predator, who represents, in its own mortality, the possibility of the burrow creature's death. There is a predictable regret at having no confidant, and the usual retrospection as to how the structure should have been laid out. Having only briefly allowed itself to register the results of displacement, the text now begins to repeat on itself compulsively like an obsessional neurosis.[9] In light of this textual cud-chewing, it is no accident that as the creature reverts to the "original" setting of the bifurcation, the burrow, it is taken with the image of its own warehouse, filled to overflowing with meat (*Fleischvorräte*, p. 340).

In the final section of the text, the creature's attempts to interpret the recurrent noise drive it to further thresholds of frenzy. Ironically, the interpretative act presupposes the bifurcated consciousness as much as it strives to contain it. The interpretative preoccupation in this segment of the text is prefigured by the animal's desire to ascertain, through observation, that it is experiencing oblivion. For all of its scientific aspirations, however, the interpretative act only succeeds in conjuring increasingly apocalyptic images of horror in explanation of the noise. As it builds upon itself, the interpretation merges into pure invention, into the arbitrary willfulness of the imagination. As interpretation reveals itself to be the activator of anarchy, not its container, the oppositions that have formed a rigorous system for reading and comprehending the construction and its situation find themselves upon a quagmire. The existence of the threat from outside and of the predator, as well as the architectural inadequacy of the construction, are subjects accounting for

Henry Sussman

vast segments of the narrative, factors which come into play, however, only as foregone conclusions of the interpretative deliberations first disclosed at the end of the text. The fate of these presuppositions, the fate of the way the text offers to read itself, is the shared fate of the interpretative act as it progresses at the end of the story. This fate is, quite simply, ongoing discomposure and apocalypse.

The progress toward arbitrary fabrication in the interpretative act found in this section of the text does not imply that the "classical" oppositions (in terms of "The Burrow") have disappeared. On the contrary, these oppositions endure as an archaeological substratum upon which the frenzy plays itself out. After once inspecting the central repository upon its return from the outside, the creature can still claim, "now that I have seen the Castle Keep I have endless time—for everything I do there is good and important and satisfies me somehow" (p. 342). Here, the unthreatened tranquillity is figured on the abstract level of the uninterrupted temporality prevailing within the construction. The unendingly accommodating time is a function of the full measure of the reward constituted by the labors of construction themselves. After the threat, in the form of noise, has asserted itself, however, time is not so generous. There is a premium on it. "Slowly I come to realize . . . that I merely disfigure the walls of my burrow, without taking time to fill up the holes again . . ." (p. 348). "I do not surrender to it, I hurry on, I do not know what I want, probably simply to put off the hour" (p. 352). The original opposition between the unarticulated ideal and the threat of articulation now plays itself out squarely along the coordinates of time. It is the same opposition which we have observed most predominantly in terms of silence and stillness.

Within the "classical" context carried over from the story's introduction and body, the development of the interpretative process itself becomes as horrific as are the successively extreme images of danger conjured by the creature. As it begins, the noise is innocent, "an almost inaudible whistling noise" (p. 343). "This noise, however, is a comparatively innocent one; I did not hear it at all when I first arrived, although it must certainly have been there; I must first feel quite at home before I could hear it; it is, so to speak, audible only to the ear of the householder" (p. 343). Although the "certainty" of the noise's being "already present" is undermined by the admission that it is audible "only" to the homeowner, at this point in the text the noise is indeed relatively innocent. The interpretation itself will deprive the noise of its benign aspect.

And what was it? A faint whistling, audible only at long intervals, a mere nothing to which I don't say that one could actually get used, for no one could get used to it, but which one could, without actually doing something about it at once, observe for a while; that is, listen every few hours, let us say, and patiently register the results, instead of, as I had done, keeping one's ear fixed to the wall and at every hint of noise tearing out a lump of earth, not really hoping to find anything, but simply so as to do something to give expression to one's inward agitation. All that will be changed now, I hope. And then, with furious shut eyes, I have to admit to myself that I hope nothing of the kind, for I am still trembling with agitation just as I was hours ago. . . . (Pp. 348–49)

The "faint whistling," hardly more, almost less than nothing is, by itself, innocuous. It is the compulsive nature of the interpretative process, the inability to let up, the drive to stay on top of the noise and to do, in the absence of deliberately formed plans, *something*, that brings on the "trembling with agitation just as I was hours ago." It is also consistent with the compulsion motivating the interpretative act that the introspection gravitates naturally toward the most horrific potentiality: "But what avail all exhortations to be calm; my imagination (*Einbildungskraft*) will not rest, and I have actually come to believe—it is useless to deny it to myself—that the whistling is made by some beast, and moreover not by a great many small ones, but by a single big one" (p. 353). This passage represents one of the creature's rare glimpses of insight, one of the few occasions when even a partial realization of the extent of the disquietude enters its discourse. In this passage, the gravitation toward progressively horrific images of the threat is linked to the unbreakable momentum of *Einbildungskraft*, imagining power. The movement of the imagination is as relentless in its drive as the noise is penetrating and unsettling. In this moment, the reader is also afforded a glimpse of what may be the narrative's only discovery, and is certainly a possibility bearing heavily on the interpretation of the construction as a whole, the discovery that the animal is the source as well as the object of the threats from outside. If this is so, the animal has erected the construction against itself, its self the powerless pawn of its imagination's compulsion. A prisoner of the imagination, the animal is equally the prisoner of the construction which it has summoned as an only occasionally watertight dam to stem the imagination.

The ability of such suggestive moments of insight to subside into oblivion before reaching a logical conclusion is fundamental to the story's temporality of obsessive repetition, to its rhythm of consciousness and sleep, anxiety and oblivion, and threat and tranquillity. One reason why the story fails to reach any culmination is precisely the mechanism of erasure built into the animal's consciousness and into the narrative structure as a whole, a mechanism of relapse preempting any overall thrust toward realization. The story is disconcerting in the absolute inconsequentiality of the incisive moments when the creature verges on realizing the full extent of the bifurcating threat. The creature returns to its former anxieties as if the insights had never taken place.

These mechanisms of erasure and the text's capacity to sustain unending repetition enable the creature to ignore that it endows the threatening noise with the same internal indifference and inarticulateness characteristic of the construction in its idyllic state. "I listen now at the walls of the Castle Keep, and wherever I listen, high or low, at the roof or the floor, at the entrance or the corners, I hear the same noise" (p. 347). Owing to the perforations in the creature's own consciousness, the categories it has established undergo a relentless reversal of which it is not even aware. The noise, the menacing sign of a predator imagined to be increasingly horrific, takes on the inarticulateness characteristic of the Edenic state of the construction. The interpretative act by which the creature hopes to localize and contain the threat becomes an attempt to discern articulations within the inarticulate. The delineation of articulation thus passes from the nature of the threat to the only means of coping with it. The creature's admission that it once entertained the possibility of the existence of a doubled sound source comprises yet another instance of unrealized insight. In postulating a double origin, the animal passes from the victim to the agent of articulation. And yet, even in articulating the noise, the animal continues to believe in its exteriority and autonomy, in the absoluteness of the partition defining the categories of opposition according to which it has arranged its everyday life.

With the creature trapped in the cycle of its unrealized insights and regressions into old fears, oblivious while the categories it has set into play in an effort to attain some stable grasp of the situation reverse upon themselves, the only progressive thrust staged by the text is toward distraction and unintelligibility. "But this time everything seems difficult, I am too distracted . . ." (p. 350). "Suddenly I cannot comprehend my former plan. I can find no slightest trace of reason in what had seemed so reasonable; once more I lay aside my work and even my listening; I have no wish to discover any further signs that the noise is growing louder; I have had enough of discoveries; I let everything slide; I would be quite content if I could only still the conflict going on within me" (p. 352). The rational plans to contain the bifurcation silence one another in a babble of unintelligibility. In the service of rationality, interpretation has succumbed to the cacophony engendered by its own schemes. The architecture of the construction, the consummate product of the attempt at containment, is itself now illegible. Numbed by the confusion unearthed in the rational effort to suppress the bifurcation, the consciousness seeks only a release from itself. Once and for all, the inner strife is identified with the animal consciousness.

It is fitting that the no longer comprehensible "plan" mentioned in the above passage was to contain the innermost repository in yet a further partition (p. 346). The idea of the ultimate partition shares the fate of the plan to erect it. The uncontained bifurcation comes closest to home near the end of the text, when the reader is finally permitted a glimpse of the creature's visualization of its predator. As should be no longer surprising, the animal that the animal visualizes is a double of itself, the very image of the animal that we extrapolate from the creature's characterization of its own activity: "It probably bores its snout into the earth with one mighty push and tears out a great lump . . ." (p. 354). In this passage the creature bases the alterity of the predator on the different sound its digging makes. Yet surely a consciousness oblivious to the near-identical relation between the nature of the hypothetical tranquillity and that of the direst threats it imagines might also be oblivious to the nature of the sound of its own digging. Here the text comes closest to the possibility that the animal has been driven to distraction by the sound of its own digging, of its own functions, breathing, eating, and running, contained, as it is, within an echo-chamber of reflection. With this possibility, the text comes closest to realizing how far the bifurcation it both stages and restrains extends: as far back as the animal self which is the oracle of the voice of the monologue, as far back as the narrative voice itself.

With the admission of the possibility that the cause of the animal's frenzy has been its own activity, that a schizoid break has occurred, the text adds complexity to passages seeming otherwise to lend a dignified air of resolution:

Between that day and this lie my years of maturity, is it not as if there were no interval at all between them? I still take long rests from my labors and listen at the wall, and the burrower (*Graber*) has changed his intention anew, he has turned back, he is returning from his journey, thinking he has given me ample time in the interval to prepare for his reception. But on my side everything is worse prepared for than it was then; the great burrow stands defenseless, and I am no longer a young apprentice, but an old architect. (P. 357)

From the standpoint of the creature's naiveté, this passage recapitulates past achievements and the fundamental opposition which alone remains unresolved. But all is not so simple if the *Graber* is the animal itself. A *Graber*, as opposed to a *Gräber*, is not merely a simple digger, but a graver/engraver. The passage simply describing the animal's anticipation of the *Graber* also characterizes the not so simple relation joining the narrative voice, the construction, and the writing which the construction is to death. The above passage describes the animal's entire adult life as having gotten lost in the transition between the undertaking of the construction and the present. The work of construction itself and attentiveness to the concerns of the deep have absorbed that life. If now is the time for some final and resolving confrontation, it is because now is the only time available. And yet, if the anticipation of the *Graber* is the anticipation of writing, the life absorbed in the work of construction, in its blindness, its progressive self-disqualification, and its incoherence, has always been subsumed by the textual sphere. If the *Graber* brings death, that death has already transpired, for the above passage defines the work of construction as the erasure of life. It may well be that death enters the narrative in the hyphens immediately succeeding the final words: "But all remained unchanged" (p. 359). Within the enclosure of the construction, death, writing, and alterity all step into the *ich* set into play by the narrative voice, their claims to that voice equally legitimate. In its final section, then, the text allows its movement of bifurcation to extend both back to the very beginning and ahead to the ultimate end. The bifurcation has penetrated the provisional system of oppositions improvised to contain it, arriving at its (equally) primal loci: Self, consciousness, the narrative voice.

In the conjunction of death, writing, and duplicity which it stages, the all-embracing metaphor, the construction, serves as a setting for the discovery of textual limit. Both representing consciousness and articulating it, the text finds itself barricaded against itself, deadlocked in its internal contortions. Strive as it may for a release from its own functions, the text finds no exit. Although constantly shifting, for the sake of legibility, certain fictive entities *outside* the metaphoric sphere to serve as "objective" indices for obscurer enigmas, these realities invariably find themselves once again contained within a realm of uniform fictionality admitting no definitive arbitration. The construction thus records a bizarre cycle. Contained within its own limits, it nonetheless opens a panorama revealing the penetration of all barriers by the bifurcation unsettling the animal soul.

In tracing the Kafkan text to its (dead) end, this text has nonetheless left certain of its own questions open. The present essay views the selection of an animal narrator in the context of an overall challenge to the notion of subjectivity. By its conclusion, however, the essay describes Kafka's text as finding itself "barricaded against itself" (p. 112) or coming close to "realizing" certain insights (p. 119). The subjectivity and self ostensibly abolished by Kafka find themselves relocated, by my text, back to Kafka's story, which evidently takes on a life of its own.

In light of the creature's obsessions and the repetitive patterns of frenzy and forgetting, the automatic mechanism of Kafka's writing can come as no surprise. The story's circumscription, the abstract simplicity of its setting, shift even the most basic conditions for its writing or enunciation back to within its texture. The self so easily dismissed on the very first page of Kafka's story appears to return in a more resilient form when the story's textuality becomes the subject of an interpretation. But it is a far different self, one so charged, as I have attempted to demonstrate, with repetition and reversal as to disfigure the concept of self-hood beyond recognition even while invoking it.

To be self-contained is not to be complete. Various levels of knowledge are delineated by my reading. Successive stages to some extent culminate or complete prior ones. As much as this may imply an overall orientation, it also initiates the endless movement of supplanting so typical of Kafka. We begin with an animal who knows less than the text of the story and a story in need of some reader or beast to whom it may disclose the differentiated knowledge. An interpretation steps forth to make this ironic situation explicit, but in order to do so, deploys constructs already rendered obsolete by the text under discussion. Like a cornered animal, the present text awaits a reader to release it from its regressions.

CODA: BOSCH AND THE VECTOR
OF DECONSTRUCTION

For Kafka, duplicity is the unavoidable onus of textuality. Whether in the play between the realms demarcated by human existence and the legal code, between the naive and penetrating attitudes occasioned by the image of the Castle, or in the multiplicity of categories finding themselves bifurcated within the negative projection of the construction, the duplicity of textual function challenges the grounds upon which the text establishes consequences and founds its legibility. In pursuing the geometry of metaphor, Kafka attempted to characterize the spatial and temporal settings in which this duplicity plays itself out.

The problem of duplicity in the Kafkan text compels us, in concluding, toward a dizzying question of priority. Like Hieronymus Bosch, the Kafka of "The Burrow" summons the deconstructed world before us as an already accomplished fact, forcing us to confront it in the absence of mediatory accounts of its coming into being. Viewed as an ongoing process whose goal is the breakdown of hierarchy, the disclosure of the monstrosity suppressed within the refined ambiances of culture, and the reduction of the sublime to its animal components, deconstructive criticism risks being subsumed by an orientation of its own, finding itself compelled toward only one pole of the horizon. Repetition is the central problem facing deconstructive criticism today. Even having transcended thematic or substantive levels of inquiry, a criticism confining itself to a single thrust, a single vector along the trajectory from mystification to penetration, brings itself dangerously close to the very progression toward a general truth which it has debunked. To argue that the synchronic dissonances of duplicity prevail and that the vector of deconstruction has played a subordinate role as a temporalizing fiction, a way of legibly articulating the disjunction along the axis of time, is a weak resolution to the problem. The horrific uncertainty which Kafka injected into the master-slave dialectic (which is perhaps most fully realized in "The Judgment") instructs us to ask whether a logic of temporalizing can ever be cast in a subordinate role.

Like the fictional characters' attempts to deal with the duplicity that has already taken hold in Kafka's novels and stories, the attempt to rationalize the simultaneous mutually negating activities staged by the literary text through a fictive temporalizing comes too late. For this reason it is so important that the world to which Kafka's characters awake has already sealed their fate. That Gregor Samsa wakes to see the world through insect-eyes, that Joseph K. awakes to find his underwear the property of the Court, are most characteristic Kafkan gestures. The Kafkan hero wields a belabored rationality to negotiate the bifurcated field of vision he has awakened to perceive. The preeminant characteristic of this double vision is its apriority, rationality, and hopeless tardiness. It is in this sense, finally, that the door of the parable was always open for the *Mann vom Lande*. It was only his pedestrian rationality that could not find the opening.

In the interest of hypothetical fairness, let us nonetheless propose a stand-off between duplicity articulated spatially and duplicity articulated temporally, let us grant the temporalizing vector of deconstruction the same priority that we accord duplicity sustained in suspense. Even here, the deconstructive movement does not permit the completion of its negative thrust. While the structure of duplicity opens itself to articulation along the supplementary axes of time and space, the vector of deconstruction is unidirectional, always leaving the dismembered, the regressive, the monstrous in its wake. In as apparently unrelated a work to "The Burrow" as Bosch's *Garden of Earthly Delights*, Western culture has also elicited an instance of negativity projected positively, has projected a model of *de*construction in the full assertion of its priority. In order for deconstruction to complete its operation, to unmask the double faces of its orientation, it must hint at the unicorns and domed castles hovering above the plane where the fragments of order, the scenarios of regression, have been set out in their ab-original form.[10]

On the timeless plane of the canvas, in a space pressing dissonant actions together within the same instant of simultaneity, Bosch, like Kafka, projects negativity positively, preempts all attempts to rationalize the awakening to metamorphosis with a story. *The Garden of Earthly Delights* is punctuated by any number of shapes that would be welcome in a contemporary science fiction film. To this day no history has rationalized their appearance. If we are to make sense of their presence, if we are to relate these spheres, translucent envelopes, and castles radiating projections to the themes of inversion, regression, and perversion prevalent in the painting, it will be less by dint of a temporalizing history than by the spatial paradoxes which these enclosures inject into the plane of the painting itself.[11] There are indeed strong affinities linking the characteristic Boschian gestures of imposing an enclosure between the viewer and the action, thus internalizing action that would otherwise be exterior, to the inversions and regressions which his paintings, at least on one level, *depict*.

The skeletal man on the right wing of *The Garden of Earthly Delights* is a case in point (figure 5.1). It is indeed fitting that this figure does not rest on solid ground (its legs, rotten tree stumps, are planted on ships), for the figure effects the juxtaposition of jarringly remote stages in the evolution of man. While the legs have the shape of dead trees, the body is an egg whose posterior end is open, permitting us to view an interior scene. All segments of this man are painted in a spectral white, identifying the substance it is made of with a skull or jawbone fragment to the immediate left of this figure. In the image of a bone-man whose body is a shell, the structural underpinnings of human existence come together. The skeletons of the natural world (tree stumps) and of the animal kingdom (the egg) join with bone in the composition of a truly skeletal man, a man whose evolutionary joints have been opened to view in a theater of dissection.

Bosch has not omitted, despite the primordial nature of this figure, to place the man within a cultural context. Atop a platter on the man's head, a musical scene goes on. Music, emitted as a vapor, arises from the top of a large pink bagpipe in the form of a bladder. Smaller than this instrument, human and not-so-human creatures dance along the rim, among them a bishop, a nun, and a naked man who is being led by a bird/man (bird head/human body). The bird/man itself represents a bizarre evolutionary crossing, but it is attuned to this music. The bird/man dancing on the cultivated human head serves notice that the cross-

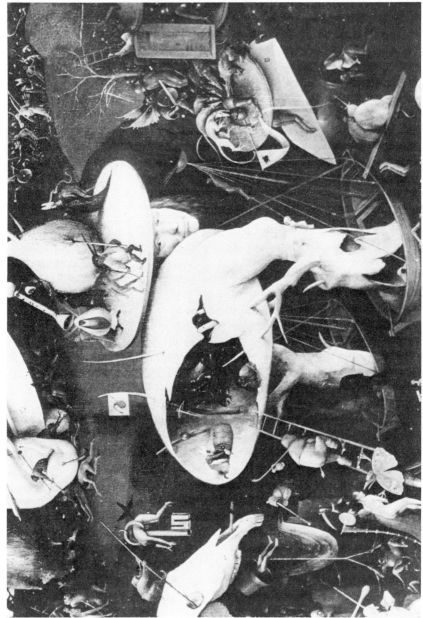

FIGURE 5.1. Detail. Right Panel. Hieronymus Bosch.

ings of diverse evolutionary stages continue in an infinite regress, whether the immediate context is corporeal or intellectual.

The figure of the skeletal man thus encompasses the entire range of human evolution, from inanimate nature to the confections of religion and art. From the standpoint of the stumps, the process promises prodigious refinement. As the representation of a man, however, this figure embodies an almost systematic fragmentation and is indeed worthy of its position as the last "complete" figure beneath the flows of black hellfire. The consummate Boschian expression of this negative thrust is the image of figures, both human and animal, swarming to enter eggs and their surrogates, crustacean shells and spheres. It is not difficult to find in this regressive sweep a context for the bizarre crossings of human and animal life peopling Bosch's canvases. It is furthermore not surprising that the egg which comprises the skeletal man's body should open upon and contain a scene of its own, a small feast illuminated by red hell-fire. There is no more appropriate expression of the negativity of the sweep toward the egg than the egg's capacity to contain, to stage the *mise en abîme*, to introduce a pane of irony within the panorama of space. To perceive through a (perforated) sphere encloses an action seeming to take place in "open" space. To observe a figure breaking out of the confinement of an egg or a crustacean shell, or to take advantage of the voyeurism offered by a translucent sheath, introduces an element of release where freedom was no issue before. The negativity injected by Bosch into the visual plane of the painting in the form of perforated and transparent spherical shapes is the same negativity elaborated thematically in the pictures he conjures of human/animal crossings, inversion, and perversion. It is, then, appropriate that an executioner should be mounting a ladder (how it stands in the water holding the ships afloat is a mystery) into the egg/body which provides a setting for this (last) supper. Death, too, joins the forces of negativity uniting in the fragmented figure of the skeletal man, forces finding their literary expression in the ironic capacity of space to contain, and hence open, space.

The Garden of Earthly Delights is a triptych, a three-part serial. Read from left to right, it extends from the theological origin to the metaphysical horizon of Western culture, from Eden to the apocalypse. Read according to this scheme, the center panel is our earthly world. Yet the left and right wings of the triptych throw wrenches into this history, or, if you like, our world, the world in which the positive and negative forces are in full play, reaches out and digests the extremities. Read thematically, the left (primordial) panel does trace a trajectory from prelapsarian tranquillity to postlapserian strife in the movement from top to bottom and from background to foreground. The benign giraffe grazing toward the back of the wing is supplanted by the vermin playing by the fetid pool in the extreme foreground. And yet, the Edenic upper portion of this wing is not so Edenic. Behind the giraffe, a lion devours a deer and a canine creature is terrorized by a wild sow. The most telling evidence that even Eden belongs to our world consists in the prevalence of the characteristic Boschian spatial ironies. A flock of flying birds emerges from an orifice in a rock-formation, but only to loop two times through the uncannily geometrical holes in the formation before reaching the freedom of the open skies. A flock of walking birds enters, in procession, an egg-shape which is also, at its far end, a crustacean shell. An owl peers out of a perforation in the spherical base of the fountain which is both the geometrical center and the world-navel of Eden. In the spatial irony extending even to the most innocent of its three fictively temporalized components, the triptych resists its preconceived historical program and concentrates on the thematic and textual imaging of negativity.

At all stages of its history, then, the painted text admits a negativity whose highest textual expression is the spatial incoherence entering in the form of the play between projection and penetration. Just as "Der Bau" stages a movement of bifurcation, passing systematically from one dimension of the construction to the next, the perforated spheres, bubbles, and bodies of water in *The Garden of Earthly Delights* enter virtually every context of thematic elaboration (figures 5.2 and 5.3). (Water joins the other Boschian tropes for internalizing exterior action and vice versa.) In the play between marine and terrestrial settings in the right foreground of the center panel, for example, a wide variety of spheres, bubbles, and shells coincides with the images of human cohabitation with the birds and fish. Afloat in the water is a red sphere, from whose window the heads of a man, a woman, and a crane emerge. A foot apparently belonging to no one extends whimsically from the far end of this sphere. The man is holding afloat a huge bunch of berries, shaped like raspberries but colored dark blue. A group of human figures has congregated around this bunch in the water. They suck at it like infants nursing at an immense breast. At the opposite end of this body of water, in its lower left corner, we find a corresponding red sphere afloat. A man peers out a porthole through a cylindrical translucent sleeve at the far end of which a black mouse crouches and peers back. Supported by the red sphere in which this reflection takes place is a clear bubble in which a man and a woman caress one another. Behind these two spheres an admixture of human figures and somewhat larger birds observes the scene. In the extreme foreground (and on terra firma) a man and a woman kiss through the hole in a flesh-colored, veined sphere. Only the

FIGURE 5.2. Detail, Center Panel, Left Foreground. Bosch, *The Garden of Earthly Delights*. Courtesy of the Prado.

FIGURE 5.3.　Detail, Center Panel, Left Foreground. Bosch,

upper body of the woman is actually enclosed by the sphere. Her head and legs are released through two separate perforations. Closer to the edge of the water, a man carries on his back an immense mussel, from the opening of which the legs of two people emerge. Below the mussel, a man, sitting in the mouth of a blue barrel on its side, is being fed a berry from the beak of a bird. In this setting, the spherical forms staging the play between interiority and exteriority also serve as architectural elements in the scenarios of fragmentation, regression, and anarchy being depicted. In a similar fashion, it is the hollow shell of the skeletal man which literally serves as the setting for a last pre-apocalyptic supper. While there is indeed a level at which anarchy enters the painting through its represented images, these images are set loose in a space which has fully acknowledged its capacity to negate and bracket itself. The spatial violence injected by the systematic application of interposed shapes cannot be precipitated out of, is indeed the textual manifestation of the apocalypse framed by the painting. Thus, for Bosch the literal negativity of the apocalypse extends into the spatial setting of the painted text.

In violating history, Bosch has, however, proven himself capable of assimilating the images of innocence held over from the prelapserian world into his apocalypse. However deceitful his image of Eden may be, he has nonetheless included a unicorn there, peacefully drinking at a pool of water. Like Kafka, Bosch summons a world fragmented by a priori deconstruction. Also like Kafka, however, for Bosch there is the possibility of moving two ways, of assimilating the pristine into the sweep toward fragmentation. Does the contemporary criticism of deconstruction entertain this reversibility? Can it discern the unicorns, the alabaster castles, the domes and statuary bespeaking sublime symmetry hovering above the plane where the Boschian mutation has broken forth in all its generosity?

NOTES

1. Franz Kafka, "The Burrow," tr. Willa and Edwin Muir, in *The Complete Short Stories*, ed. Nahum N. Glatzer (New York: Schocken, 1976), pp. 325–59. In a few cases it will be necessary to refer to the German edition. These will be designated "Fischer" and will refer to Franz Kafka, *Sämtliche Erzählungen*, ed. Paul Raabe (Frankfurt am Main and Hamburg: S. Fischer, 1972), pp. 412–44.

2. See Gilles Deleuze and Félix Guattari, *Kafka: Pour une littérature mineure* (Paris: Seuil, 1975), pp. 15, 23–28, 32–33, and 40–41. In their treat-of Kafka as a writer of "minor literature," Deleuze and Guattari have given Kafka's animalism its widest range of implications thus far. "Devenir animal" is an instance of the deterritorialization or disenfranchisement which consti-

Henry Sussman

tutes perhaps the key element of minor literature. By implication, animalism joins a complex including the literature of the politically oppressed, bureaucratic phantasm (Kafka as prophet of future totalitarian and technocratic repression), and, on a sexual level, sadism and masochism.

3. *Der Große Duden: Herkunftswörterbuch*, Volume 7 (Mannheim, Vienna, and Zurich: Bibliographisches Institut, 1963), p. 230.

4. Aborted autobiographical references are to be found on pp. 327–28, 330, 332, 346, and 347.

5. In slapstick comedy as in the cartoon, physical motion seizes control of the subjects of the narrative, shattering the illusion of their subjectivity. Before his identity is revealed, Uncle Jacob appears as a Chaplin figure, "the man with the bamboo cane" (*Amerika* [New York: Schocken, 1974], pp. 14, 20). It cannot also be purely coincidental that the Nature Theater of Oklahoma episode in *Amerika* corresponds exactly, in its position and its scenario of an ironic afterlife in which the entire cast of characters appears in this world as angels, to a wishful dream of Charlie's at the end of "The Kid."

6. The creature describes itself as a "master" (*Herr* or *Hausherr*) on pp. 333 and 335. The most extended application of a rhetoric of ownership appears on pp. 354–55, where within eight lines, "own" and "possess" appear four times. In the German, this rhetoric is even more pronounced, all terms of ownership being based on the substantive *Besitz* and its forms.

7. *Der Große Duden: Herkunftswörterbuch*, Volume 7, pp. 252–53.

8. In a completely different context, Jacques Derrida describes the splitting of another construct initially representing itself as self-present. The construct is, of course, the voice. The disquieting notion of auto-affection indicates a division, a primordial opposition, within the self-presence accompanying the voice. See Jacques Derrida, *La voix et le phénomène* (Paris: Presses Universitaires de France, 1967), p. 92, translated as *Speech and Phenomena*, tr. David B. Allison (Evanston, Ill.: Northwestern University Press, 1973), p. 82:

And here again we find all the incidences of primordial nonpresence whose emergence we have already noted on several occasions. Even while repressing difference by assigning it to the exteriority of the signifiers, Husserl could not fail to recognize its work at the origin of sense and presence. Taking auto-affection as the exercise of the voice, auto-affection supposed that a pure difference comes to divide self-presence. In this pure difference is rooted the possibility of everything we think we can exclude from auto-affection: space, the outside, the world, the body, etc. As soon as it is admitted that auto-affection is the condition for self-presence, no pure transcendental reduction is possible. But it was necessary to pass through the transcendental reduction in order to grasp this difference in what is closest to it. . . . We come closest to it in the movement of difference.

9. Although Klaus Wagenbach informs us of Kafka's "early" (c. 1912) awareness of psychoanalysis (*Eine Biographie seiner Jugend* [Bern: Franke, 1958], p. 199), certain similarities between the creature's behavior and Freud's characterization of obsessional neurosis are so striking as to be uncanny. To begin, there is the gross similarity between our rodent hero and the pivotal obsessional image in one of Freud's celebrated case histories, "The Rat Man"

(1909), in Sigmund Freud, *Three Case Histories*, ed. Philip Rieff (New York: Collier, 1973), pp. 15–102. In this case as in the more speculative *Totem and Taboo* (1913), tr. James Strachey (New York: Norton, 1950), Freud views obsession primarily as a function of failed instinctual repression and ambivalence. Particularly relevant to my reading of Kafka's story are Freud's description of the displacement, transference, and substitution of obsessional prohibitions (*Totem and Taboo*, pp. 27–30), projection of hostility onto potentially malevolent spirits (ibid., p. 64), and a "scrupulous conscientiousness" (ibid., p. 68). I have demonstrated how the disconcerting threat displaces itself from the interior to the exterior of the burrow, and it is self-evident that the creature is overly "scrupulous." As will be hypothesized below, the fullest realization of the story's duplicity comes in the faint suggestion that the creature's lifelong threat may have been all along a projection.

10. What follows is a preposterous speculation, a reversal imposed upon a deconstructive movement that is itself hardly alien to reversal. It should be noted from the outset that this "critique" applies at least as much to a potential and not yet written body of formalized deconstructive literature as it does to any current work—and certainly cannot be addressed to Jacques Derrida, who particularly in *Positions* (Paris: Seuil, 1972), pp. 21, 31, spells out the need for transformation (Kafkan metamorphosis?) within the contrapuntal accompaniment offered by deconstruction. And yet, the falling of a continuously transformative deconstruction in and out of formalization is symptomatic of a certain impasse, one which may also be a factor in the appearance of *Glyph*. In his recent exploratory analysis of the function of the teaching of philosophy in France, Derrida may himself be charting a possible way out of the same impasse. See Jacques Derrida, "Où commence et comment finit un corps enseignant," in *Politiques de la philosophie*, ed. and intr. Dominique Grisoni (Paris: Bernard Grasset, 1976), pp. 55–97.

11. Art criticism has generally interpreted Bosch's paintings in two ways: either as theologico-moral allegories or in terms of contemporary religious or mystical movements and practices. For readings which do attempt to relate the themes of *The Garden of Earthly Delights* to the spatial play incorporated into the painted texture, see Charles de Tolnay, *Hieronymus Bosch* (Baden-Baden: Holle, 1965), pp. 31–34, rpt. in *Bosch in Perspective*, ed. James Snyder (Englewood Cliffs, N.J.: Prentice-Hall, 1973), pp. 57–61, and Robert L. Delevoy, *Bosch* (Cleveland: World, 1960), pp. 94–98.

SIX

WALDEN'S FALSE BOTTOMS
Walter Benn Michaels

Walden has traditionally been regarded as both a simple and a difficult text, simple in that readers have achieved a remarkable unanimity in identifying the values Thoreau is understood to urge upon them, difficult in that they have been persistently perplexed and occasionally even annoyed by the form his exhortations take. Thoreau's Aunt Maria (the one who bailed him out of jail in the poll tax controversy) understood this as a problem in intellectual history and blamed it all on the Transcendental *Zeitgeist*: "I do love to hear things called by their right names," she said, "and these *Transcendentalists* do so transmogrophy . . . their words and pervert common sense that I have no patience with them."[1] Thoreau's Transcendentalist mentor, Emerson, found, naturally enough, another explanation, blaming instead what he called Henry's "old fault of unlimited contradiction. The trick of his rhetoric is soon learned: it consists in substituting for the obvious word and thought its diametrical antagonist. . . . It makes me," he concluded, "nervous and wretched to read it."[2] That old fault of contradiction is in one sense the subject of this essay, so is wretchedness and especially nervousness, so, in some degree, are the strategies readers have devised for feeling neither wretched nor nervous.

The primary strategy, it seems to me, has been to follow a policy of benign neglect in regard to the question of what *Walden* means; thus, as Charles Anderson noted some ten years ago, critics have concerned themselves largely with "style," agreeing from the start that the book's distinction lies "more in its manner than its matter."[3] Anderson was referring mainly to the tradition of essentially formalist studies ushered in by F.O. Matthiessen's monumental *American Renaissance* in 1941, in which Thoreau is assimilated to the American tradition of the "native craftsman," and *Walden* itself is compared to the "artifacts of the cabinet maker, the potter and the founder."[4] Anderson himself has no real quarrel with this procedure; his chief complaint is that Matthiessen's successors have not taken their enterprise seriously enough. The concern with *Walden's* style, he says, "has not usually been pursued beyond a general eulogy. Perhaps it is through language that all the seemingly disparate subjects of this book are integrated into wholeness." "Why not try an entirely new approach," he suggests, "and read *Walden* as a poem?"[5]

From our present perspective, of course, it is hard to see how reading *Walden* "as a poem" constitutes an entirely new approach; it seems, if anything, a refinement of the old approaches, a way of continuing to bracket the question of *Walden's* meaning in at least two different ways. The first is by introducing a distinction between form and content which simultaneously focuses attention on the question of form and reduces content to little more than a banality, typically, in the case of *Walden*, a statement to the effect that the book is fundamentally "a fable of the renewal of life."[6] But from this first move follows a second, more interesting and more pervasive: the preoccupation with *Walden's* formal qualities turns out to involve a more than tacit collaboration with the assumption that *Walden's* meaning (what Anderson might call its content and what Stanley Cavell will explicitly call its "doctrine") is in a certain sense simple and univocal. The assertion implicit in this approach is that to examine the form of any literary "artifact" (in fact, even to define the artifact) is precisely to identify its essential unity, thus the continuity between Matthiessen's concern with *Walden's* "structural wholeness" and Anderson's project of showing how well "integrated" the book is. Where nineteenth-century critics tended to regard *Walden* as an anthology of spectacular fragments and to explain it in terms of the brilliant but disordered personality of its author (his "critical power," wrote James Russell Lowell, was "from want of continuity of mind, very limited and inadequate"),[7] more recent criticism, by focusing directly on the art of *Walden*, has tended to emphasize the rhetorical power of its "paradoxes," finding elegant formal patterns in what were once thought to be mere haphazard blunders. Thus, in accepting unity and coherence not simply as *desiderata* but as the characteristic identifying marks of the work of art, these critics have begun by answering the question I should like to begin by asking, the question of *Walden*'s contradictions.

Thoreau himself might well have been skeptical of some of the claims made on behalf of *Walden*'s aesthetic integrity. He imagined himself addressing "poor students," leading "mean and sneaking lives," "lying, flattering, voting."[8] "The best works of art," he said, "are the expression of man's struggle to free himself from this condition, but the effect of our art is merely to make this low state comfortable and that higher state to be forgotten" (p. 25). In this context, what we might begin to see emerging as the central problem of reading *Walden* is the persistence of our own attempts to identify and understand its unity, to dispel our nervousness by resolving or at least containing the contradictions which create it. It is just this temptation, Thoreau seems to suggest, which must be refused. And in this respect, the naïve perspective of someone like Lowell, who saw in Thoreau the absolute lack of any "artistic mastery" and in his works the total absence of any "mutual relation" between one part and another, may still be of some provisional use, not as a point of view to be reclaimed but as a reminder that resolution need not be inevitable, that we need not read to make ourselves more comfortable.

One way to begin nurturing discomfort is to focus on some of the tasks Thoreau set himself as part of his program for living a life of what he called "epic integrity." There were, of course, a good many of them, mostly along the lines of his own advice to the unhappily symbolic farmer John Field—"Grow wild according to thy nature," Thoreau urged him, "Rise free from care before the dawn. Let the noon find thee by other lakes and the night overtake thee everywhere at home" (p. 138). Some other projects, however, were conceived in less hortatory terms and the possibility of their completion was more explicitly imaginable. One, "To find the bottom of Walden Pond and what inlet and outlet it might have,"[9] worked its way eventually out of Thoreau's *Journal* and into a central position in the experiment of *Walden* itself. What gave this quest a certain piquancy were the rumours that the pond had no bottom, that, as some said, "it reached quite through to the other side of the globe." "These many stories about the bottom, or rather no bottom, of this Pond," had, Thoreau said, "no foundation for themselves." In fact, the pond was "exactly one hundred and two feet deep," his own "soundings" proved it. This is, he admits, "a remarkable depth for so small an area; yet not an inch of it can be spared by the imagination. What if all ponds were shallow? Would it not react on the minds of men? While men believe in the infinite some ponds will be thought to be bottomless" (p. 189).

If Thoreau's final position on bottoms seems to come out a little blurred here, this has an interest of its own which may be worth pursuing. On the one hand, the passage seems to be asserting that a belief in the potential bottomlessness of ponds is a Bad Thing. The villagers predisposed in this direction who set out to measure Walden with a fifty-six-pound weight and a wagon load of rope were already entrapped by their own delusions, for "while the fifty-six was resting by the way," Thoreau says, "they were paying out the rope in the vain attempt to fathom their truly immeasurable capacity for marvellousness" (p. 189). On the other hand, it isn't enough that the pond is revealed to have a "tight bottom," or even that it turns out symbolically "deep and pure"; it must be imagined bottomless to encourage men's belief in the "infinite." Thus, the passage introduces two not entirely complementary sets of dichotomies. In the first, the virtues of a pond with a "tight bottom" are contrasted with the folly of believing in bottomless ponds. But then the terms shift: the tight bottom metamorphoses into the merely "shallow" and the bottomless becomes the "infinite." The hierarchies are inverted here: on the one hand, a "tight bottom" is clearly preferable to delusory bottomlessness, on the other hand, the merely "shallow" is clearly not so good as the symbolically suggestive "infinite." Finally, the narrator is thankful that the pond was made deep, but "deep" is a little ambiguous: is he glad that the pond is *only* deep so that tough-minded men like himself can sound it and discover its hard bottom, or is he glad that the pond is so deep that it deceives men into thinking of it as bottomless and so leads them into meditations on the infinite? This second explanation seems more convincing, but then the account of the experiment seems to end with a gesture which undermines the logic according to which it was undertaken in the first place.

Sounding the depths of the pond, however, is by no means the only experimental excavation in *Walden*. There is perhaps a better-known passage near the end of the chapter called "Where I Lived and What I Lived For" which helps to clarify what is at stake in the whole bottom-hunting enterprise. "Let us settle ourselves," Thoreau says, "and work and wedge our feet downward through the mud and slush of opinion, and prejudice, and tradition, and delusion, and appearance . . . through church and state, through poetry and philosophy and religion, till we come to a hard bottom and rocks in place which we can call *reality*, and say This is, and no mistake; and then begin, having a *point d'appui* . . . a place where you might found a wall or a state" (p. 66). Measurement here is irrelevant—the issue is solidity, not depth, and the metaphysical status of hard bottoms seems a good deal less problematic. They are real, and "Be it life or death," Thoreau says, "we crave only reality." It is only when we have put ourselves in touch with such a *point d'appui* that we really begin to lead our lives and not be led by them, and the analogy with the *Walden* experiment itself is obvious—it becomes a kind of ontological scavenger-hunt—the prize is reality.

But there is at least one more hard bottom story which unhappily complicates things again. It comes several hundred pages later in the "Conclusion," and tucked in as it is between the flashier and more portentous parables of the artist from Kouroo and of the "strong and beautiful bug," it has been more or less ignored by critics. "It affords me no satisfaction to commence to spring an arch before I have got a solid foundation," Thoreau begins in the now familiar rhetoric of the moral imperative to get to the bottom of things. "Let us not play at kittly-benders," he says, "There is a solid bottom everywhere." But now the story proper gets underway and things begin to go a little haywire. "We read that the traveller asked the boy if the swamp before him had a hard bottom. The boy replied that it had. But presently the traveller's horse sank in up to the girths, and he observed to the boy, "I thought you said that this bog had a hard bottom.' 'So it has,' answered the latter, 'but you have not got half way to it yet.' " And "so it is with the bogs and quicksands of society," Thoreau piously concludes, "but he is an old boy that knows it" (p. 219).

This puts the earlier story in a somewhat different light, I think, and for several reasons. For one thing, the tone is so different; the exalted rhetoric of the evangelist has been replaced by the fireside manner of the teller of tall tales. But more fundamentally, although the theme of the two stories has remained the same—the explorer in search of the solid foundation—the point has been rather dramatically changed. The exhortation has become a warning. The exemplary figure of the heroic traveller, "tied to his mast like Ulysses," Thoreau says, who accepts no substitutes in his quest for the real, has been replaced by the equally exemplary but much less heroic figure of the suppositious traveller drowned in his own pretension. In the first version, Thoreau recognized death as a possibility, but it was a suitably heroic one: "If you stand right fronting and face to face to a fact," he wrote in a justly famous passage, "you will see the sun glimmer on both its surfaces, as if it were a cimeter, and feel its sweet edge dividing you through the heart and marrow, and so you will happily conclude your mortal career" (p. 66). The vanishing traveller of the "conclusion" knows no such happy ending, when he hits the hard bottom he will just be dead, his only claim to immortality his skill in the art of sinking, dispiritedly, in prose.

The juxtaposition of these three passages does not in itself prove anything very startling but it does suggest what may be a useful line of inquiry. What, after all, is at stake in the search for a solid bottom? Why is the concept or the project of foundation so central to *Walden* and at the same time so problematic? At least a preliminary answer would seem justified in focusing on the almost Cartesian process of peeling away until we reach that point of ontological certainty where we can say "This is, and no mistake." The peeling away is itself a kind of questioning: what justification do we have for our opinions, for our traditions? What authorizes church and state, poetry, philosophy, religion? The *point d'appui* has been reached only when we have asked all the questions we know how to ask and so at last have the sense of an answer we are unable ourselves to give. "After a still winter night," Thoreau says, "I awoke with the impression that some question had been put to me, which I had been endeavouring in vain to answer in my sleep, as what— how—when—where? But there was dawning Nature in whom all crea- tures live . . . and no question on *her* lips. I awoke to an answered question, to Nature . . ." (p. 187). The *point d'appui* then, is a place we locate by asking questions. We know that we've found it when one of our questions is answered. The name we give to this place is Nature. The search for the solid bottom is a search for justification in Nature, wedging our way through "appearance," that is to say human institu- tions, like church and state and philosophy, until we hit what is real, that is, natural, and not human.

That nature in its purest form should exclude humanity is perhaps a somewhat peculiar doctrine, and one which runs counter to much of what Thoreau often says, and to much of what we think about him and his enterprise. But the logic and the desires which generate this concep- tion are made clear in *Civil Disobedience* when Thoreau attacks the "statesmen and legislators" who, "standing so completely within the in- stitution, never distinctly and nakedly behold it" (p. 241). In an essay called "What Is Authority?" Hannah Arendt has described what she calls "the dichotomy between seeing truth in solitude and remoteness and being caught in the relationships and relativities of human affairs" as "authoritative for the (Western) tradition of political thought,"[10] and it is precisely this privilege of distance and detachment to which Thoreau seems to be appealing in *Civil Disobedience*. He goes on, however, to diagnose more specifically what is wrong with the legislators: "They speak of moving society, but have no resting-place without it." Webster, for instance, "never goes behind government and so cannot speak with authority about it." The appeal here is to the example of Archimedes— "Give me a place to stand and I will move the earth"—and the sugges- tion in *Walden* is that nature must be much more than a place of retreat. She is a "resting-place" only in the sense of the "*point d'appui*," the place to stand, and she is an authoritative *point d'appui* only insofar as she is truly "behind," first, separate, and other. Thus, through most of *Walden*, when Thoreau is addressing himself to the problem of his search for a *cogito*, a political and philosophical hard bottom, the human and the natural are conceived as standing in implicit opposition to each other. Nature has a kind of literal authority precisely because she is not one of men's institutions. She serves as the location of values which are real insofar as they are not human creations. She is exemplary. "If we would restore mankind," Thoreau says, "let us first be as simple and as well as Nature ourselves" (p. 53). The force of this conception is expressed most directly, perhaps, in the short essay "Slavery in Massachusetts," written to protest the state's cooperation with the Fugitive Slave Law of 1850. The image of Nature here is a white water-lily, an emblem, like Walden Pond itself, of "purity." "It suggests what kind of laws have prevailed longest," Thoreau writes, ". . . and that there is virtue even in man, too, who is fitted to perceive and love it."[11] And, he goes on to say, "It reminds me that Nature has been partner to no Missouri Compromise. I scent no compromise in the fragrance of the water-lily." The point again is that it is Nature's independence which makes her exemplary, which, from this standpoint, justifies the retreat to Walden and authorizes the hope that something of real value may be found and hence founded there.

But this conception of nature, as attractive and useful as it is, turns out to be in some ways a misleading one. In "Slavery in Massachusetts," the encomium on the lily is preceded by a brief excursion in search of solace to "one of our ponds" (it might as well be Walden). But there is no solace to be found there. "We walk to lakes to see our serenity reflected in them," Thoreau says, "when we are not serene we go not to them."[12] For "what signifies the beauty of nature when men are base?" If the water-lily is a symbol of nature free and clear, sufficient unto itself, the pond in its role as reflector symbolizes a nature implicated in human affairs. It fails as a source of consolation because, unlike the water-lily, it participates in the world of Missouri Compromises and Fugitive Slave Laws. And this vision of nature compromised finds a significant position in *Walden* as well. In the chapter called "Sounds," Thoreau devotes the beginning of one paragraph to a sound he claims he never heard, the sound of the cock crowing. This is no doubt a kind of back-handed reference to his own declaration at the beginning of the book: "I do not propose to write an ode to dejection, but to brag as lustily as chanticleer in the morning . . . if only to wake my neighbors up" (p. 1). The writing of *Walden* makes up for the absent cock-crow. But he goes on to speak of the cock as a "once wild Indian pheasant" and to wonder if it could ever be "naturalized without being domesticated" (pp. 85–86). Here *Walden*'s customary opposition between nature and civilization turns into an opposition between wilderness and civilization, and nature ("naturalized") appears as a third term, at one remove from "wild" and in constant danger of being domesticated and so rendered useless. Furthermore, this danger appears most pronounced at a moment which has been defined as that of writing, the cock-crow. The dismay at seeing only one's face reflected in the pond repeats itself here for a moment as the text imagines itself as a once wild voice now tamed and defused.

These two accounts suggest, then, the kind of problem that is being defined. The attraction of Nature as a bottom line is precisely its otherness—"Nature puts no question and answers none which we mortals ask" (p. 187)—and touching bottom is thus (paradoxically) a moment of recognition; we see what "really is" and our relation to it is basically one of appreciation (and perhaps emulation). The paradox, of course, is our ability to recognize something which is defined precisely by its strangeness to us, a difficulty Thoreau urges upon us when he insists that "Nature has no human inhabitant who appreciates her" (p. 134), and that "she flourishes most alone." But, as I have said, this aloneness is the chief guarantee of authenticity—when we have reached the bottom, we know at least that what we are seeing is not just ourselves. And yet this is also what is most problematic in the symbolic character of Walden Pond itself; looking into it, we find ourselves sounding the depths of our own "nature," and so the reflection makes a mockery of our enterprise. "For his genius to be effective," one critic has written, Thoreau recognized that he "had to slough off his civilized self and regain his natural self,"[13] and this seems innocuous enough. But the cosmological continuity which would authorize a notion like the "natural self" is exactly what is being questioned here. For us to recognize ourselves in Nature, Nature must be no longer herself, no longer the *point d'appui* we were looking for when we started.

But even if Nature proves inadequate as a final category, an absolute, *Walden*'s response is not to repudiate the notion of intrinsic value. The pond remains a precious stone, "too pure," he says, to have "a market value" (p. 134), and so it provides at least a symbolic alternative to the commercial values of the first chapter, "Economy." "Economy" has usually been read as a witty and bitter attack on materialism, perhaps undertaken, as Charles Anderson has suggested,[14] in response to Mill's *Political Economy* and/or Marx's *Manifesto* (both published in 1848), motivated, in any event, by a New Testament perception: "Men labor under a mistake. . . . They are employed . . . laying up treasures

Walter Benn Michaels

which moth and rust will corrupt and thieves break through and steal"
(p. 3). But it isn't simply a mistake in emphasis—too much on the
material and not enough on the spiritual—that Thoreau is concerned
with here, for the focal point of "Economy's" attack is not wealth *per se*
but "exchange," the principle of the marketplace. Thus, he questions not
merely the value of material goods but the process through which the
values are determined; "trade curses everything it handles," he says,
"and though you trade in messages from heaven, the whole curse of
trade attaches to the business" (p. 47). In some degree this can be
explained as a nineteenth-century expression of a long-standing ideological debate between the political conceptions of virtue and commerce,
which depended in turn upon an opposition between what J.G.A.
Pocock has called "real, inheritable, and, so to speak, natural property in
land,"[15] and property understood to have only what Pocock calls a
"symbolic value, expressed in coin or in credit." One of the phenomena
Pocock describes is the persistence with which various social groups
attempted to convince themselves that their credit economies were
"based on the exchange of real goods and the perception of real values."
Failing this, he says, "the individual could exist, even in his own sight,
only at the fluctuating value imposed upon him by his fellows."[16]

Thoreau was obviously one of those unconvinced and unhappy
about it. Not only did he repudiate what he perceived as false methods
of determining value, not only did he rail against the maintenance of a
standing army and even reject at times the validity of the entire concept
of representative government (all these, as Pocock depicts them, classical political positions); he also attacked real, so-called natural property
as well, and precisely at the point which was intended to provide its
justification, its inheritability. "I see young men," he says at the very
beginning of *Walden*, "my townsmen, whose misfortune it is to have
inherited farms, houses . . . for these are more easily acquired than got
rid of" (p. 2). Here he blurs the customary distinction between real or
natural and symbolic or artificial property, insisting that all property is
artificial and so exposing laws of inheritance as mere fictions of continuity, designed to naturalize values which in themselves are purely arbitrary.

This points toward a rather peculiar dilemma—Thoreau's doggedly
ascetic insistence on distinguishing natural values from artificial ones
leads him to reject the tokens of natural value which his society provides, and so the category of the natural becomes an empty one. But this
doesn't mean that the natural/arbitrary distinction breaks down. Quite
the contrary: the more difficult that it becomes to identify natural principles, the more privilege attaches to a position which can be defined

only in theoretical opposition to the conventional or institutional. The "resting-place without" society that Thoreau speaks of in *Civil Disobedience* now turns out to be located neither in nature nor in culture but in that empty space he sometimes calls "wilderness." This is perhaps what he means when he describes himself once as a "sojourner in civilized life" and another time as a "sojourner in nature." To be a sojourner everywhere is by one account (Thoreau's own in "Walking") to be "at home everywhere." In *Walden*, however, this vision of man at home in the world is undermined by the Prophetic voice which proclaims it. He denounces his contemporaries who "no longer camp as for a night but have settled down on earth and forgotten heaven" by comparing them unfavorably to the primitive nomads who "dwelt . . . in a tent in this world" (p. 25), thus invoking one of the oldest of western topoi, the moral authority of the already atavistic Hebrew nomads, the Rechabites, relating the commandments of their father to the prophet Jeremiah: "Neither shall ye build house, nor sow seed, nor plant vineyard, nor have any: but all your days ye shall dwell in tents; that ye may live many days in the land where ye be strangers" (*Jeremiah* 35:7). The Rechabites were at home nowhere, not everywhere. Jeremiah cites them as exemplars not of a healthy rusticity but of a deep-seated and devout alienation which understands every experience except that of Yahweh as empty and meaningless.[17] Thus, to be, like Thoreau, a self-appointed stranger in the land is to repudiate the values of a domesticated pastoral by recognizing the need for a resting-place beyond culture and nature both, and to accept the figurative necessity of living always in one's tent is to recognize the impossibility of ever actually locating that resting-place.

Another way to deal with this search for authority is to imagine it emanating not only from a place but from a time. In *Walden*, the notion of foundation brings these two categories uneasily together. The solid bottom is a place where you might "found a wall or a state," but the foundation of a state is perhaps more appropriately conceived as a time —July 4, for example, the day Thoreau says he moved to the woods. This constitutes an appeal to the authority of precedent which would justify also the exemplary claims *Walden* makes on behalf of itself. The precedent has force as the record of a previous "experiment," and since "No way of thinking or doing, however ancient, can be trusted without proof" (p. 5), the "experiment" of *Walden* can apparently be understood as an attempt to repeat the results originally achieved by the Founding Fathers. But the scientific term "experiment," precisely because it relies on the notion of repeatability, that is, on an unchanging natural order, turns out to work much less well in the historical context of human events. "Here is life," Thoreau says, "an experiment to a great extent untried by me; but it does not avail me that they have tried it" (p. 5). This now is a peculiar kind of empiricism which stresses not only the primacy of experience but its unrepeatability, its uniqueness. (What good is *Walden* if not as a precedent?) The revolutionary appeal to foundation as a new beginning seems to be incompatible with the empiricist notion of foundation as the experience of an immediate but principled (i.e., repeatable) reality. The historical and the scientific ideas of foundation are clearly at odds here, and Thoreau seems to recognize this when he speaks of his desire "to anticipate not the sunrise and the dawn merely, but if possible Nature herself," that is, to achieve a priority which belongs to the historical but not the natural world. Coleridge had written some twenty years before that "No natural thing or act can be called an originate" since "the moment we assume an origin in nature, a true beginning, that moment we rise above nature."[18] Thoreau speaks of coming before rather than rising above, but the sense of incompatibility is the same. Once again the desire for the solid bottom is made clear, but the attempt to locate it or specify its characteristics involves the writer in a tangle of contradictions.

What I have tried to describe thus far is a series of relationships in the text of *Walden*—between nature and culture, the finite and the infinite, and (still to come) literal and figurative language—each of which is imagined at all times hierarchically, that is, the terms don't simply coexist, one is always thought of as more basic or more important than the other. The catch is that the hierarchies are always breaking down. Sometimes nature is the ground which authorizes culture, sometimes it is merely another of culture's creations. Sometimes the search for a hard bottom is presented as the central activity of a moral life, sometimes that same search will only make a Keystone-cop martyr out of the searcher. These unresolved contradictions are, I think, what makes us nervous reading *Walden*, and the urge to resolve them seems to me a major motivating factor in most *Walden* criticism. Early, more or less explicitly biographical criticism tended to understand the inconsistencies as personal ones, stemming, in Lowell's words, from Thoreau's "want of continuity of mind." But as the history of literary criticism began to deflect its attention from authors to texts, this type of explanation naturally began to seem unsatisfactory. Allusions to Thoreau's psychological instability were now replaced by references to *Walden*'s "literary design," and paradox, hitherto understood as a more or less technical device, was now seen to lie near the very center of *Walden*'s "literariness." In one essay, by Joseph Moldenhauer,[19] Thoreau's techniques are seen in easy analogy to those of Sir Thomas Browne, Donne, and the other English Metaphysicals, and generally the "presentation of truth through paradox" is identified as Thoreau's characteristic goal, although sometimes the truth is mythical, sometimes psychological, sometimes a little of both. In any event, the formalist demand that the text be understood as a unified whole (mechanical or organic) is normative; what Moldenhauer calls the "heightened language of paradox" is seen as shocking the reader into new perceptions of ancient truths.

More recently, the question of *Walden*'s hierarchies has been raised again by Stanley Cavell in a new and interesting way. Cavell recounts what he calls the "low myth of the reader" in *Walden*. "It may be thought of," he says, as a one-sentence fabliau:

The writer has been describing the early spring days in which he went down to the woods to cut down timber for his intended house; he depicts himself carrying along his dinner of bread and butter wrapped in a newspaper which while he was resting he read. A little later, he says: "In those days when my hands were much employed, I read but little, but the least scraps of paper which lay on the ground . . . afforded me as much entertainment, in fact answered the same purpose as the *Iliad*."

If you do not know what reading can be, you might as well use the pages of the *Iliad* for the purpose for which newspaper is used after a meal in the woods. If, however, you are prepared to read, then a fragment of newspaper, discovered words, are sufficient promptings . . . The events in a newspaper, our current lives are epic, and point morals, if we know how to interpret them.[20]

The moral of this interpretation, as I understand it, is that just as the hierarchical relation between nature and culture is uncertain and problematic, so there is no necessary hierarchy among texts—a Baltimore *Morning Sun* is as good as an *Iliad* if you know how to read it. But it is interesting that one of the passages Cavell elsewhere refers to (from *Walden*'s chapter on "Reading") is concerned precisely to specify a hierarchy of texts. "I kept Homer's *Iliad* on my table through the summer," Thoreau writes, "though I looked at his page only now and then. . . . Yet I sustained myself by the prospect of such reading in the future. I read one or two shallow books of travel in the intervals of my work, till that employment made me ashamed of myself, and I asked where it was then that *I* lived" (p. 67). The contrast here is between the epic and the travelogue, and for Thoreau the latter was a particularly vexing genre. "I would fain say something, not so much concerning the Chinese and Sandwich Islanders as you who read these pages, who are said to live in New England" (p. 2), he proclaims in *Walden*'s first chapter, and in its last chapter he renounces any "exploration" beyond one's "private sea, the Atlantic and Pacific Ocean of one's being alone" (p. 212). In his personal life, too, he shied away from voyages; until his last years, he never got any farther from Concord than Staten Island, and it took only several youthful weeks on that barbaric shore to send him scurrying for home. But he was at the same time inordinately fond of travel books; one scholar's account has him reading a certifiable minimum of 172 of them,[21] and as any reader of *Walden* knows, these accounts make frequent appearances there. In fact, in "Economy," no sooner has Thoreau announced his intention to ignore the lure of Oriental exoticisms than he plunges into a series of stories about the miraculous exploits of certain heroic "Bramins." *Walden* is, in fact, chock full of the wisdom of the mysterious East. The epics which Thoreau opposes to "shallow books of travel" are, in almost the same breath, described as "books which circulate around the world," that is, they are themselves travelling books.

All this serves mainly to reinforce Cavell's point; judging by subject matter at least, epics and travelogues turn out to look pretty much the same—the significant distinctions must then be not so much in the books themselves as in the way we read them. And along these lines, Thoreau suggests in "Reading" another, perhaps more pertinent way of distinguishing between the two genres: travel books are "shallow," epics presumably are not, which is to say that in reading epics, we must be prepared to conjecture "a larger sense than common use permits" (pp. 67–68). The mark of the epic is thus that it can be, indeed must be, read figuratively, whereas the travel book lends itself only to a shallow or literal reading. Thoreau goes on to imagine the contrast between classical literature and what he calls a "cheap, contemporary literature" (p. 68) as a contrast between the eloquence of the writer who "speaks to the intellect and heart of mankind, to all in any age who can *understand* him" and the lesser eloquence of the orator who "yields to the inspiration of a transient occasion, and speaks to the mob before him, to those who can *hear* him" (p. 69). Thus the opposition between the epic and travelogue has modulated into an opposition between the figurative and the literal and then between the written and the oral. In each case, the first term of the opposition is privileged, and if we turn again to the attempt to sound the depths of Walden Pond, we can see that these are all values of what I have called 'bottomlessness.' A shallow pond would be like a shallow book, that is, a travel book, one meant to be read literally. *Walden* is written "deep and pure for a symbol."

But this pattern of valorization, although convincing, is by no means ubiquitous or final. The chapter on "Reading" is followed by one called "Sounds," which systematically reconsiders the categories already introduced and which reasserts the values of the hard bottom. Here the written word is contrasted unfavorably with the magical "noise" of nature. The 'intimacy' and 'universality' for which Thoreau had praised it in the first chapter are now metamorphosed into 'confinement' and a new kind of 'provincialism.' But not only is the hierarchical relation between the written and the oral inverted, so is what we have seen to be the corresponding relation between the figurative and the literal. What in the chapter on "Reading" was seen to be the greatest virtue of the classic texts, their susceptibility to interpretation, to the conjecturing of a larger sense "too significant," Thoreau says, "to be heard by the ear," a sense which "we must be born again to speak" (p. 68), all this is set aside in favor of the "one articulation of Nature" (p. 83), the "language which all things and events speak without metaphor" (p. 75). In "Sounds," Nature's voice is known precisely because it resists interpretation. The polysemous becomes perverse; the models of communication are the Puri Indians who, having only one word for yesterday, today, and tomorrow, "express the variety of meaning by pointing backward for yesterday, forward for tomorrow, and overhead for the passing day" (p. 75). Where the classic texts were distinguished by their underdetermined quality—since the language they were written in was "dead," their "sense" was generated only by the reader's own interpretive "wisdom," "valor," and "generosity"—nature's language in "Sounds," the song of the birds, the stirring of the trees, is eminently alive and, as the example of the Indians shows, correspondingly overdetermined. Theirs is a system of words modified only by gestures and so devised that they will allow only a single meaning. No room is left for the reader's conjectures; the goal is rather a kind of indigenous and monosyllabic literalism, so many words for so many things by the shores of Gitcheegoomee. This means, of course, that the values of bottomlessness are all drained away. The deep is replaced by the shallow, the symbolic by the actual—what we need now, Thoreau says, are "tales.of real life, high and low, and founded on fact" (p. 81).

This particular set of inversions helps us to relocate, I think, the problem of reading *Walden*, which we have already defined as the problem of resolving, or at least containing, its contradictions, of establishing a certain unity. Critics like Lowell domesticated the contradictions by understanding them as personal ones; to point out Thoreau's (no doubt lamentable) inconsistencies was not, after all, to accuse him of schizophrenia—the parts where he seemed to forget himself or ignore what he had said before were evidence only of certain lapses of attention. The formalists, turning their attention from the author to the text, transformed Thoreau's faults into *Walden*'s virtues; theirs was already the language of paradox, apparent inconsistencies pointing toward final literary (i.e., not necessarily logical) truths. Now Cavell takes this process of resolution, of replacement, as far, in one direction, as it can go; the unity which was claimed first for the personality of the author, then for the formal structure of the text itself, now devolves upon the reader. *Walden's* contradictions are resolved, he says, "if you know how to interpret them." The reader who knows how, it turns out, can discern in *Walden* "a revelation in which the paradoxes and ambiguities of its doctrine achieve a visionary union."[22] And more recent writers like Lawrence Buell have extended this principle to others among the Transcendentalists. "Emerson's contribution," Buell writes, "is to show through his paradoxical style the inoperability of doctrine, to force the auditor to read him figuratively, as he believes that scriptures should be read."[23]

But Cavell's position has its own peculiarity, for while it recognizes and even insists upon the difficulty of maintaining hierarchies in the text of *Walden*, it goes on simply to reinscribe those hierarchies in *Walden's* readers. Knowing how to read for Cavell and for Buell is knowing how to read figuratively, and this is one of the things, Cavell says, that *Walden* teaches us. Thus the coherence that the formalists understood as the defining characteristic of the text becomes instead the defining characteristic of the reader, and the unity which was once claimed for the object itself is now claimed for the reader's experience of it. But, as we have just seen, the power of figurative reading is not the only thing *Walden* teaches us; it also urges upon us the necessity of reading literally, not so much in addition to reading figuratively as *instead of* reading figuratively. In the movement from "Reading" to "Sounds," the figurative and the literal do not coexist, they are not seen as complementary; rather the arguments Thoreau gives in support of the one take the form of attacks on the other. If, following Thoreau's guide, we conceive the literal as a meaning available to us without interpretation (i.e., the unmediated language of nature) and the figurative as a meaning generated by our own interpretive "wisdom," we find that the very act of reading commits us to a choice, not simply between different meanings, but between different stances toward reality, different versions of the self. Thus books must inevitably be "read as deliberately and reservedly as they were written" because to read *is* to deliberate, to consider and decide. "Our whole life is startlingly moral," Thoreau says, "There is never an instant's truce between virtue and vice" (p. 145). This is a call to action in the most direct sense, and the action it imagines is reading, conceived as an explicitly moral activity. Elsewhere he writes, "it appears as if men had deliberately chosen the common mode of living because they preferred it to others. Yet they honestly think there is no choice left" (p. 5). Thoreau's concern in *Walden* is, of course, to show us that we do have choices left and, by breaking down hierarchies into contradictory alternatives, to insist upon our making them. But this breakdown, which creates the opportunity, or rather the necessity for choosing, serves at the same time to undermine the rationale we might give for any particular choice. If there is no hierarchy of values, what authority can we appeal to in accounting for our decisions? What makes one choice better than another?

This is what the search for a solid bottom is all about, a location for authority, a ground upon which we can make a decision. *Walden* insists upon the necessity for such a search at the same time that it dramatizes the theoretical impossibility of succeeding in it. In this sense, the category of the bottomless is like the category of the natural, final but empty, and when Cavell urges upon us the desirability of a figurative reading, he is just removing the hard bottom from the text and relocating it in the reader. The concept remains equally problematic, our choices equally unmotivated. The result is what has been described in a different context, precisely and pejoratively, as "literary anarchy,"[24] a complaint which serves, like Emerson's attack of nerves, as a record of the response *Walden* seems to me to demand. In a political context, of course, the question of authority is an old one. Thoreau raises it himself in *Civil Disobedience*. "One would think," he writes, "that a deliberate and practical denial of its authority was the only offence never contemplated by a government" (p. 231). The form this denial takes in *Civil Disobedience* is "action from principle—the perception and the performance of right," but the perception of right is exactly what *Walden* makes most equivocal, and the possibility of action from principle is exactly what *Walden* denies, since the principles it identifies are always competing ones and hence inevitably inadequate as guidelines.

To be a citizen or to be a reader of *Walden* is to participate always in an act of foundation or interpretation which is inevitably arbitrary— there is as much to be said against it as there is for it. The role of the citizen/reader then, as Thoreau said in *Civil Disobedience*, is "essentially revolutionary," it "changes things and relations . . . and does not consist wholly with anything that was." But not only is it revolutionary, it is divisive: it "divides states and churches, it divides families," it even "divides the *individual*," that is, it divides the reader himself—he is repeatedly confronted with interpretive decisions which call into question both his notion of the coherence of the text and of himself. In *Civil Disobedience*, however, as in most of the explicitly political texts, Thoreau professes no difficulty in locating and identifying legitimate principles of action. It is only in *Walden* itself that the principle of uncertainty is built in. "Let us not play at kittlybenders," he wrote in

Walden's "Conclusion," "There is a solid bottom everywhere." Kittly-benders is a children's game; it involves running or skating on thin ice as quickly as you can so that you don't fall through. If the ice breaks, of course, you're liable to find the solid bottom and so, like the traveller in the story, "conclude your mortal career." The traveller is an image of the writer and, as we can now see, of the reader too. *Walden*, as it has been all along, is a book. To read it, as Thoreau suggested some hundred pages earlier, you "lie at your length on ice only an inch thick, like a skater insect on the surface of the water, and study the bottom at your leisure" (p. 163). But, he goes on to say, "the ice itself is the object of most interest." To read *Walden*, then, is precisely to play at kittly-benders, to run the simultaneous risks of touching and not touching bottom. If our reading claims to find a solid bottom, it can only do so according to principles which the text has both authorized and repudiated; thus we run the risk of drowning in our own certainties. If it doesn't, if we embrace the idea of bottomlessness and the interest of the ice itself, we've failed *Walden*'s first test, the acceptance of our moral responsibility as deliberate readers. It's heads I win, tails you lose. No wonder the game makes us nervous.

NOTES

1. Quoted in H. S. Canby, *Thoreau* (Boston: Houghton Mifflin, 1939), p. 243.

2. Quoted in Charles R. Anderson, *The Magic Circle of Walden* (New York: Holt, Rinehart, and Winston, 1968), p. 55.

3. Anderson, *The Magic Circle of Walden*, p. 14.

4. F. O. Matthiessen, *American Renaissance* (New York: Oxford University Press, 1968), p. 172.

5. Anderson, *The Magic Circle of Walden*, p. 14.

6. This particular quotation is from Sherman Paul, *The Shores of America* (Urbana: University of Illinois Press, 1958, 1972), p. 293, but the sentiment is almost unanimous, and it is perhaps a little misleading to single out Paul, whose book is probably the single most important work of Thoreau scholarship and whose assumptions are in many ways different from those of Matthiessen, Moldenhauer, Broderick, Anderson, *et al.*

7. James Russell Lowell, "Thoreau," reprinted in *Walden and Civil Disobedience*, ed. Owen Thomas (New York: W. W. Norton, 1966), p. 286.

8. Henry David Thoreau, *Walden and Civil Disobedience*, ed. Owen Thomas (New York: W. W. Norton, 1966), p. 4. All future references to *Walden* are to this edition and are included in parentheses in the text.

9. H. D. Thoreau, *Journal*, eds. Bradford Torrey and Francis H. Allen (New York: Dover, 1962), p. 127, entry 435.

10. Hannah Arendt, *Between Past and Future* (New York: Viking, 1961), p. 115.

11. H. D. Thoreau, "Slavery in Massachusetts," reprinted in *Thoreau:*

The Major Essays, ed. with an introduction by Jeffrey L. Duncan (New York: E. P. Dutton, 1972), p. 144.

12. Ibid.

13. Melvin E. Lyon, "Walden Pond as Symbol," *PMLA* 82 (1967): 289.

14. Anderson, *The Magic Circle of Walden*, p. 19.

15. J. G. A. Pocock, *The Machiavellian Moment* (Princeton: Princeton University Press, 1975), p. 463.

16. Ibid., p. 464.

17. On this point, see Herbert N. Schneidau, *Sacred Discontent*, forthcoming from Louisiana State University Press.

18. Quoted in Geoffrey Hartman, *The Fate of Reading* (Chicago: University of Chicago Press, 1975), p. 259.

19. Joseph J. Moldenhauer, "Paradox in *Walden*," in *Twentieth Century Interpretations of Walden*, ed. with an introduction by Richard Ruland (Englewood Cliffs, N.J.: Prentice-Hall, 1968), pp. 73–84.

20. Stanley Cavell, *The Senses of Walden* (New York: Viking, 1972), p. 67.

21. John Aldrich Christie, *Thoreau as World Traveller* (New York: Columbia University Press, 1965), p. 44.

22. Cavell, *The Senses of Walden*, p. 109.

23. Lawrence Buell, *Literary Transcendentalism* (Ithaca: Cornell University Press, 1973), pp. 118–19.

24. Charles Feidelson, Jr., *Symbolism and American Literature* (Chicago: University of Chicago Press, 1953, 1966), p. 149. Feidelson is actually discussing Emerson's own "literary doctrines."

SEVEN
THE SCENE OF WRITING:
A DEFERRED OUTSET
Rodolphe Gasché

"Time, too, is a function of Shadow."
Roger Zelazny, *The Guns of Avalon*

To BRING INTO FOCUS a chapter such as the one entitled "Cetology" in Herman Melville's *Moby-Dick* presupposes a certain approach to the novel which needs from the outset a justification of sorts. The narrator, Ishmael, suggests that "at the outset it is but well to attend to a matter almost indispensable to a thorough appreciative understanding of the leviathanic revelations and allusions of all sorts which are to follow."[1] The incipience in question however, is a beginning caught in the network of the text, for we are already, as the narrator states, "boldly launched upon the deep."[2] The chapter, "Cetology," consequently, cannot be conceived as a privileged entrance into the body of the text because the outset in question emerges after the narration itself has already proceeded for a long while. But if the narration evolves by postponing its outset, or let us say one of its outsets, until it becomes almost indispensable to the understanding of what is to follow—"when the Pequod's weedy hull rolls side by side with the barnacled hulls of the leviathan"—then this outset which is necessarily produced *après-coup* by the coercion of narration gains a fictitious status which through its ambiguity allows an inside view into the production of the text.

Ambiguous inception, for Cetology is both a branch of a positivistic, apparently non-fictitious science and an entangled, intrinsic part of the writing of *Moby-Dick* itself. As a positivistic science Cetology is exterior to the narration, however as part of the fiction it partakes of it, is encompassed by it and inscribed in it. A movement which undoubtedly will not leave Cetology as a science untouched. Thus, what the narration postpones as an outset until it becomes indispensable to be mentioned is a kind of language, the language of science dealing with whales. In the framework of the narration this language has no privilege, for it is one of the various languages displayed by Melville in *Moby-Dick*, but not in order to expose the failure of language coping with what James Guetti calls the "ineffable."[3] As he ascertains himself, the procedure in question "also refutes the idea that . . . inadequacy may become suggestive of anything beyond language and thus of meaningful failure itself."[4] Neither does Melville, by introducing the artificial language of science, tend to "the scholarship of imagination: the only kind, after all, at home in a work of fiction," as Harold Beaver writes in his commentary on *Moby-Dick*, for this keeps the relation between scientific inquiry, the language of science, and the language of fiction unquestioned.[5] If the display of various languages in *Moby-Dick* displaces equally the language of univocity as in the case of Ahab's discourse, as James Guetti convincingly has shown, then this is altogether true for the unequivocal language par excellence, scientific discourse. Asserting that the *mise en scène* of the multitude of possible rhetorics aims at the expression of the failure of getting hold of the "ineffable" means to miss the fact that the discourse on the "ineffable" is itself a rhetoric inserted in the tissue of the text.

In *Moby-Dick*, to the extent that the novel displays different linguistic codes, these various codes are unsettled with respect to their referential aspect, the referent being either the empiric object of science or the "ineffable" of a certain kind of literature or philosophy. To undo all possible linguistic codes also implicates the fictionalization of their referents. So, if the movements of the text do not permit its approach by means of a concept such as the "ineffable," if its movements seem to be what is essential to fiction, then its very object might be, perhaps, the entirety of these movements. Displacing the concept of the "ineffable" I tend, for the limited purpose of this approach, to call "ineffable" these very movements of the text. For, as far as the "ineffable" concerns what cannot be expressed in words, orally, it has to do only with the operations of writing which find their result exclusively in the handling and shifting of words and codes. Our reading of the chapter entitled "Cetology" is an attempt to put forth, by insisting on certain metaphors, this "ineffable": the scene and the necessity of writing. Such a point of view reinterprets the deferred outset mentioned above. It is no longer this pseudo-scientific matter which Ishmael has to settle before the narration can encounter the whale, on the contrary, it is the *mise en scène* of the scene of writing,[6] its inevitability and its impossible enunciation. Thus, this particular scene which tries "to grope down" into the very beginnings of writing is not definitive, but indispensable as it may be, it cannot be fixed once and for all and is repeated throughout the text. For its *mise en scène* obeys the movements of writing itself which displace its final expression constantly. This expression is deferred backwards and forwards along the line of the text in order to find an enlarged exposition in the chapters "Stubb's Supper," "A Squeeze of the Hand," and more particularly "The Blanket," chapters which I will not take into consideration here.

I will begin to outline this "draught of a draught": the systematized presentation of Cetology, dealing first with its preliminaries by stepping into "the very vestibule" of its uncompleted architecture.

The "systematized exhibition of the whale" is, as the narrator advances, "no easy task," "it is a ponderous task" instead. For what is to be revealed, "the whale in his broad genera," is veiled by the deep. And "what befell the weakling youth lifting the dread goddess's veil at Sais,"[7] sorrow and a premature death, is the "fearful thing" at stake. "To grope down into the bottom of the sea after them; to have one's hand among the unspeakable foundation, ribs, and very pelvis of the world" is what has to be achieved in order to undertake "the classification of a chaos." Thus, the architect of the building, of the system, feels about blindly for the already drafted but hidden, speechless, and mute foundations on the bottom of the sea, having his hand in the basin-shaped structure of a uterus-like cavity. The architect, blinded from the very outset,[8] is meant to outline in his draft nothing less than the chaotic structure of this already given architecture. The object of the architect is then reduced to simply *projecting* the draft of a systematization of cetology, using the process or technique of reproducing a spatial object upon a plane surface by projecting its points, thus precipitating the deepness of the sea, its cavity, onto its surface. The hand at the bottom of the sea is the hand which casts or drafts a net in order to bring up onto the surface the particular constituents of the before mentioned chaos. At the surface of the sea appear fragments of the divided, shattered foundations of the world. Henceforth, nothing complete is to be expected, because these fragments are but classified.

As we saw, by projecting the deep into the horizontal surface of the sea, the volume of the deep is scattered upon "its unshored, harborless immensities." This operation can be understood as the dividing of an original totality by means of its precipitation into a plane surface, disseminating this primary whole into isolated constituents so as to produce this basically unencompassable chaos. But on the other hand, the chaos to be classified is a primary chaos too: a voluminous chaos whose architecture paradoxically denies its architectural nature, for it is a moving structure loosely binding its already always scattered constituents. Because the division is original and because the whale in its broad genera is from the very outset partaking in this primary diffusion, its projection into the flat surface of the sea—a projection by which what had been hidden now becomes visible—doubles the original dissemination in such a way as to render hopeless all secondary attempts to divide the original division in order to classify it. "On this rock every one of the whale-naturalists has split," claims the narrator, suggesting that any kind of naturalistic approach to this matter is in vain. For "the true matter of dividing" sought by the naturalist obliterates the fact that the whale is a constituent of a primary dispersion and an agent of the force of division itself.

Science has at its disposal a twofold method of division: first, the detachment of the exterior particularities from the body of the object, and secondly the dissection of this body in order to establish a set of inner distinctions. On behalf of the first taxonomic approach, the narrator states that it "is in vain to attempt a clear classification of the leviathan, founded upon either his baleen, or hump, or fin, or teeth; notwithstanding that those marked parts or features very obviously seem better adapted to afford the basis for a regular system of Cetology than any other detached bodily distinctions, which the whale in his kind, presents." For "these are things whose particularities are indiscriminately dispersed among all sorts of whales." More decisive is the fact that these features common to the entire genera of whales do not permit their division and classification relative to their particular arrangement. "In various sorts of whales, they (these features) form such irregular combination; or, in the case of any one of them detached, such an irregular isolation; as utterly to defy all general methodization formed upon such a basis." These distinctive features form no regular pattern because they are disseminated all over the body of the whales: as much over the body of the entire species as over the body of any one single individual. Neither the combination nor the isolation of the singular traits allows their being marshalled into a figure, especially in view of the fact that the individuals of one kind of species are basically to be understood as deviations from the fictitious species or family. Dispersed in irreducible and irregular combinations or prominent to such a degree that their isolation allows no classification either, the seemingly distinc-

Rodolphe Gasché

tive features characterizing whales repeat the original dispersion of the whales themselves. The irregular combinations or the outstanding aspects in their irreducible isolation are no deviation from a standard rule in view of which they could be determined as exceptions to this rule, but, on the contrary, the irregular patterns of features or their overruling isolation mark a sweeping away of all possible rules. It is the movement of deviation (itself).

What happens if science descends "into the bowels of the various leviathan?" "Why there you will not find distinctions a fiftieth part as available to the systematizer as those external one's already enumerated." The dissecting-knife of science cuts into a volume, into a space rolling upon itself. The representation of mass in architecture, the word *volume* proceeds from the same movement which characterizes the etymological root of the word *whale*, and which Melville, in his preface on Etymology, does not omit to quote: "Whale. Sw. and Dan. *hval.* This animal is named from roundness or rolling; for in Dan. *hvalt* is arched or vaulted."[9] The dissecting-knife cutting into this volume rolling upon itself, displacing it in itself, cuts into sheer nothingness. As this voluminous space is one of disseminating spacing it also represents the movement of a primary cutting compared to which the scientific operation of dissecting is but a powerless poking about. This is especially on account of the fact that science fancies itself cutting into an uncut volume, into a substantial object identical with itself. Ishmael, "waiving all argument" exclaims: "Dissect him how I may, I but go skin deep: I know him not, and never will."[10] For the "impenetrable veil" which conceals the whale is the fathomless skin which yields to the knife only to give way to another layer or leaf of skin. Leaf upon leaf, the volume of the whale scatters its pages "in its lost, harborless immensities."

But supposing that science, by gathering distinctive features and by dissecting the whale, would proceed to explain the whale by means of these detached traits—it would then delve in sheer cannibalism, in a scientific cannibalism feeding on the whale which feeds the light of science. The distinctive feature detached, cut off the body of the fish, is that by which science enlightens the body of the fish. On this same light as a flame, similar to the burning spermaceti by means of which Stubb prepares his whalesteak, the fish is stewed until it may be served as a dish to the devouring appetite of science. Thus Ishmael rejects the explanatory procedures of science on behalf of this auto-affective and tautological rotation.[11] But does the theoretical auto-affection not simulate the rolling of the volume of the whale on itself? No, for the rolling of the whale is a movement of unfolding, rolling away from a merely fictitious identity unflaggingly deferring its occurence. Undermining every possible outset of its movement, the volume of the whale is a pure displacement of this movement itself: the constant disruption of the circuit so as to produce its unfolding into space and the projection of its volume into the scattering and scattered surface. The implications of these apparently abstract developments will become more evident as we proceed.

Now, if the scientific approach thus characterized fails to give an account of the whale, "what then remains?" What remains is an irreducible residue concerning the nature of the hitherto unmastered whale and the only remaining possibility in dealing with it. Both remnants are congenital to each other. What remains is "nothing but to take hold of the whales bodily, in their entire liberal volume, and boldly sort them that way."

"But it is a ponderous task," "a fearful thing," "no ordinary letter-sorter in the post-office is equal to it." Why this is the case may soon become clear. Who is the subject that can undertake the endeavor of such an essay? The subject in question will have to make a covenant with the Leviathan, otherwise "the hope of him is in vain." A covenant, in other words, a written agreement binding both the Leviathan and the narrator, inserting them as subjects in a textual tissue. The possibility of such a contract had to be earned and the narrator had to swim "through libraries" and to sail "through oceans." The narrator, Ishmael, had to assume his being an outcast: the outcast son of Abraham and Hagar according to the account in *Genesis*, had to stray about the same *Scriptures* where the other outcast, the Leviathan, resides. The covenant between the two outcasts can be only concluded in the sense that both of them are wandering through the textual network of the same body of writing. Both of them are letters in this scriptural body. The covenant inscribes the narrator into a tissue which surrounds him in such a way as to unsettle his identity entirely. This is the fearful thing to which no ordinary letter-sorter in the post-office is equal. The letter-sorter hinted at by Ishmael here reminds us of course of Bartleby, who had to deal with those letters which "on errands of life . . . speed to death."[12] Bartleby undoubtedly is an ordinary letter-sorter who is not equal to his task, for he is overcome by the letters which pull him to death. Bartleby as an ordinary letter-sorter is no exegete of the letters, he does not take hold of the letters bodily, in their entire volume, in order to sort them boldly that way. Bartleby does not assume from the outset the dispersing movement of the letters which circulate only to leave behind them the traces of death. Taking hold of the letters bodily entails one's facing being crossed out by their movement. Taking hold of the letter implies assuming the mark of the letter in one's own body, being outcast from one's own identity and thus being thrown into the deadly movement of its straying. Bartleby, by not having faced this inevitable destiny of the letters, without destination, is henceforth their ultimate receiver in the Dead Letter Office: he has to die, not having made a covenant with these letters by means of which he would have become one of them himself. These letters have no addressee, and only the contract by means of which he is struck dead would have made him circulate endlessly, marked by the sign of death. Ishmael, on the contrary, assumes that he is an outcast and faces being crossed out by the letter. Thus, he is able to continue his circulation. Narrating the story of Ahab and the Whale, he adds himself as a letter to the floating library containing the undelivered books.

No surprise, then, if the narrator, offering his endeavors to establish at least "some sort of popular comprehensive classification," cannot pretend to anything complete. "Any human thing being supposed to be complete, must for that very reason infallibly be faulty," claims Ishmael. The architecture of the attempted classification is, as we saw, only a projection into a plane surface of the always already scattered deep. Compared to the abyss, the bottomless bottom of the worlds, the human attempt to banish it into a plane surface remains inadequate, but as the deep is already the movement of eternal dispersion, it defers completeness forever. Of this primary incompleteness no definite account is possible. So, finally, after having exposed his system, Ishmael can assert that he kept his promise: "I now leave my cetological system standing thus unfinished, even as the great Cathedral of Cologne was left, with the crane still standing upon the top of the uncompleted tower. For small erections may be finished by their first architects; grand ones, ever leave the copestone to posterity. God keep me from ever completing anything." Two other reasons why the system of Cetology cannot be finished need to be mentioned. First: Moby-Dick, the white whale, is in no way its copestone, but on the contrary, shatters the whole system. Notwithstanding his belonging to the family of the Sperm Whale, he circumvents the entire group in the sense that he is the pure movement of deviation. The Sperm Whale's head surpasses by the singularity and isolation of his outstanding features, the whiteness of his skin, his grandeur, etc. his entire class so as to shake radically its thorough definition. With him Cetology as a systematized exhibition of the whale is unshored, spread out again into harborless immensities. The movement of dispersion which verifies the whole genera is true of its head: a chapter can undo a book if the book strives for completeness. Secondly: Ishmael elaborates his classification solely in order to dethrone a usurper upon the throne of the sea, that is to say, the Greenland Whale. Thus,

Ishmael's system is "Charing Cross," the geometric center of the circumference of old London where public hangings used to be held. The decapitation of the former monarch is not only the effect of the Sperm Whale's grandeur, of its magnificence, but of the utmost ferocity which defines it as the agency of beheading itself, as the agency of smashing all orders to such a degree that his own head cannot be erected any more as a marshalling principle.

Two books have hitherto tried "to put the living sperm whale" before the reader which "at the same time in the remotest degree succeed in the attempt." So it happens that "the sperm whale, scientific or poetic, lives not complete in any literature. Far above all other hunted Whales, his is an unwritten life." *Moby-Dick*, consequently, is Ishmael's *essai* to write this unwritten life, to make the Sperm Whale live complete in literature. Ishmael, however, did not promise anything complete. How is this to be understood? The Sperm Whale's life is yet an unwritten life. Only by writing this life does it become complete in literature. The two books which pretend to put it before us, write *on* the whale. By writing *on* the whale they prove to have little knowledge of it. For the Sperm Whale lives in literature only insofar as it becomes the book itself, as its voluminous grandeur coincides with the volume of the book. A white leaf as long as its life has not been written. The Sperm Whale comes to life only by tracing into this white sheet the furrows or the wrinkles of its trajectory. Inseminating the white surface, writing opens in its space the volume constituted by disseminated marks left as traces of the whale's movement. Through this deadly path the Sperm Whale lives its life, its only possible life, a life in literature which coincides with an unflagging crosscut and crossing out. Only in such a way does the Sperm Whale live complete in literature. His course, however, like those letters which continue speeding to death without any destinator, cannot be mastered. A book, even if it is the written life of the Sperm Whale, is unable to comprehend his uncontrollable movement. Therefore, Ishmael cannot pretend to write anything complete because both the cetological system, as well as *Moby-Dick*, are but the traces left of the Sperm Whale's irreducible movement. Both the cetological system and "this whole book" are "but a draught—nay, but the draught of a draught."

If the Sperm Whale lives solely in literature and if a single book cannot comprehend its untameable motion, its complete life manifests itself in endless substitutions of one book for another. So it happens that "though of real knowledge there be little, yet of books there are plenty." As the whale's nature is such that you can only make it live by letting it write its life, and as this life cannot be comprehended in one book, one

Rodolphe Gasché

book opens in its volume the necessities of its further supplementation by other books. The hidden chaotic architecture concealed in the bottom of the sea, whose foundations Ishmael strives blindly to elucidate, is this never to be perfected library he swims through. Projecting it up to the surface, making its books emerge, Ishmael produces only a draft of a draft, because the primary library, without regard to its secondary scattering by means of its projection, is in itself nothing but an incomplete structure. The draft of the draft corresponds to the forever tentative "popular comprehensive classification," to the "easy outline for the present, hereafter to be filled in all its departments by subsequent laborers." These subsequent laborers are not only supposed to fill out the departments which Ishmael has left unfilled, since he writes only the life of the Sperm Whale, but to incorporate unknown whales into the system hereafter, to be "caught and marked." Because they strive for the impossible exhibition of the whale's complete life, they are forced to subdue themselves to the necessity of writing: the endless supplementing of one book by another. As writing is the proper object of literature, the always escaping whale or the never to be mastered movement of writing cannot once and for all be caught in one volume. The unfinished architecture is the unlimited structure of the *architexture*, of the primary text, of the original movements of writing which, as the unique object of literature, permits only its endless repetition through supplementary supplements. An inherent movement of writing, it leaves no hope of ever getting hold of this primary object of literature. Returning to what remains if neither exterior nor interior distinctive features are apt for the classification of whales, the remaining necessity "to take hold of the whale bodily, in his entire liberal volume," entails the elaboration of "the Bibliographical System here adopted." This Bibliographical System consists in the copying of books, mainly by tearing out pages of the Scriptures to rewrite them, but also in producing, in view of what has already been written, new books to be inserted into the library. The Bibliographical System suggests that there are only original books in regard to which one can only do supplementary and subsequent work. As the whale lives only as literature, in the ambiguous way previously mentioned, writing on the whale implies starting off fatally with former books on this matter: the original book as the Holy Scriptures.[13] But as the Bibliographcal System serves to support a classification of books in a library, it implies their being ordered in regard to their magnitude. But before entering the provisional draft of the architecture to follow, we cannot help staying for the present a while longer in its vestibule. Before whales can be classified in such an order, further reasons for their liberal volume must be presented.

"First: The uncertain, unsettled condition of this science of Cetology is in the very vestibule attested by the fact, that in some quarters it still remains a moot point whether a whale be a fish." By definition Cetology can only be a science, a logical discourse, if it deals with *Cetacea*, which, according to their etymological root deriving from the Latin *cetus* and the Greek *ketos* are sea monsters or huge fish. As long as this has not been established once and for all, cetology remains in "utter confusion." Defining the whale to be a mammal, as Linnaeus does, entails its banishment "from the water," the water which is the element of the whale, which thus is a fish. Without this fundamental acknowledgment, Cetology remains a pure aberration and hence lacks all scientific and logical value. Waiving all pseudo-scientific arguments which do not assume the etymological significance of Cetology as a science of huge sea monsters, and which are erroneous since they presuppose a non-fictitious status of the whale as something exterior to a scientific or poetic approach, Ishmael takes "the good old fashioned ground that the whale is a fish, and call(s) holy Jonah to back" him. Here we have to deal with another aspect of the already mentioned covenant: Jonah provides a certain substantiating assistance, the Bible being the ultimate source of Cetology. By this token Jonah, or the first literary emergence of the Leviathan, furnishes Ishmael with a back: Ishmael's belief in Jonah's being devoured by a sea-monster. Moreover, a phantasmatic or fictitious dimension of Cetology as a science, as a well ordered system, is revealed here. For the anticipation of the draft of the architecture to follow does not only need the support of a former architecture, of a previous writing to give consistency to a systematic elaboration, but every fiction seems to rest upon an irreducible tissue of a primary yet unfinished fiction that it has to rewrite and to supplement. This is true too of science as a positivistic discourse which constitutes itself solely through the repression of its fictitious character, which nevertheless continues its haunting, as it were, in the form of a blind spot in the scientific discourse which being unthought nevertheless orders its structure.

Now, "this fundamental thing settled (that the whale be a fish), the next point is, in what internal respect does the whale differ from other fish . . . Linnaeus has given you those terms. But in brief, they are these: lungs and warm blood; whereas all other fish are lungless and cold blooded." Putting forth this difference in the species of fish in general, difference which sorts fish into common fish and sea-monsters of ambiguous natures, Ishmael reinscribes the scientific discourse with its positivistic knowledge into the fictitious network of Cetology, encompassing science by the element in its discourse which has been suppressed as repellent: the phantasmatical source of its birth.

Rodolphe Gasché

We are already familiar with the idea that the interior differences of the whale are of no great value in its understanding. Science consequently offers little resistance to its reinscription into Cetology. How about the exterior features which distinguish whales? I quote: "Next: how shall we define the whale, by his obvious externals, so as conspicuously to label him for all time to come? To be short, then, a whale is a spouting fish with a horizontal tail." It should first be emphasized that what enters into this definition are the obvious externals of the whale which one can take hold of if the whale appears at the surface of the sea, as the result of its projection into the surface which separates the depth and the surface above the sea. In regard to what is seen of the whale, this definition labels it as an axial section constituted by the horizontal surface of the sea and the vertical dimension of the depth and the height. Labelling it that way, the whale becomes the instance of disrupting the surface. Being a label, this linguistic definition, as J. Guetti puts it, binds the whale for all time to come into language according to the archaic meaning of label: band, fillet. Caught forever in the net of language, the whale, in regard to its determination as an axial section, cannot be considered anymore as an object exterior to language. For disrupting the plane surface is nothing less than the inscription of a mark into its hitherto virgin space, the opening of a gap in a surface. And indeed what does the definition, "a spouting fish with a horizontal tail," signify but the movement of this interruption and the created blank space, the label, ready for the entry of subsequent data? This blank space is a featureless place, a dash substituting for an impossible exteriority of language, which as we shall yet see, is to be filled with names. It is a featureless space insofar as the definition retains of the whale only those features which although exterior ones, nevertheless draw simply the interrupting gesture. What science has distinguished as specific features of the whale is going to be subsequently distributed in the ripped up space.

Ishmael goes on as follows: "However contracted that definition it is the result of an expanded meditation." By reducing the features to a mere axial section, the definition draws the whale together into a movement whose monstrosity, however, is hardly diminished in light of its ripping the immaculate surface. This contracted definition, as the minimal *Tractatus Cetaceus*, is established according to the initial contract, the binding agreement which Ishmael has made with the Leviathan, who is the haunting movement of writing in the Scriptures. As the "result of an expanded meditation," of Ishmael's cruising through the libraries, of a meditation taking the "measure of what is to be defined," the contracted definition is "cogent" as it couples two terms: tail and spout. "But the last term of the definition is still more cogent, as coupled with the first." The definition is convincing, for it contracts two terms thus paired together by means of a copula. The expanded meditation thus extends outwardly the sexual overdetermination of the interrupting movement which takes place in the axial section, and it emphasizes the congenitality of sexuality and writing.

Once "this ground-plan of Cetology" is established as an empty space ripped in an unspotted surface, then "come the grand divisions of the entire whale host." Now that the necessity of dissecting the whale or of looking for its exterior features has been overcome, the multitude of the whales can be inscribed into the blank of the definition. "First: According to magnitude I divide the whales into primary BOOKS (sub-divisible into CHAPTERS), and these shall comprehend them all, both small and large." If such be the case, it remains, however, dubious, for as Ishmael *finally* states this system, it is left unfinished, uncompleted. It remains questionable, uncertain that the system will comprehend the entire host, both the guests that it accomodates *and* the strangers who are perhaps its enemies. But let's leave this undecided. In view of the before mentioned definition opening up the twofold di-vision of the space in which the entire whale host is now to be inscribed, the obvious and decisive externals of the whale are the spout and the horizontal tail. They are in sequel, not supplemented by other distinctive features which could be used as implements of the classification. On the contrary, Ishmael draws the grand divisions only with regard to the magnitude of the initial externals which constitute the definition. So it happens that the whales are only classified according to their size. If the contracted definition labels a primary aspect of writing, a decisive aspect of the scene of writing which we still have to render more precise by further details, the opened gap in the surface has to be filled out with books which, according to the magnitude of their object and the ferocity of their writing subject, are to be classified in view of their proximity to the initial ripping act constituting writing.

The three primary BOOKS are classified in such an order. It is re-markable, however, that these three BOOKS ordered on the basis of the hugeness of their agent should infringe on this rule in the classification of the chapters of the third BOOK, where the porpoise is itemized in an inverse or counterclockwise order. For Ishmael classifies the chapters of the third BOOK in such a way as to end with "the largest kind of Por-poise." The porpoise now, and this might be a first hint of an explana-tion, is either "the great Sperm Whale himself in miniature," or "he is chiefly found in the vicinity of that FOLIO." The CHAPTERS in which the BOOKS are divided live as *capitulli* and as canons under the rule of each

Rodolphe Gasché

BOOK. But as the CHAPTERS of the third BOOK are ordered in an inverse direction and as the Porpoise refers in its aspects to the whales of the first BOOK, the third one is re-bound into the first one and included in its Volume. Or is this rebinding to be understood as a counterclockwise movement which erases, in a to and fro movement, all the distinctions which have been established, so as to leave this cetological system incomplete for all time? There are three primary BOOKS: the FOLIO, the OCTAVO, and the DUODECIMO whale. This order does not include the Quarto. As is observed in a footnote, the whales of the second BOOK, "though smaller than those of the former order, nevertheless retain a proportionate likeness to them in figure, yet the bookbinder's Quarto volume in its diminished form does not preserve the shape of the Folio volume, but the Octavo volume does." The OCTAVO and DUODECIMO whales are but diminished sizes of the FOLIO whale, which is a result of the corresponding folding of the original folio leaf: a folio leaf representing a once-folded page, thus not only the leaf of the first and greatest book but also the leaf containing the elementary fold. As a folio is also a manuscript of a book, it might, according to the Bibliographical System adopted by the narrator, be a copied page of the Scriptures, a single page dealing with the Leviathan, torn out of the Holy Bible and folded successively in such a way as to give birth to all the books required to comprehend the entire whale host. The Leviathan as the one elementary large and formidable fold engenders the volume of its yet unfolded multiple folds.

What these three primary BOOKS contain according to their division into CHAPTERS are merely names. In the first CHAPTER of the first BOOK, where the narrator situates the Sperm Whale, no particularities of this whale are set forth. "All his peculiarities will, in many other places, be enlarged upon. It is chiefly with his name that I now have to do." The CHAPTERS, as the heads of the BOOKS, are filled out with names which represent somehow the heads of the whales such that they constitute a gallery of appellations. These names, moreover, are bestowed on the whales. To bestow, from *stow*, to *stowen* (ME) derives from the Greek *stylos*: pillar. Functioning as pillars, the names support the vaulting volume of the Cetological System as well as of the body of the whale, so as to form the before-mentioned gallery. The attribution of the names to the various whales needs some further investment of our attention, for the names are supposed to distinguish sufficiently the creatures to be classified. First it has to be remarked that the names bestowed on the various species derive from those particular features which until now had not been taken into account: the Sperm Whale is denominated according to the spermaceti which is derived from it, the Fin-Back derives his appellation from his "grand distinguishing feature," and so on, from features which are conspicuous objects. The distinguishing traits, however, which positivistic science has used to construct the sole "theoretic species" are, since only the most outstanding ones from each species are used in the nomenclature, isolated so as to overrule all other ones. In doing so, Ishmael sticks to his former declaration that no system can be established on the ground of a marshalling of the different features. Only the irregular isolation of one obvious feature serves as the nomenclature. Secondly: as the whales are already named, especially "by their forecastle appellation," and as there are plenty of these names, utter confusion reigns regarding the identity of the species they are meant to denote. Concerning the Right Whale for instance, the narrator states as follows: "There is a deal of obscurity concerning the identity of the species thus multitudinously baptized." All the titles attributed to the whale which is to be included in the second species of the FOLIO are "indiscriminately" attributed. Partially because, and this is altogether true for most of the "forecastle names," the whales are "curiously named," or their names are inadequate insofar as they denote features common to all whales (this is the case of the Hump Back and the Black Fish), or their names are "indistinct" (in the case of the Killer), and so forth. Thus, Ishmael ascertains that "where any name happens to be vague and inexpressive" he "shall say so, and suggest another." But notwithstanding their indistinctness, "the popular fisherman names for all these fish . . . generally . . . are the best," and actually in only one special case, in the case of the Huzza Porpoise, does the narrator attribute a name of his "own bestowal, for there are more than one sort of porpoises, and something must be done to distinguish them." In all the other cases, Ishmael chooses one name among the crowd of already given names or he conserves the only popular name available.

Now what takes place by inscribing names as CHAPTERS into the three primary BOOKS is a contraction of the swarm of words and names into one single appellation to designate the volume of each species. What is intended here is an appropriate nomenclature which designates the whale relative to its "more essential particulars," which are its isolated outstanding features. But even if Ishmael does not thoroughly succeed in this attempt, its purpose remains to reduce the multiplicity of the swarming appellations. Consequently, the question might be asked if this failure is not inevitable, for does one name suffice to encompass the volume of its signified? Does not the manifold nature itself of the monstrous creature to be designated produce the profusion of its appellations? For as one name cannot exhaust the whale's volume, the supplementary creation of names might be more appropriate to its nature. Undoubtedly this is true to a certain degree, but the name, however appropriate, incorporated into the system, does not pretend to sound the deep, a sounding which produces only sounds, names. It does not intend to grasp for an essence of the volume insofar as the volume is its own constant and continuous deferring. The names attributed to the CHAPTERS are, as we saw, only formed in view of an outstanding irregular feature. This feature, and thus the name, in no way designates the totality of its object. In relation to an eventual essence of the whale even the best names remain inappropriate. For as a book or writing displaces constantly the occurrence of something as its meaning, and thus opens up the tradition of endless exegesis, its title, as the titles of its chapters, renders salient only superficial marks which in no case exhaust its movement. And as most of the names of the enumerated whales are drawn from features common to all whales, the specific names have no necessary reference to a salient character, such that, strictly speaking, they designate nothing at all. Which is all the more true of the relation of the name to the entire volume of what it signifies.

What, then, is the function of the name, if it has no necessary link to what it designates? Its role is merely to call a first articulation into the volume constituted by the ripped up surface, to inscribe it in this volume as a rumour, and more specifically, to reinscribe the verbal sound of a name into the scene of writing. Those fabulous and "wild rumours" which abound in maritime life,[14] tied and inscribed in the opened gap, become, in the contracted form of a name, the impelling instances or tokens of an anticipated unravelling of the writing of the CHAPTERS of the BOOKS. The CHAPTERS of the BOOKS, containing only names which by means of their insertion into the volume have recovered their initial written nature, are potential books. Linked to the specific scene of interrupting the blank surface, they are miniatures of the volume they designate, or more precisely, arbitrary signs constituting the core of a further filling out of the space, having been inserted in it in accordance to the law which rules the gap. Originating initially in the scene of primary writing (the circulating rumours spring forth from the inscription of the name of Leviathan in the Holy Scriptures), they are names which seem to have an independent life without regard to any concrete object. Actually, the Sperm Whale's name "philologically considered" is absurd, for in ancient times spermaceti "was popularly supposed to be derived from . . . the Greenland or Right Whale." Only when "the true nature of spermaceti became known," "the appellation must at last have come to be bestowed upon the whale from which this spermaceti was really derived." Thus, the Sperm Whale's name existed before it was known. Only later it obtained the name which from the very beginning was its name. As a result of this formerly existing name, the Sperm Whale's nominal originality, the implicit assertion of its being the true monarch of the seas, is the result of a movement of *Nachträglichkeit*, of an *après coup*. The name consequently lives an independent life and is in a position to be shifted from one object to another.

Moreover, there are still whales of whom "little is known but . . . (their) name," which suits the Razor Back for instance. Hardly known and rarely seen, this whale exists only as a name.

But strangely enough, there are further names having no referent at all which wait as letters in the Dead Letter Office to be attributed to a receiver. There are plenty of these names. Ishmael, the narrator, comes to them after having developed his uncompleted cetological system. They remain as an irreducible remainder not comprehended by the system. "Above, you have all the Leviathan of note. But there are a rabble of uncertain, fugitive, half fabulous whales, which as an American whaleman, I know by reputation, but not personally." And so, he starts enlisting an endless number of still hovering appellations, names in want of their referent, enabling the narrator to say that "if any of the following whales, shall hereafter be caught and marked, then he can readily be incorporated into this system." But if for any of these names there is still a small chance to be inserted or reduced by the system, there remain others left over which apparently have no chance of ever being attributed: "From the Icelandic, Dutch and English authorities, there might be quoted lists of uncertain whales, blessed with all manner of uncouth names. But I omit them as altogether obsolete; and can hardly help suspecting them for mere sounds, full of Leviathanism, but signifying nothing." These uncouth names, uncaught, as it were, in the net of the system, are mere sounds yet full of Leviathanism. Leviathanism is thus linked to sounds or rumours, independent of a concrete referent. Of Leviathanic names there are more than Leviathans. These names are hovering, as another scattered volume, to be engraved into the liberal volume of the whale. As floating marks, as mere signifiers signifying nothing, they respond to the primary leviathanic operation, the act of ripping up the surface, an operation which itself cannot be caught entirely in words. Among all the floating names crossing the chapter entitled "Cetology," only a small list is inserted, incorporated into its manifold gaps. Here they function, as we suggested, as the seeds of stories to be unfolded. But at the same time, in order to signify, they reduce Leviathanism to an order of signifieds so as to produce the effect, however ambiguous, of creatures having an existence exterior to language. But the deep veils the whale and the mere sounds of Leviathanism loom in the heights, or in other words, the whale as the mighty signifier, in the sense that it is the agency of ripping up the immaculate surface, glides underneath the realm of names, this other secondary order of signifiers. Only where the whale in its Leviathanic majesty protrudes do the words tumble down on the page in order to signify him. A small number of them succeed in fixing themselves to the outstanding features and to form the system of Cetology. But the names which thus "hook the nose" of the Leviathan are vague, indistinct, inappropriate. Most of the time they don't even designate as much as one outstanding feature. Hence the system they form is not perfect, and further encounters of sounds full of Leviathanism accompanying the irruption of the Leviathan announce an erasing of its order in a new, but just as much provisory, re-ordering of the system. This unsettling and erasing movement of what has been written is, as we shall see now, the very scene of writing at stake in the concept of the Bibliographical System adopted.

What is to follow is no theory of writing, and our assertion will show its foundations. For as a matter of fact the scene of writing incorporated in the text *represents* only this scene. The scene of writing condenses the act of writing into a figure which itself is a result of this same action. Every representation of the scene of writing, and this is equally true for its theoretical comprehension, is subordinated to the process of writing so as to be a mere coming to halt of a writing nevertheless undoing this figure again in its movement. No wonder, then, if the scene we shall pin down for a moment is a simile, a quotation from an already written book, the Bible. The scene of writing to be evoked is therefore not only a representation produced by the unmasterable movement of writing itself, but a transformation of a formerly given scene. The simile in question appears in CHAPTER III, entitled "*Fin-Back* of the first BOOK."

Even if not the slightest other part of the creature be visible, this isolated fin will at times, be plainly seen projecting from the surface. When the sea is moderately calm and slightly marked with spherical ripples, and this gnomon-like fin stands up and casts shadows upon the wrinkled surface, it may well be supposed that the watery circle surrounding it somewhat resembles a dial, with its style and wavy hour-lines graved on it. On that Ahaz-dial the shadow often goes back.

Before attempting an analysis of this passage, let's first make sure that the generalization of sorts we intend to make is justifiable. The rising fin is indeed the main axis around which our interpretation turns. The question is whether it is warranted to extend what can be derived from this peculiar mark of the Fin-Back to the other bodies of the whales. Certainly, for as has been observed already, the fin is a common trait of all whales (except the porpoise). The Fin-Back's fin is only appropriate to such a degree as to be the outstanding feature of its kind and to be used as a name in order to distinguish it from the other species. But more profoundly, as the fin is the instance of rising to the surface of the sea which counts for our interpretation, the following developments could be centered equally around the hump, the tail, the spout, or the whales "tossing themselves to heaven." The fin, however, "some three or four feet long, growing vertically from the hinder part of the back, of an angular shape, and with a very sharp pointed end," or with a razorlike protrusion, is better qualified for the *mise en scène* of writing, and Ishmael does not casually link this outstanding feature with the simile.

To be brief then, in what way does the above-mentioned passage inscribe the scene of writing into the text? Analogous to "his straight and single lofty jet rising like a tall misanthropic spear upon a barren plain," the Fin-Back's fin projects at times from the surface. The sharp blade of the fin tears and splits the barren surface of the water apart, producing the ripples which mark the Fin-Back's area. Previously, we asserted that this action of ripping up an immaculate surface or of tracing folds into a surface could be understood as the very effect of writing. Moreover, the outstanding feature, the fin, bestowed on the body of this whale as his name, is not only the before-mentioned column, but the stylus too, that is to say, the instrument of writing, of marking and incision. Thus, the cutting tool of the fin marks at times, at intervals, not only elementary characters into the barren surface, but its dividing action produces tidal movements as well, which are the elementary letters of time. Time indeed comes from *tide* which is derived from the Greek *daiesthai*, to divide. The stylus-like fin consequently links letter and time in the process of primary writing. At intervals, however, which are either measurable, as in the case of the Sperm Whale, whose diving and reemerging could serve as a measure of time for "an undeviating rhyme (can be observed) between the periods of his jet and the ordinary periods of respiration,"[15] or completely unexpected, as for the Fin-Back. At intervals time and letters coincide. The style or the stylus of the sharp-pointed fin produces time and letters simultaneously to erase them again as soon as the outstanding feature disappears in the deep. Thus, the elementary writing produces its own erasures through the intervals punctuating time.

The fin projects itself from the surface, the whales "keep tossing themselves to heaven," "out of the bottomless profundities the gigantic tail seems spasmodically snatching at the highest heaven,"[16] for the whales are sun-worshippers. "Standing at the mast-head of my ship during a sunrise that crimsoned sky and sea, I once saw a large herd of whales in the east, all heading towards the sun, and for a moment vibrating in concert with peaked flukes."[17] But these sun-worshippers interpret the sun in a rather curious way. They interpret it with their upstanding gnomon-like fin. The stylus of the sundial refracts the light of the sun, extinguishes it, and projects it as a shadow onto the wavy hour-lines engraved on it. On these hour-lines the sun sinks into its grave. The sun, or what it stands for, the donor of all life, the *logos spermatikos*, sees its semen being put to death by its extinction, the shadow. The moving shadow, as a result of this casting down of the sun, marks the derived scene of writing which does not only put to death the fertilizing semen but unsettles equally the logos, the meaning, the semantic unities by scattering them and splitting them, like the slitting razòr-sharp point of the style upon the surface, as dark spots. The *logos spermatikos* is projected onto an already "wrinkled surface," a surface already ripped up, twisted and wrenched into spherical ripples. So there is no previous immaculate surface where the seeding *logos spermatikos* could strew its semantic unities. The furrows engendered by the rising style close upon the quenched sema. An already primary scene of writing in which the unspotted surface has been stained catches the inky traces of the extinguished sunbeams and at the same time renders possible this derived scene of writing.

What hovers in the height are the floating names, the bearers of significance which fell themselves down in order to attach themselves to the uprising objects. But on the sharp edge of the style they become diffracted and only their shadow comes to designate the objects; at this threshold between depth and height, signifier and signified, they become utterly indistinguishable. The mere sounds full of Leviathanism but signifying nothing, after having tumbled down and hit the style where their shadow signifies an object, become the names functioning from now on as signifiers for the signified objects. Their former nature, however, as sounds full of Leviathanism, qualify them as sounds signifying nothing because they suffice in themselves: thus, they can also be understood as initial signifieds. The whales represent the gliding movement of the signifier, which is only fixed by the name after its transformation into a signifier, and which acquires hence the status of a signified. The derived scene of writing, rendered possible on the already always deflowered white leaf of paper, is consequently the scene of the transformation of the signifier into the signified and conversely: a transformation however, whose effects are always undone again by the primary agency of writing. It undoes what the secondary scene of writing implies: the attribution of names to objects and their systematized marshalling.

At times this erasure is the effect of the diving of the whales and of the subsequent rebounding of the names toward the realm of the mere sounds of Leviathanism. But in the derived scene this movement of effacing is already at work. It can only be thought, of course, as being linked to the primary erasing of the wrinkles or ripples on the surface. If the dial is the apparatus of writing in which both scenes are articulated, producing the letter subject to time and the letter of time, then the shadow which often goes back on this dial and which undoes its former writing has to be understood as a counterclockwise movement originated by the effacing of the primary writing.[18]

Ahaz, King of Judah, introduced the sundial with which he had become acquainted through the Assyrians. Hezekiah, his son, ascended to the throne and got sick unto death. The Lord admonished him to set his house in order and so Hezekiah did and he prayed to the Lord. But the word of the Lord came to Isaiah saying that he would heal Hezekiah for he had heard his prayer.

And Hezekiah said unto Isaiah, What *shall* be the sign that the *Lord* will heal me. . . . And Isaiah said, This sign shalt you have of the *Lord*, that the *Lord* will do the thing that he hath spoken: shall the shadow go forward ten degrees, or go back ten degrees?

And Hezekiah answered, It is a light thing for the shadow to go down ten degrees: nay let the shadow return backwards ten degrees. And Isaiah the prophet cried unto the *Lord*: and he brought the shadow ten degrees backward, by which it had gone down in the dial of Ahaz. (*King James Version,* II Kings XX:8–11)

The episode is related once more in Isaiah XXXVIII:8:

Behold, I will bring again the shadow of the degrees, which is gone down in the sundial of Ahaz, ten degrees backward. So the sun returned ten degrees, by which degrees it was gone down.

The whole passage undoubtedly gives evidence of the omnipotence of God to undo what he has done, to turn back the course of time, to erase the signs of time in order to defer death and give a supplementary present to life. In the context of the chapter on Cetology, however, the counterclockwise erasing of the marks of time and of the letters of writing engenders an inverse effect: for it is the result of the turning of the style about itself in the slashed wound of the surface which makes the shadow go back. The twisting, projected style erases what has been written by means of the diffraction of sunlight. By this movement of putting to death these impregnated letters on its wavy hourlines, the style re-enforces the extinction of the beams of the *logos spermatikos* which came down on itself. The agency of liquidating and erasing is here imparted to the powers of depth.[19] Their sign, the gnomon-like fin, prevents and ruins every attempt of the *logos spermatikos* to inseminate once and for all the barren plain of the surface. Projected on the already-ravished surface, the shadow is the drifted-off fetus of the logos, of the procreating sun.

And this is true too of the "single lofty jet rising like a tall misanthropic spear upon the barren plain." For even if "that vapour" is sometimes "glorified by a rainbow, as if Heaven had put its seal upon" it,[20] the rainbow formed opposite the sun, by reflection and refraction of the sun's rays in raindrops, marks the dissemination of its beams. Even if the rainbow announces the return of the sun, like the shadow that goes back on the sundial, the sun rises only to be diffracted again on the erected style. That style projecting from the surface, however, might be an indelible mark itself, a mark to protect its bearer as the mark the Lord set upon Cain. Of the Fin-Back Ishmael writes:

This Leviathan seems the banished and unconquerable Cain of his race, bearing for his mark that style upon his back.

Should thus an even more profound scene of writing, encompassed by a theological horizon, be at the origin of the already developed ones? Should it be the Lord who engendered himself as style, as a primary mark? The text we are reading could suggest that such may be the case. But the style, this primary incision, is the tool of writing and the tool of its striking out at the same time. This mark set upon the forehead of Cain by the Lord in order that nobody should slay him is a rather ambiguous mark, for on its sharp-pointed edge the Word of the Lord comes down to be extinguished, to be inscribed into the wavy patterns of the ravished surface. As the mark turns into an instrument of writing, it undoes its own celestial origin, it unsettles its being derived from an origin previous to itself by engraving this origin into its written patterns, which it subsequently erases again. Annulling its origin, deferring it by inscribing it as one figure into its text, writing postpones its outset. The style which engraves the letters on the withered leaf subordinates every priority to itself: there is no time prior to it. Writing, being without an origin except the one which it ascribes to itself in an everlasting movement of supplementation, sets with its letters the time-marks which open up the dimensions of temporality in the tissue of its textuality. A time machine, a dial on which the shadow often goes back, writing engenders time only to put it to death.

NOTES

1. If not otherwise mentioned all the quotes come from the chapter "Cetology" in Herman Melville, *Moby-Dick*, eds. Harrison Hayford and Hershel Parker (New York: W. W. Norton, 1967), pp. 116–28.

2. For a detailed discussion of the chapter "Cetology" in regard to the whole of *Moby-Dick*, see Howard P. Vincent, *The Trying Out of Moby-Dick* (Carbondale and Edwardsville: Southern Illinois University Press, 1949), pp. 121–42.

3. James Guetti, *The Limits of Metaphor* (Ithaca: Cornell University Press, 1969).

4. Ibid., p. 112.

5. Harold Beaver, "Introduction," in *Moby-Dick: or The Whale* (Harmondsworth: Penguin Books, 1972).

6. Edgar A. Dryden, *Melville's Thematics of Form* (Baltimore: The Johns Hopkins Press, 1968), p. 95.

7. Melville, *Moby-Dick*, p. 286.

8. For the relation between descent and dismemberment, see H. Bruce Franklin, *The Wake of the Gods: Melville's Mythology* (Stanford: Stanford University Press, 1963), pp. 53–98.

9. Melville, *Moby-Dick*, p. 1.

10. Ibid., p. 318.

11. Dryden, p. 96, defines Ishmael's relation to cannibalism differently.

12. Herman Melville, "Bartleby," in *Piazza Tales* (New York: Hendricks House, 1948).

13. For the preadamite sources Melville refers to, see Franklin.

14. For instance, Melville, *Moby-Dick*, p. 156.

15. Ibid., p. 312.

16. Ibid., p. 317.

17. Ibid., p. 317.

18. About the "terrors of gyratory time" in Melville's *Moby-Dick*, see Georges Poulet, *Studies in Human Time* (Baltimore: The Johns Hopkins Press, 1956), pp. 338–39.

19. The two whales distinguished by Robert Zoellner, the whale of Ishmael and the one of Ahab, come to substitute each other here, for as he writes: "In the actual text of *Moby-Dick*, of course, these distinctions tend to coalesce to produce a single all-encompassing symbol, Leviathanism. It makes no difference whether we are dealing with Ahab's or Ishmael's whale, with Moby Dick in particular or whales in general—the affirmative fact is Leviathanism's prodigious bulk and power." Robert Zoellner, *The Salt-Sea Mastodon: A Reading of Moby-Dick* (Berkeley and Los Angeles: University of California Press, 1973), pp. 150–51.

20. Melville, *Moby-Dick*, p. 314.

EIGHT

SIGNATURE EVENT CONTEXT*
Jacques Derrida

"Still confining ourselves for simplicity to *spoken* utterance."
Austin, *How to Do Things with Words*

Is IT CERTAIN that to the word *communication* corresponds a concept that is unique, univocal, rigorously controllable, and transmittable: in a word, communicable? Thus, in accordance with a strange figure of discourse, one must first of all ask oneself whether or not the word or signifier "communication" communicates a determinate content, an identifiable meaning, or a describable value. However, even to articulate and to propose this question I have had to anticipate the meaning of the word *communication*: I have been constrained to predetermine communication as a vehicle, a means of transport or transitional medium of a *meaning*, and moreover of a *unified* meaning. If *communication* possessed several meanings and if this plurality should prove to be irreducible, it would not be justifiable to define communication *a priori* as the transmission of a *meaning*, even supposing that we could agree on

* Paper read at the Congrès international des Sociétés de philosophie de langue française, Montreal, August 1971. The theme of the conference was "Communication." Published in Jacques Derrida, *Marges de la Philosophie* (Paris: Editions de Minuit, 1972), pp. 365–93. The English translation of *Marges* will be published by the Harvard University Press, which has kindly permitted us to publish this text, which was translated by Samuel Weber and Jeffrey Mehlman.—Eds.

what each of these words (transmission, meaning, etc.) involved. And yet, we have no prior authorization for neglecting *communication* as a word, or for impoverishing its polysemic aspects; indeed, this word opens up a semantic domain that precisely does not limit itself to semantics, semiotics, and even less to linguistics. For one characteristic of the semantic field of the word *communication* is that it designates non-semantic movements as well. Here, even a provisional recourse to ordinary language and to the equivocations of natural language instructs us that one can, for instance, *communicate a movement* or that a tremor [*ébranlement*], a shock, a displacement of force can be communicated —that is, propogated, transmitted. We also speak of different or remote places communicating with each other by means of a passage or opening. What takes place, in this sense, what is transmitted, communicated, does not involve phenomena of meaning or signification. In such cases we are dealing neither with a semantic or conceptual content, nor with a semiotic operation, and even less with a linguistic exchange.

We would not, however, assert that this non-semiotic meaning of the word *communication*, as it works in ordinary language, in one or more of the so-called natural languages, constitutes the *literal* or *primary* [*primitif*] meaning and that consequently the semantic, semiotic, or linguistic meaning corresponds to a derivation, extension, or reduction, a metaphoric displacement. We would not assert, as one might be tempted to do, that semio-linguistic communication acquired its title *more metaphorico*, by analogy with "physical" or "real" communication, inasmuch as it also serves as a passage, transporting and transmitting something, rendering it accessible. We will not assert this for the following reasons:

1) because the value of the notion of *literal meaning* [*sens propre*] appears more problematical than ever, and

2) because the value of displacement, of transport, etc., is precisely constitutive of the concept of metaphor with which one claims to comprehend the semantic displacement that is brought about from communication as a non-semio-linguistic phenomenon to communication as a semio-linguistic phenomenon.

(Let me note parenthetically that this communication is going to concern, indeed already concerns, the problem of polysemy and of communication, of dissemination—which I shall oppose to polysemy— and of communication. In a moment a certain concept of writing cannot fail to arise that may transform itself and perhaps transform the problematic under consideration.)

It seems self-evident that the ambiguous field of the word "communication" can be massively reduced by the limits of what is called a

Jacques Derrida

context (and I give notice, again parenthetically, that this particular communication will be concerned with the problem of context and with the question of determining exactly how writing relates to context in general). For example, in a philosophic *colloquium* on philosophy in the *French language*, a conventional context—produced by a kind of consensus that is implicit but structurally vague—seems to prescribe that one propose "communications" concerning communication, communications in a discursive form, colloquial communications, oral communications destined to be listened to, and to engage or to pursue dialogues within the horizon of an intelligibility and truth that is meaningful, such that ultimately general agreement may, in principle, be attained. These communications are supposed to confine themselves to the element of a determinate, "natural" language, here designated as French, which commands certain very particular uses of the word *communication*. Above all, the object of such communications is supposed, by priority or by privilege, to organize itself around communication *qua discourse*, or in any case *qua* signification. Without exhausting all the implications and the entire structure of an "event" such as this one, an effort that would require extended preliminary analysis, the conditions that I have just recalled seem to be evident; and those who doubt it need only consult our program to be convinced.

But are the conditions [*les réquisits*] of a context ever absolutely determinable? This is, fundamentally, the most general question that I shall endeavor to elaborate. Is there a rigorous and scientific concept of *context*? Or does the notion of context not conceal, behind a certain confusion, philosophical presuppositions of a very determinate nature? Stating it in the most summary manner possible, I shall try to demonstrate why a context is never absolutely determinable, or rather, why its determination can never be entirely certain or saturated. This structural non-saturation would have a double effect:

1) it would mark the theoretical inadequacy *of the current concept of context* (linguistic or non-linguistic), as it is accepted in numerous domains of research, including all the concepts with which it is systematically associated;

2) it would necessitate a certain generalization and a certain displacement of the concept of writing. This concept would no longer be comprehensible in terms of communication, at least in the limited sense of a transmission of meaning. Inversely, it is within the general domain of writing, defined in this way, that the effects of semantic communication can be determined as effects that are particular, secondary, inscribed, and supplementary.

If we take the notion of writing in its currently accepted sense—one which should not—and that is essential—be considered innocent, primitive, or natural, it can only be seen as a *means of communication*. Indeed, one is compelled to regard it as an especially potent means of communication, *extending* enormously, if not infinitely, the domain of oral or gestural communication. This seems obvious, a matter of general agreement. I shall not describe all the *modes* of this extension in time and in space. I shall, however, pause for a moment to consider the import [*valeur*] of *extension* to which I have just referred. To say that writing *extends* the field and the powers of locutory or gestural communication presupposes, does it not, a sort of *homogeneous* space of communication? Of course the compass of voice or of gesture would encounter therein a factual limit, an empirical boundary of space and of time; while writing, in the same time and in the same space, would be capable of relaxing those limits and of opening the *same field* to a very much larger scope. The meaning or contents of the semantic message would thus be transmitted, *communicated*, by different *means*, by more powerful technical mediations, over a far greater distance, but still within a medium that remains fundamentally continuous and self-identical, a homogeneous element through which the unity and wholeness of meaning would not be affected in its essence. Any alteration would therefore be accidental.

The system of this interpretation (which is also, in a certain manner, *the* system of interpretation, or in any case of all hermeneutical interpretation), however currently accepted it may be, or inasmuch as it is current, like common sense, has been *represented* through the history of philosophy. I would even go so far as to say that it is the interpretation of writing that is peculiar and proper to philosophy. I shall limit myself to a single example, but I do not believe that a single counter-example can be found in the entire history of philosophy as such; I know of no analysis that contradicts, essentially, the one proposed by Condillac, under the direct influence of Warburton, in the *Essay on the Origin of Human Knowledge* (*Essai sur l'origine des connaissances humaines*). I have chosen this example because it contains an *explicit* reflection on the origin and function of the written text (this explicitness is not to be found in every philosophy, and the particular conditions both of its emergence and of its eclipse must be analyzed) which organizes itself here within a philosophical discourse that, in this case and throughout philosophy, presupposes the simplicity of the origin, the continuity of all derivation, of all production, of all analysis, and

Jacques Derrida

the homogeneity of all dimensions [*ordres*]. Analogy is a major concept in the thought of Condillac. I have also chosen this example because the analysis, "retracing" the origin and function of writing, is placed, in a rather uncritical manner, *under the authority of the category of communication.*[1] If men write it is: (1) because they have to communicate; (2) because what they have to communicate is their "thought," their "ideas," their representations. Thought, as representation, precedes and governs communication, which transports the "idea," the signified content; (3) because men are *already* in a state that allows them to communicate their thought to themselves and to each other when, in a continuous manner, they invent the particular means of communication, writing. Here is a passage from chapter XIII of the Second Part ("On Language and Method"), First Section ("On the Origins and Progress of Language") (Writing is thus a modality of language and marks a continual progression in an essentially linguistic communication), paragraph XIII, "On Writing": "Men in a state of communicating their thoughts by means of sounds, felt the necessity of imagining new signs capable of perpetuating those thoughts and of making them *known* to persons who are *absent*" (I underscore this value of *absence*, which, if submitted to renewed questioning, will risk introducing a certain break in the homogeneity of the system). Once men are already in the state of "communicating their thoughts," and of doing it by means of sounds (which is, according to Condillac, a second step, when articulated language has come to "supplant" [*suppléer*] the language of action, which is the single and radical principle of all language), the birth and progress of writing will follow in a line that is direct, simple, and continuous. The history of writing will conform to a law of mechanical economy: to gain or save the most space and time possible by means of the most convenient abbreviation; hence writing will never have the slightest effect on either the structure or the contents of the meaning (the ideas) that it is supposed to transmit [*véhiculer*]. The same content, formerly communicated by gestures and sounds, will henceforth be transmitted by writing, by successively different modes of notation, from pictographic writing to alphabetic writing, collaterally by the hieroglyphic writing of the Egyptians and the ideographic writing of the Chinese. Condillac continues: "Thus, the imagination will represent to them only the very *same* images that they had already expressed through actions and words, and which had, from the very beginning, rendered language figural and metaphorical. *The most natural means* was thus to depict [*dessiner*] images of things. *To express the idea* of a man or of a horse, one represented the form of the one or of the other, and the first attempt at writing was nothing but a simple painting" (my emphasis—J. D.).

The representational character of the written communication—writing as picture, reproduction, imitation of its content—will be the invariant trait of all progress to come. The concept of *representation* is here indissociable from those of *communication* and of *expression* that I have emphasized in Condillac's text. Representation, of course, will become more complex, will develop supplementary ramifications and degrees; it will become the representation of a representation in various systems of writing, hieroglyphic, ideographic, or phonetic-alphabetical, but the representative structure which marks the first degree of expressive communication, the relation idea/sign, will never be either annulled or transformed. Describing the history of the types of writing, their continuous derivation from a common root that is never displaced and which establishes a sort of community of analogical participation among all the species of writing, Condillac concludes (in what is virtually a citation of Warburton, as is most of this chapter): "Thus, the general history of writing proceeds by simple gradation from the state of painting to that of the letter; for letters are the final steps that are left to be taken after the Chinese marks which, on the one hand, participate in the nature of Egyptian hieroglyphics, and on the other, participate in that of letters just as the hieroglyphs participate both in Mexican paintings and Chinese characters. These characters are so close to our writing that an alphabet simply diminishes the inconvenience of their great number and is their succinct abbreviation."

Having thus confirmed the motif of economic reduction in its *homogeneous and mechanical* character, let us now return to the notion of *absence* that I underscored, in passing, in the text of Condillac. How is that notion determined there?

1) It is first of all the absence of the addressee. One writes in order to communicate something to those who are absent. The absence of the sender, of the receiver [*destinateur*], from the mark that he abandons, and which cuts itself off from him and continues to produce effects independently of his presence and of the present actuality of his intentions [*vouloir-dire*], indeed even after his death, his absence, which moreover belongs to the structure of all writing—and I shall add further on, of all language in general—this absence is not examined by Condillac.

2) The absence of which Condillac speaks is determined in the most classic manner as a continuous modification and progressive extenuation of presence. Representation regularly *supplants* [*supplée*] presence. However, articulating all the moments of experience insofar as it is involved in signification ("to supplant," *suppléer*, is one of the most decisive and most frequent operational concepts in Condillac's *Essay*[2]), this operation of supplementation is not exhibited as a break in presence

Jacques Derrida

but rather as a continuous and homogeneous reparation and modification of presence in the representation.

I am not able to analyze, here, everything presupposed in Condillac's philosophy and elsewhere, by this concept of absence as the modification of presence. Let us note only that this concept governs another operational notion (for the sake of convenience I invoke the classical opposition between *operational* and *thematic*) which is no less decisive for the *Essay: tracing* and *retracing*. Like the concept of supplanting [*suppléance*], the concept of trace would permit an interpretation quite different from Condillac's. According to him, tracing means "expressing," "representing," "recalling," "rendering present" ("Thus painting probably owes its origin to the necessity of tracing our thoughts in the manner described, and this necessity has doubtless contributed to preserving the language of action as that which is most readily depictable" ["On Writing," p. 128]. The sign comes into being at the same time as imagination and memory, the moment it is necessitated by the absence of the object from present perception [*la perception présente*] ("Memory, as we have seen, consists in nothing but the power of recalling the signs of our ideas, or the circumstances that accompanied them; and this power only takes place by virtue of the *analogy of the signs* [my emphasis—J. D.: the concept of analogy, which organizes the entire system of Condillac, provides the general guarantee of all the continuities and in particular that linking presence to absence] that we have chosen; and by the order that we have instituted among our ideas, the objects that we wish to retrace are bound up with several of our present needs" 1, 11 ch. iv, # 39]). This holds true for all the orders of signs distinguished by Condillac (arbitrary, accidental, and even natural, distinctions that Condillac qualifies and, on certain points, even calls into question in his letters to Cramer). The philosophical operation that Condillac also calls "retracing" consists in reversing, by a process of analysis and continuous decomposition, the movement of genetic derivation that leads from simple sensation and present perception to the complex edifice of representation: from ordinary presence to the language of the most formal calculus [*calcul*].

It would be easy to demonstrate that, fundamentally, this type of analysis of written signification neither begins nor ends with Condillac. If I call this analysis "ideological," I do so neither to oppose its notions to "scientific" concepts nor to appeal to the dogmatic—one might also say ideological—usage to which the term "ideology" is often put, while seldom subjecting either the various possibilities or the history of the word to serious consideration. If I define notions such as those of Condillac as "ideological" it is because, against the background [*sur le fond*] of a vast, powerful, and systematic philosophical tradition dominated by the prominence of the *idea* (*eidos, idea*), they delineate the field of reflection of the French "ideologues," who in the wake of Condillac elaborated a theory of the sign as representation of the idea which itself represented the object perceived. From that point on, communication is that which circulates a representation as an ideal content (meaning); and writing is a species of this general communication. A species: a communication admitting a relative specificity within a genre.

If we now ask ourselves what, in this analysis, is the essential predicate of this *specific difference*, we rediscover *absence*.

I offer here the following two propositions or hypotheses:

1) since every sign, whether in the "language of action" or in articulated language (before even the intervention of writing in the classical sense), presupposes a certain absence (to be determined), the absence within the particular field of writing will have to be of an original type if one intends to grant any specificity whatsoever to the written sign;

2) if perchance the predicate thus introduced to characterize the absence peculiar and proper to writing were to find itself no less appropriate to every species of sign and of communication, the consequence would be a general shift: writing would no longer be one species of communication, and all the concepts to whose generality writing had been subordinated (including the *concept* itself *qua* meaning, idea or grasp of meaning and of idea, the concept of communication, of the sign, etc.) would appear to be non-critical, ill-formed, or destined, rather, to insure the authority and the force of a certain historical discourse.

Let us attempt, then, while still continuing to take this classical discourse as our point of departure, to characterize the absence that seems to intervene in a specific manner in the functioning of writing.

A written sign is proferred in the absence of the receiver. How to style this absence? One could say that at the moment when I am writing, the receiver may be absent from my field of present perception. But is not this absence merely a distant presence, one which is delayed or which, in one form or another, is idealized in its representation? This does not seem to be the case, or at least this distance, divergence, delay, this deferral [différance] must be capable of being carried to a certain absoluteness of absence if the structure of writing, assuming that writing exists, is to constitute itself. It is at that point that the *différance* [difference and deferral, *trans.*] as writing could no longer (be) an (ontological) modification of presence. In order for my "written communication" to retain its function as writing, i.e., its readability, it must remain readable despite the absolute disappearance of any receiver, determined in general. My communication must be repeatable—iterable—in the absolute absence of the receiver or of any empirically determinable collectiv-

Jacques Derrida

ity of receivers. Such iterability—(*iter*, again, probably comes from *itara, other* in Sanskrit, and everything that follows can be read as the working out of the logic that ties repetition to alterity) structures the mark of writing itself, no matter what particular type of writing is involved (whether pictographical, hieroglyphic, ideographic, phonetic, alphabetic, to cite the old categories). A writing that is not structurally readable—iterable—beyond the death of the addressee would not be writing. Although this would seem to be obvious, I do not want it accepted as such, and I shall examine the final objection that could be made to this proposition. Imagine a writing whose code would be so idiomatic as to be established and known, as secret cipher, by only two "subjects." Could we maintain that, following the death of the receiver, or even of both partners, the mark left by one of them is still writing? Yes, to the extent that, organized by a code, even an unknown and non-linguistic one, it is constituted in its identity as mark by its iterability, in the absence of such and such a person, and hence ultimately of every empirically determined "subject." This implies that there is no such thing as a code—organon of iterability—which could be structurally secret. The possibility of repeating and thus of identifying the marks is implicit in every code, making it into a network [*une grille*] that is communicable, transmittable, decipherable, iterable for a third, and hence for every possible user in general. To be what it is, all writing must, therefore, be capable of functioning in the radical absence of every empirically determined receiver in general. And this absence is not a continuous modification of presence, it is a rupture in presence, the "death" or the possibility of the "death" of the receiver inscribed in the structure of the mark (I note in passing that this is the point where the value or the "effect" of transcendentality is linked necessarily to the possibility of writing and of "death" as analyzed). The perhaps paradoxical consequence of my here having recourse to iteration and to code: the disruption, in the last analysis, of the authority of the code as a finite system of rules; at the same time, the radical destruction of any context as the protocol of code. We will come to this in a moment.

What holds for the receiver holds also, for the same reasons, for the sender or the producer. To write is to produce a mark that will constitute a sort of machine which is productive in turn, and which my future disappearance will not, in principle, hinder in its functioning, offering things and itself to be read and to be rewritten. When I say "my future disappearance" [*disparition*: also, demise, *trans.*], it is in order to render this proposition more immediately acceptable. I ought to be able to say my disappearance, pure and simple, my non-presence in general, for instance the non-presence of my intention of saying something meaningful [*mon vouloir-dire, mon intention-de-signification*], of my wish to communicate, from the emission or production of the mark. For a writing to be a writing it must continue to "act" and to be readable even when what is called the author of the writing no longer answers for what he has written, for what he seems to have signed, be it because of a temporary absence, because he is dead or, more generally, because he has not employed his absolutely actual and present intention or attention, the plenitude of his desire to say what he means, in order to sustain what seems to be written "in his name." One could repeat at this point the analysis outlined above this time with regard to the addressee. The situation of the writer and of the underwriter [*du souscripteur*: the signatory, *trans.*] is, concerning the written text, basically the same as that of the reader. This essential drift [dérive] bearing on writing as an iterative structure, cut off from all absolute responsibility, from *consciousness* as the ultimate authority, orphaned and separated at birth from the assistance of its father, is precisely what Plato condemns in the *Phaedrus*. If Plato's gesture is, as I believe, the philosophical movement par excellence, one can measure what is at stake here.

Before elaborating more precisely the inevitable consequences of these nuclear traits of all writing (that is: (1) the break with the horizon of communication as communication of consciousnesses or of presences and as linguistical or semantic transport of the desire to mean what one says [*vouloir-dire*]; (2) the disengagement of all writing from the semantic or hermeneutic horizons which, inasmuch as they are horizons of meaning, are riven [*crever*] by writing; (3) the necessity of disengaging from the concept of polysemics what I have elsewhere called *dissemination*, which is also the concept of writing; (4) the disqualification or the limiting of the concept of context, whether "real" or "linguistic," inasmuch as its rigorous theoretical determination as well as its empirical saturation is rendered impossible or insufficient by writing), I would like to demonstrate that the traits that can be recognized in the classical, narrowly defined concept of writing, are generalizable. They are valid not only for all orders of "signs" and for all languages in general but moreover, beyond semio-linguistic communication, for the entire field of what philosophy would call experience, even the experience of being: the above-mentioned "presence."

What are in effect the essential predicates in a minimal determination of the classical concept of writing?

1) A written sign, in the current meaning of this word, is a mark that subsists, one which does not exhaust itself in the moment of its inscription and which can give rise to an iteration in the absence and beyond the presence of the empirically determined subject who, in a

given context, has emitted or produced it. This is what has enabled us, at least traditionally, to distinguish a "written" from an "oral" communication.

2) At the same time, a written sign carries with it a force that breaks with its context, that is, with the collectivity of presences organizing the moment of its inscription. This breaking force [*force de rupture*] is not an accidental predicate but the very structure of the written text. In the case of a so-called "real" context, what I have just asserted is all too evident. This allegedly real context includes a certain "present" of the inscription, the presence of the writer to what he has written, the entire environment and the horizon of his experience, and above all the intention, the wanting-to-say-what-he-means, which animates his inscription at a given moment. But the sign possesses the characteristic of being readable even if the moment of its production is irrevocably lost and even if I do not know what its alleged author-scriptor consciously intended to say at the moment he wrote it, i.e. abandoned it to its essential drift. As far as the internal semiotic context is concerned, the force of the rupture is no less important: by virtue of its essential iterability, a written syntagma can always be detached from the chain in which it is inserted or given without causing it to lose all possibility of functioning, if not all possibility of "communicating," precisely. One can perhaps come to recognize other possibilities in it by inscribing it or *grafting* it onto other chains. No context can entirely enclose it. Nor any code, the code here being both the possibility and impossibility of writing, of its essential iterability (repetition/alterity).

3) This force of rupture is tied to the spacing [*espacement*] that constitutes the written sign: spacing which separates it from other elements of the internal contextual chain (the always open possibility of its disengagement and graft), but also from all forms of present reference (whether past or future in the modified form of the present that is past or to come), objective or subjective. This spacing is not the simple negativity of a lacuna but rather the emergence of the mark. It does not remain, however, as the labor of the negative in the service of meaning, of the living concept, of the *telos*, supersedable and reducible in the *Aufhebung* of a dialectic.

Are these three predicates, together with the entire system they entail, limited, as is often believed, strictly to "written" communication in the narrow sense of this word? Are they not to be found in all language, in spoken language for instance, and ultimately in the totality of "experience" insofar as it is inseparable from this field of the mark, which is to say, from the network of effacement and of difference, of units of iterability, which are separable from their internal and external context and also from themselves, inasmuch as the very iterability which constituted their identity does not permit them ever to be a unity that is identical to itself?

Let us consider any element of spoken language, be it a small or large unit. The first condition of its functioning is its delineation with regard to a certain code; but I prefer not to become too involved here with this concept of code which does not seem very reliable to me; let us say that a certain self-identity of this element (mark, sign, etc.) is required to permit its recognition and repetition. Through empirical variations of tone, voice, etc., possibly of a certain accent, for example, we must be able to recognize the identity, roughly speaking, of a signifying form. Why is this identity paradoxically the division or dissociation of itself, which will make of this phonic sign a grapheme? Because this unity of the signifying form only constitutes itself by virtue of its iterability, by the possibility of its being repeated in the absence not only of its "referent," which is self-evident, but in the absence of a determinate signified or of the intention of actual signification, as well as of all intention of present communication. This structural possibility of being weaned from the referent or from the signified (hence from communication and from its context) seems to me to make every mark, including those which are oral, a grapheme in general; which is to say, as we have seen, the non-present *remainder* [*restance*] of a differential mark cut off from its putative "production" or origin. And I shall even extend this law to all "experience" in general if it is conceded that there is no experience consisting of *pure* presence but only of chains of differential marks.

Let us dwell for a moment on this point and return to that absence of the referent and even of the signified meaning, and hence of the correlative intention to signify. The absence of referent is a possibility easily enough admitted today. This possibility is not only an empirical eventuality. It constructs the mark; and the potential presence of the referent at the moment it is designated does not modify in the slightest the structure of the mark, which implies that the mark can do without the referent. Husserl, in his *Logical Investigations*, analyzed this possibility very rigorously, and in a two-fold manner:

1) An utterance [*énoncé*] whose object is not impossible but only possible can very well be made and understood without its real object (its referent) being present, either to the person who produced the statement or to the one who receives it. If while looking out the window, I say: "The sky is blue," this utterance will be intelligible (let us say, provisionally if you like, communicable) even if the interlocutor does not see the sky; even if I do not see it myself, if I see it badly, if I am mistaken or if I wish to mislead my interlocutor. Not that this is always

Jacques Derrida

the case; but the structure of possibility of this utterance includes the capability to be formed and to function as a reference that is empty or cut off from its referent. Without this possibility, which is also that of iterability in general, "generable," and generative of all marks, there would be no utterance.

2) The absence of the signified. Husserl analyzes this as well. He judges it to be always possible even if, according to the axiology and teleology that governs his analysis, he judges this possibility to be inferior, dangerous, or "critical": it opens the phenomenon of the *crisis* of meaning. This absence of meaning can take three forms:

A) I can manipulate symbols without animating them, in an active and actual manner, with the attention and intention of signification (crisis of mathematical symbolism, according to Husserl). Husserl insists on the fact that this does not prevent the sign from functioning: the crisis or the emptiness of mathematical meaning does not limit its technical progress (the intervention of writing is decisive here, as Husserl himself remarks in *The Origin of Geometry*).

B) Certain utterances can have a meaning although they are deprived of *objective* signification. "The circle is squared" is a proposition endowed with meaning. It has sufficient meaning at least for me to judge it false or contradictory (*widersinnig* and not *sinnlos*, Husserl says). I place this example under the category of the absence of the signified, although in this case the tripartite division into signifier/signified/referent is not adequate to a discussion of the Husserlian analysis. "Squared circle" marks the absence of a referent, certainly, as well as that of a certain signified, but not the absence of meaning. In these two cases, the crisis of meaning (non-presence in general, absence as the absence of the referent—of the perception—or of the meaning—of the intention of actual signification) is still bound to the essential possibility of writing; and this crisis is not an accident, a factual and empirical anomaly of spoken language, it is also its positive possibility and its "internal" structure, in the form of a certain outside [*dehors*].

C) Finally there is what Husserl calls *Sinnlosigkeit* or agrammaticality. For instance, "the green is either" or "abracadabra" [*le vert est ou*; the ambiguity of *ou* or *où* is noted below, *trans.*]. In such cases Husserl considers that there is no language any more, or at least no "logical" language, no cognitive language such as Husserl construes in a teleological manner, no language accorded the possibility of the intuition of objects given in person and signified in *truth*. We are confronted here with a decisive difficulty. Before stopping to deal with it, I note a point that touches our discussion of communication, namely that the primary interest of the Husserlian analysis to which I am referring here (while

precisely detaching it up to a certain point, from its context or its teleological and metaphysical horizon, an operation which itself ought to
provoke us to ask how and why it is always possible), is its claim
rigorously to dissociate (not without a certain degree of success) from
every phenomenon of communication the analysis of the sign or the
expression (*Ausdruck*) as signifying sign, the seeking to say something
(*bedeutsames Zeichen*).[3]

Let us return to the case of agrammatical *Sinnlosigkeit*. What
interests Husserl in the *Logical Investigations* is the system of rules of a
universal grammar, not from a linguistic point of view but from a logical
and epistemological one. In an important note to the second edition,[4] he
specifies that his concern is with a pure *logical* grammar, that is, with
the universal conditions of possibility for a morphology of significations
in their cognitive relation to a possible object, not with a pure grammar
in *general*, considered from a psychological or linguistic point of view.
Thus, it is solely in a context determined by a will to know, by an
epistemic intention, by a conscious relation to the object as cognitive
object within a horizon of truth, solely in this oriented contextual field is
"the green is either" unacceptable. But as "the green is either" or "abracadabra" do not constitute their context by themselves, nothing prevents
them from functioning in another context as signifying marks (or indices, as Husserl would say). Not only in contingent cases such as a
translation from German into French, which would endow "the green is
either" with grammaticality, since "either" (*oder*) becomes for the ear
"where" [*où*] (a spatial mark). "Where has the green gone (of the
lawn: the green is where)," "Where is the glass gone in which I wanted
to give you something to drink?" ["Où est passé le verre dans lequel je
voulais vous donner à boire?"] But·even "the green is either" itself still
signifies an *example of agrammaticality*. And this is the possibility on
which I want to insist: the possibility of disengagement and citational
graft which belongs to the structure of every mark, spoken or written,
and which constitutes every mark in writing before and outside of every
horizon of semio-linguistic communication; in writing, which is to say in
the possibility of its functioning being cut off, at a certain point, from its
"original" desire-to-say-what-one-means [*vouloir-dire*] and from its participation in a saturable and constraining context. Every sign, linguistic
or non-linguistic, spoken or written (in the current sense of this opposition), in a small or large unit, can be *cited*, put between quotation marks;
in so doing it can break with every given context, engendering an in-
finity of new contexts in a manner which is absolutely illimitable. This
does not imply that the mark is valid outside of a context, but on the

Jacques Derrida

contrary that there are only contexts without any center or absolute anchoring [*ancrage*]. This citationality, this duplication or duplicity, this iterability of the mark is neither an accident nor an anomaly, it is that (normal/abnormal) without which a mark could not even have a function called "normal." What would a mark be that could not be cited? Or one whose origins would not get lost along the way?

PARASITES. ITER, OF WRITING: THAT IT PERHAPS DOES NOT EXIST

I now propose to elaborate a bit further this question with special attention to—but in order, as well, to pass beyond—the problematic of the *performative*. It concerns us here for several reasons:

1) First of all, Austin, through his emphasis on an analysis of perlocution and above all of illocution, appears to consider speech acts only as acts of communication. The author of the introduction to the French edition of *How To Do Things With Words*, quoting Austin, notes as much: "It is by comparing *constative* utterances (i.e., classical 'assertions, generally considered as true or false 'descriptions' of facts) with *performative* utterances (from the English 'performative,' i.e., allowing to accomplish something through speech itself) that Austin is led to consider *every* utterance worthy of the name (i.e., intended to communicate—thus excluding, for example, reflex-exclamations) as being primarily and above all a speech act produced in the *total* situation in which the interlocutors find themselves" (*How To Do Things With Words*, p. 147, G. Lane, Introduction to the French translation, p. 19).

2) This category of communication is relatively new. Austin's notions of illocution and perlocution do not designate the transference or passage of a thought-content, but, in some way, the communication of an original movement (to be defined within a *general theory of action*), an operation and the production of an effect. Communicating, in the case of the performative, if such a thing, in all rigor and in all purity, should exist (for the moment, I am working within that hypothesis and at that stage of the analysis), would be tantamount to communicating a force through the impetus [*impulsion*] of a mark.

3) As opposed to the classical assertion, to the constative utterance, the performative does not have its referent (but here that word is certainly no longer appropriate, and this precisely is the interest of the discovery) outside of itself or, in any event, before and in front of itself. It does not describe something that exists outside of language and prior to it. It produces or transforms a situation, it effects; and even if it can be said that a constative utterance also effectuates something and always

transforms a situation, it cannot be maintained that that constitutes its internal structure, its manifest function or destination, as in the case of the performative.

4) Austin was obliged to free the analysis of the performative from the authority of the truth *value*, from the true/false opposition,[5] at least in its classical form, and to substitute for it at times the value of force, of difference of force (*illocutionary* or *perlocutionary force*). (In this line of thought, which is nothing less than Nietzschean, this in particular strikes me as moving in the direction of Nietzsche himself, who often acknowledged a certain affinity for a vein of English thought.)

For these four reasons, at least, it might seem that Austin has shattered the concept of communication as a purely semiotic, linguistic, or symbolic concept. The performative is a "communication" which is not limited strictly to the transference of a semantic content that is already constituted and dominated by an orientation toward truth (be it the *unveiling* of what is in its being or the *adequation-congruence* between a judicative utterance and the thing itself).

And yet—such at least is what I should like to attempt to indicate now—all the difficulties encountered by Austin in an analysis which is patient, open, aporetical, in constant transformation, often more fruitful in the acknowledgement of its impasses than in its positions, strike me as having a common root. Austin has not taken account of what—in the structure of *locution* (thus before any illocutory or perlocutory determination)—already entails that system of predicates I call *graphematic in general* and consequently blurs [*brouille*] all the oppositions which follow, oppositions whose pertinence, purity, and rigor Austin has unsuccessfully attempted to establish.

In order to demonstrate this, I shall take for granted the fact that Austin's analyses at all times require a value of *context*, and even of a context exhaustively determined, in theory or teleologically; the long list of "infelicities" which in their variety may affect the performative event always comes back to an element in what Austin calls the total context.[6] One of those essential elements—and not one among others—remains, classically, consciousness, the conscious presence of the intention of the speaking subject in the totality of his speech act. As a result, performative communication becomes once more the communication of an intentional meaning,[7] even if that meaning has no referent in the form of a thing or of a prior or exterior state of things. The conscious presence of speakers or receivers participating in the accomplishment of a performative, their conscious and intentional presence in the totality of the operation, implies teleologically that no *residue* [*reste*] escapes the present totalization. No residue, either in the definition of the requisite conventions, or in the internal and linguistic context, or in the grammatical form, or in the semantic determination of the words employed; no irreducible polysemy, that is, no "dissemination" escaping the horizon of the unity of meaning. I quote from the first two lectures of *How to Do Things with Words*:

> Speaking generally, it is always necessary that the *circumstances* in which the words are uttered should be in some way, or ways, *appropriate*, and it is very commonly necessary that either the speaker himself or other persons should *also* perform certain *other* actions, whether 'physical' or 'mental' actions or even acts of uttering further words. Thus, for naming the ship, it is essential that I should be the person appointed to name her; for (Christian) marrying, it is essential that I should not be already married with a wife living, sane and undivorced, and so on; for a bet to have been made, it is generally necessary for the offer of the bet to have been accepted by a taker (who must have done something, such as to say 'Done'), and it is hardly a gift if I *say* 'I give it you' but never hand it over.
> So far, well and good. (Pp. 8–9)

In the Second Lecture, after eliminating the grammatical criterion in his customary manner, Austin examines the possibility and the origin of failures or "infelicities" of performative utterance. He then defines the six indispensable—if not sufficient—conditions of success. Through the values of "conventional procedure," "correctness," and "completeness," which occur in the definition, we necessarily find once more those of an exhaustively definable context, of a free consciousness present to the totality of the operation, and of absolutely meaningful speech [*vouloir-dire*] master of itself: the teleological jurisdiction of an entire field whose organizing center remains *intention*.[8] Austin's procedure is rather remarkable and typical of that philosophical tradition with which he would like to have so few ties. It consists in recognizing that the possibility of the negative (in this case, of infelicities) is in fact a structural possibility, that failure is an essential risk of the operations under consideration; then, in a move which is almost *immediately simultaneous*, in the name of a kind of ideal regulation, it excludes that risk as accidental, exterior, one which teaches us nothing about the linguistic phenomenon being considered. This is all the more curious—and, strictly speaking, untenable—in view of Austin's ironic denunciation of the "fetishized" opposition: *value/fact*.

Thus, for example, concerning the conventionality without which there is no performative, Austin acknowledges that *all* conventional acts are exposed to failure: "it seems clear in the first place that, although it has excited us (or failed to excite us) in connexion with certain acts which are or are in part acts of *uttering words*, infelicity is an ill to which *all* acts are heir which have the general character of ritual or ceremonial, all *conventional* acts: not indeed that *every* ritual is liable to every form of infelicity (but then nor is every performative utterance)" (pp. 18–19, Austin's emphasis).

In addition to the questions posed by a notion as historically sedimented as "convention," it should be noted at this point:

1) that Austin, at this juncture, appears to consider solely the conventionality constituting the *circumstance* of the utterance [*énoncé*], its contextual surroundings, and not a certain conventionality intrinsic to what constitutes the speech act [*locution*] itself, all that might be summarized rapidly under the problematical rubric of "the arbitrary nature of the sign," which extends, aggravates, and radicalizes the difficulty. "Ritual" is not a possible occurrence [*éventualité*], but rather, *as* iterability, a structural characteristic of every mark.

2) that the value of risk or exposure to infelicity, even though, as Austin recognizes, it can affect *a priori* the totality of conventional acts, is not interrogated as an essential predicate or as a *law*. Austin does not ponder the consequences issuing from the fact that a possibility—a possible risk—is *always* possible, and is in some sense a necessary possibility. Nor whether—once such a necessary possibility of infelicity is recognized—infelicity still constitutes an accident. What is a success when the possibility of infelicity [*échec*] continues to constitute its structure?

The opposition success/failure [*échec*] in illocution and in perlocution thus seems quite insufficient and extremely secondary [*dérivée*]. It presupposes a general and systematic elaboration of the structure of locution that would avoid an endless alternation of essence and accident. Now it is highly significant that Austin rejects and defers that "general theory" on at least two occasions, specifically in the Second Lecture. I leave aside the first exclusion.

I am not going into the general doctrine here: in many such cases we may even say the act was 'void' (or voidable for duress or undue influence) and so forth. Now I suppose some very general high-level doctrine might embrace both what we have called infelicities *and* these other 'unhappy' features of the doing of actions—in our case actions containing a performative utterance—in a single doctrine: but we are not including this kind of unhappiness—we must just remember, though, that features of this sort can and do constantly obtrude into any case we are discussing. Features of this sort would normally come under the heading of 'extenuating circumstances' or of 'factors reducing or abrogating the agent's responsibility,' and so on. (P. 21, my emphasis)

The second case of this exclusion concerns our subject more directly. It involves precisely the possibility for every performative utterance (and a priori every other utterance) to be "quoted." Now Austin excludes this possibility (and the general theory which would account for it) with a kind of lateral insistence, all the more significant in its off-handedness. He insists on the fact that this possibility remains *abnormal, parasitic*, that it constitutes a kind of extenuation or agonized succumbing of language that we should strenuously distance ourselves from and resolutely ignore. And the concept of the "ordinary," thus of "ordinary language," to which he has recourse is clearly marked by this exclusion. As a result, the concept becomes all the more problematical, and before demonstrating as much, it would no doubt be best for me simply to read a paragraph from the Second Lecture:

(ii) Secondly, as *utterances* our performances are *also* heir to certain other kinds of ill, which infect *all* utterances. And these likewise though again they might be brought into a more general account, we are deliberately at present excluding. I mean, for example, the following: a performative utterance will, for example, be *in a peculiar way* hollow or void if said by an actor on the stage, or if introduced in a poem, or spoken in soliloquy. This applies in a similar manner to any and every utterance—a sea-change in special circumstances. Language in such circumstances is in special ways—intelligibly—used not *seriously*, [my emphasis, J. D.] but in many ways *parasitic* upon its normal use—ways which fall under the doctrine of the *etiolations* of language. All this we are *excluding* from consideration. Our performative utterances, felicitous or not, are to be understood as issued in ordinary circumstances. (Pp. 21–22)

Austin thus excludes, along with what he calls a "sea-change," the "non-serious," "parasitism," "etiolation," "the non-ordinary" (along with the whole general theory which, if it succeeded in accounting for them, would no longer be governed by those oppositions), all of which he nevertheless recognizes as the possibility available to every act of utterance. It is as just such a "parasite" that writing has always been treated by the philosophical tradition, and the connection in this case is by no means coincidental.

I would therefore pose the following question: is this general possibility necessarily one of a failure or trap into which language may *fall* or lose itself as in an abyss situated outside of or in front of itself? What is the status of this *parasitism*? In other words, does the quality of risk admitted by Austin *surround* language like a kind of *ditch* or external place of perdition which speech [*la locution*] could never hope to leave, but which it can escape by remaining "at home," by and in itself, in the shelter of its essence or *telos*? Or, on the contrary, is this risk rather its internal and positive condition of possibility? Is that outside its inside, the very force and law of its emergence? In this last case, what would be meant by an "ordinary" language defined by the exclusion of the very law of language? In excluding the general theory of this structural parasitism, does not Austin, who nevertheless claims to describe the facts and events of ordinary language, pass off as ordinary an ethical and teleological determination (the univocity of the utterance [*énoncé*]— that he acknowledges elsewhere [pp. 72–73] remains a philosophical "ideal"—, the presence to self of a total context, the transparency of intentions, the presence of meaning [*vouloir-dire*] to the absolutely singular uniqueness of a speech act, etc.)?

For, ultimately, isn't it true that what Austin excludes as anomaly, exception, "non-serious,"[9] *citation* (on stage, in a poem, or a soliloquy) is the determined modification of a general citationality—or rather, a general iterability—without which there would not even be a "success-ful" performative? So that—a paradoxical but unavoidable conclusion— a successful performative is necessarily an "impure" performative, to adopt the word advanced later on by Austin when he acknowledges that there is no "pure" performative.[10]

I take things up here from the perspective of positive possibility and not simply as instances of failure or infelicity: would a performative utterance be possible if a citational doubling [*doublure*] did not come to split and dissociate from itself the pure singularity of the event? I pose the question in this form in order to prevent an objection. For it might be said: you cannot claim to account for the so-called graphe-matic structure of locution merely on the basis of the occurrence of failures of the performative, however real those failures may be and however effective or general their possibility. You cannot deny that there are also performatives that succeed, and one has to account for them: meetings are called to order (Paul Ricoeur did as much yesterday); people say: "I pose a question"; they bet, challenge, christen ships, and sometimes even marry. It would seem that such events have occurred. And even if only one had taken place only once, we would still be obliged to account for it.

I'll answer: "Perhaps." We should first be clear on what constitutes the status of "occurrence" or the eventhood of an event that entails in its allegedly present and singular emergence the intervention of an utter-ance [*énoncé*] that in itself can be only repetitive or citational in its structure, or rather, since those two words may lead to confusion: iter-able. I return then to a point that strikes me as fundamental and that now concerns the status of events in general, of events of speech or by speech, of the strange logic they entail and that often passes unseen.

Could a performative utterance succeed if its formulation did not repeat a "coded" or iterable utterance, or in other words, if the formula I pronounce in order to open a meeting, launch a ship or a marriage were not identifiable as *conforming* with an iterable model, if it were not then identifiable in some way as a "citation." Not that citationality in this case is of the same sort as in a theatrical play, a philosophical reference, or the recitation of a poem. That is why there is a relative specificity, as Austin says, a "relative purity" of performatives. But this relative purity does not emerge *in opposition to* citationality or iterability, but in opposition to other kinds of iteration within a general iterability which constitutes a violation of the allegedly rigorous purity of every event of discourse or every *speech act*. Rather than oppose citation or iteration to the non-iteration of an event, one ought to construct a differential typology of forms of iteration, assuming that such a project is tenable and can result in an exhaustive program, a question I hold in abeyance here. In such a typology, the category of intention will not disappear; it will have its place, but from that place it will no longer be able to govern the entire scene and system of utterance [*l'énonciation*]. Above all, at that point, we will be dealing with different kinds of marks or chains of iterable marks and not with an opposition between citational utterances, on the one hand, and singular and original event-utterances, on the other. The first consequence of this will be the following: given that structure of iteration, the intention animating the utterance will never be through and through present to itself and to its content. The iteration structuring it *a priori* introduces into it a dehiscence and a cleft [*brisure*] which are essential. The "non-serious," the *oratio obliqua* will no longer be able to be excluded, as Austin wished, from "ordinary" language. And if one maintains that such ordinary language, or the ordinary circumstances of language, excludes a general citationality or iterability, does that not mean that the "ordinariness" in question—the thing and the notion—shelter a lure, the teleological lure of consciousness (whose motivations, indestructible necessity, and systematic effects would be subject to analysis)? Above all, this essential absence of intending the actuality of utterance, this structural unconsciousness, if you like, prohibits any saturation of the context. In order for a context to be exhaustively determinable, in the sense required by Austin, conscious intention would at the very least have to be totally present and immediately transparent to itself and to others, since it is a determining center [*foyer*] of context. The concept of—or the search for—the context thus seems to suffer at this point from the same theoretical and "interested" uncertainty as the concept of the "ordinary," from the same metaphysical origins: the ethical and teleological discourse of consciousness. A reading of the connotations, this time, of Austin's text, would confirm the reading of the descriptions; I have just indicated its principle.

Différance, the irreducible absence of intention or attendance to the performative utterance, the most "event-ridden" utterance there is, is what authorizes me, taking account of the predicates just recalled, to posit the general graphematic structure of every "communication." By no means do I draw the conclusion that there is no relative specificity of effects of consciousness, or of effects of speech (as opposed to writing in the traditional sense), that there is no performative effect, no effect of ordinary language, no effect of presence or of discursive event (speech act). It is simply that those effects do not exclude what is generally opposed to them, term by term; on the contrary, they presuppose it, in an asymmetrical way, as the general space of their possibility.

SIGNATURES

That general space, is first of all spacing as a disruption of presence in a mark, what I here call writing. That all the difficulties encountered by Austin intersect in the place where both writing and presence are in question is for me indicated in a passage such as that in Lecture V in which the divided instance of the juridic signature [*seing*] emerges.

Is it an accident if Austin is there obliged to note: "I must explain again that we are floundering here. To feel the firm ground of prejudice slipping away is exhilarating, but brings its revenges" (p. 61). Shortly before, an "impasse" had appeared, resulting from the search for "any *single simple* criterion of grammar and vocabulary" in distinguishing between performative or constative utterances. (I should say that it is this critique of linguisticism and of the authority of the code, a critique based on an analysis of language, that most interested and convinced me in Austin's undertaking.) He then attempts to justify, with non-linguistic reasons, the preference he has shown in the analysis of performatives for the forms of the first person, the present indicative, the active voice. The justification, in the final instance, is the reference made therein to what Austin calls the *source* (p. 60)* of the utterance. This notion of *source*—and what is at stake in it is clear—frequently reappears in what follows and governs the entire analysis in the phase we are examining. Not only does Austin not doubt that the source of an oral utterance in the present indicative active is *present* to the utterance [*énonciation*] and its statement [*énoncé*] (I have attempted to explain why we had reasons not to believe so), but he does not even doubt that the equivalent of this tie to the source utterance is simply evident in and assured by a *signature*:

Where there is *not*, in the verbal formula of the utterance, a reference to the person doing the uttering, and so the acting, by means of the pronoun 'I'

---

* Austin's term is "utterance-*origin*"; Derrida's term (*source*) is hereafter translated as "source."—Eds.

Jacques Derrida

(or by his personal name), then in fact he will be 'referred to' in one of two ways:

(a) In verbal utterances, *by his being the person who does* the uttering—what we may call the utterance-*origin* which is used generally in any system of verbal reference-co-ordinates.

(b) In written utterances (or 'inscriptions'), *by his appending his signature* (this has to be done because, of course, written utterances are not tethered to their origin in the way spoken ones are). (Pp. 60–61)

An analogous function is attributed by Austin to the formula "hereby" in official documents.

From this point of view, let us attempt to analyze signatures, their relation to the present and to the source. I shall consider it as an implication of the analysis that every predicate established will be equally valid for that oral "signature" constituted—or aspired to—by the presence of the "author" as a "person who utters," as a "source," to the production of the utterance.

By definition, a written signature implies the actual or empirical non-presence of the signer. But, it will be claimed, the signature also marks and retains his having-been present in a past *now* or present [*maintenant*] which will remain a future *now* or present [*maintenant*], thus in a general *maintenant*, in the transcendental form of presentness [*maintenance*]. That general *maintenance* is in some way inscribed, pinpointed in the always evident and singular present punctuality of the form of the signature. Such is the enigmatic originality of every paraph. In order for the tethering to the source to occur, what must be retained is the absolute singularity of a signature-event and a signature-form: the pure reproducibility of a pure event.

Is there such a thing? Does the absolute singularity of signature as event ever occur? Are there signatures?

Yes, of course, every day. Effects of signature are the most common thing in the world. But the condition of possibility of those effects is simultaneously, once again, the condition of their impossibility, of the impossibility of their rigorous purity. In order to function, that is, to be readable, a signature must have a repeatable, iterable, imitable form; it must be able to be detached from the present and singular intention of its production. It is its sameness which, by corrupting its identity and its singularity, divides its seal [*sceau*]. I have already indicated above the principle of this analysis.

To conclude this very *dry* discussion:

1) as writing, communication, if we retain that word, is not the means of transference of meaning, the exchange of intentions and meanings [*vouloir-dire*], discourse and the "communication of consciousnesses." We are witnessing not an end of writing that would restore, in

accord with McLuhan's ideological representation, a transparency or an immediacy to social relations; but rather the increasingly powerful historical expansion of a general writing, of which the system of speech, consciousness, meaning, presence, truth, etc., would be only an effect, and should be analyzed as such. It is the exposure of this effect that I have called elsewhere logocentrism;

2) the semantic horizon that habitually governs the notion of communication is exceeded or split by the intervention of writing, that is, by a *dissemination* irreducible to *polysemy*. Writing is read; it is not the site, "in the last instance," of a hermeneutic deciphering, the decoding of a meaning or truth;

3) despite the general displacement of the classical, "philosophical," occidental concept of writing, it seems necessary to retain, provisionally and strategically, *the old name*. This entails an entire logic of *paleonymics* that I cannot develop here.[11] Very schematically: an opposition of metaphysical concepts (e.g., speech/writing, presence/absence, etc.) is never the confrontation of two terms, but a hierarchy and the order of a subordination. Deconstruction cannot be restricted or immediately pass to a neutralization: it must, through a double gesture, a double science, a double writing—put into practice a *reversal* of the classical opposition *and* a general *displacement* of the system. It is on that condition alone that deconstruction will provide the means of *intervening* in the field of oppositions it criticizes and that is also a field of non-discursive forces. Every concept, moreover, belongs to a systematic chain and constitutes in itself a system of predicates. There is no concept that is metaphysical in itself. There is a labor—metaphysical or not— performed on conceptual systems. Deconstruction does not consist in moving from one concept to another, but in reversing and displacing a conceptual order as well as the non-conceptual order with which it is articulated. For example, writing, as a classical concept, entails predicates that have been subordinated, excluded, or held in abeyance by forces and according to necessities to be analyzed. It is those predicates (I have recalled several of them) whose force of generality, generalization, and generativity is liberated, grafted onto a "new" concept of writing that corresponds as well to what has always *resisted* the prior organization of forces, always constituted the *residue* irreducible to the dominant force organizing the hierarchy that we may refer to, in brief, as logocentric. To leave to this new concept the old name of writing is tantamount to maintaining the structure of the *graft*, the transition and indispensable adherence to an effective *intervention* in the constituted historical field. It is to give to everything at stake in the operations of deconstruction the chance and the force, the power of *communication*.

Jacques Derrida

But this will have been understood, as a matter of course, especially in a philosophical colloquium: a disseminating operation *removed* from the presence (of being) according to all its modifications; writing, if there is any, perhaps communicates, but certainly does not exist. Or barely, hereby, in the form of the most improbable signature.

(Remark: the—written—text of this—oral— communication was to be delivered to the *Association des sociétés de philosophie de langue française* before the meeting. That dispatch should thus have been signed. Which I do, and counterfeit, here. Where? There. J.D.)

J. DERRIDA.

NOTES

1. The Rousseauist theory of language and of writing is also introduced under the general title of *communication* ("On the diverse means of communicating our thoughts" is the title of the first chapter of the *Essay on the Origin of Languages*).

2. Language supplants action or perception: articulated language supplants the language of action: writing supplants articulated language, etc. [The word, *supplée*, used by Derrida and here by Rousseau, implies the double notion of supplanting, replacing, and also supplementing, bringing to completion, remedying—Trans.]

3. "Up to now, we have considered expressions in their communicative function. This derives essentially from the fact that expressions operate as indexes. But a large role is also assigned to expressions in the life of the soul inasmuch as it is not engaged in a relation of communication. It is clear that this modification of the function does not affect what makes expressions expressions. They have, as before, their *Bedeutungen* and the same *Bedeutungen* as in collocution." *Logical Investigations I*, ch. I, #8). What I assert here implies the interpretation that I have offered of the Husserlian procedure on this point. I therefore refer the reader to *Speech and Phenomenon (La voix et le phénomène)*.

4. "In the first edition I spoke of 'pure grammar,' a name that was conceived on the analogy of 'pure science of nature' in Kant, and expressly designated as such. But to the extent that it cannot be affirmed that the pure morphology of *Bedeutungen* englobes all grammatical a prioris in their universality, since for example relations of communication between psychic subjects, which are so important for grammar, entail their own a prioris, the expression of *pure logical grammar* deserves priority . . ." (*LI II*, part 2, ch. iv).

5. Austin names the "two fetishes which I admit to an inclination to play Old Harry with, viz. (1) the true/false fetish, (2) the value/fact fetish" (p. 150).

6. He says, for example, that "The total speech act in the total speech situation is the *only actual* phenomenon which, in the last resort, we are engaged in elucidating" (p. 147).

7. Which occasionally requires Austin to reintroduce the criterion of

truth in his description of performatives. Cf., for example, pp. 50–52 and pp. 89–90.

8. Pp. 10–15.

9. Austin often refers to the suspicious status of the "non-serious" (cf., for example, pp. 104, 121). This is fundamentally linked to what he says elsewhere about *oratio obliqua* (pp. 70–71) and mime.

10. From this standpoint, one might question the fact, recognized by Austin, that "very commonly the *same* sentence is used on different occasions of utterance in *both ways*, performative and constative. The thing seems hopeless from the start, if we are to leave utterances *as they stand* and seek for a criterion." The graphematic root of citationality (iterability) is what creates this embarrassment and makes it impossible, as Austin says, "to lay down even a list of all possible criteria."

11. Cf. *La dissémination and Positions*.

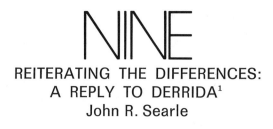

NINE

REITERATING THE DIFFERENCES:
A REPLY TO DERRIDA[1]
John R. Searle

IT WOULD BE a mistake, I think, to regard Derrida's discussion of Austin as a confrontation between two prominent philosophical traditions. This is not so much because Derrida has failed to discuss the central theses in Austin's theory of language, but rather because he has misunderstood and misstated Austin's position at several crucial points, as I shall attempt to show, and thus the confrontation never quite takes place.

His paper divides naturally into two parts: In the first part he discusses writing and its relation to context and communication. In the second, applying various of the conclusions of the first part, he discusses some features of Austin's theory of speech acts. He concludes with a discussion of the role of signatures. In my reply I will not attempt to deal with all or even very many of the points he raises, but will concentrate on those that seem to me to the most important and especially on those where I disagree with his conclusions. I should say at the outset that I did not find his arguments very clear and it is possible that I may have misinterpreted him as profoundly as I believe he has misinterpreted Austin.

A Reply to Derrida

I. WRITING, PERMANENCE, AND ITERABILITY

In the first part he mounts an attack on the idea of writing as the communication of intended meaning. The argument is that since writing can and must be able to function in the radical absence of the sender, the receiver, and the context of production, it cannot be the communication of the sender's meaning to the receiver. Since my writing can continue to function after I and all my intended readers are dead, and since the context of the writing may be totally forgotten or unknown, the horizon of communication is not the communication of consciousnesses or presences nor is it the transport of the intended meaning (*vouloir dire*) of the author. "My communication must be repeatable—iterable—in the absolute absence of the receiver or of any empirically determinable collectivity of receivers" (pp. 179–80).

He then extends this discussion to the "classical concept" of writing about which he argues that the differentiating features that the classical concept attributes to writing are generalizable. Indeed, they are "valid not only for all orders of 'signs' and for all languages in general but moreover, beyond semio-linguistic communication, for the entire field of what philosophy would call experience . . ." (p. 181). This conclusion is then in turn used to support his general attack on the idea of communication as the communication of intended meanings. His claim is that the three essential features in the classical conception of writing—that writing remains (*reste*) after its inscription, that it has "*une force de rupture*" with its context of production, and that it has an "*espacement*" which constitutes the written sign—are to be found in all language because of the *iterability* of linguistic elements. Iterability looms large in both of these arguments, and I will have more to say about it later.

In order to get at what is wrong with these arguments let us begin by asking what is it exactly that distinguishes written from spoken language. Is it iterability, the repeatability of the linguistic elements? Clearly not. As Derrida is aware, any linguistic element written or spoken, indeed any rule-governed element in any system of representation at all must be repeatable, otherwise the rules would have no scope of application. To say this is just to say that the logician's type-token distinction must apply generally to all the rule-governed elements of language in order that the rules can be applied to new occurrences of the phenomena specified by the rules. Without this feature of iterability there could not be the possibility of producing an infinite number of sentences with a finite list of elements; and this, as philosophers since Frege have recognized, is one of the crucial features of any language.

Is it absence, the absence of the receiver from the sender? Again,

John R. Searle

clearly not. Writing makes it possible to communicate with an absent receiver, but it is not necessary for the receiver to be absent. Written communication can exist in the presence of the receiver, as for example, when I compose a shopping list for myself or pass notes to my companion during a concert or lecture.

No doubt it would be possible to specify many features which distinguish writing from spoken utterances—for example, writing is visual and speaking is aural—but for the purposes of this discussion the most important distinguishing feature is the (relative) permanence of the written text over the spoken word. Even in an era of tape recordings and record playing machines, the primary device for preserving utterances is the written (or printed) word. This relative permanence in turn allows for both the absence of the receiver and, equally important, the accumulation of linguistic acts in an extended text. I can read an author's words after he has died, and even while he is alive he himself cannot tell me the entire contents of all his books, only his books can do that. Now the first confusion that Derrida makes, and it is important for the argument that follows, is that he confuses iterability with the permanence of the text. He thinks the reason that I can read dead authors is because their works are repeatable or iterable. Well, no doubt the fact that different copies are made of their books makes it a lot easier, but the phenomenon of the survival of the text is not the same as the phenomenon of repeatability: the type-token distinction is logically independent of the fact of the permanence of certain tokens. One and the same text (token) can be read by many different readers long after the death of the author, and it is this phenomenon of the permanence of the text that makes it possible to separate the utterance from its origin, and distinguishes the written from the spoken word.

This confusion of permanence with iterability lies at the heart of his argument for assimilating features of the written text with features of spoken words. He writes, "This structural possibility of being weaned from the referent or from the signified (hence from communication and from its context) seems to me to make every mark, including those which are oral, a grapheme in general; which is to say, as we have seen, the non-present *remainder* [*restance*] of a differential mark cut off from its putative 'production' or origin" (p. 183).

But there is an ambiguity in this argument that is fatal to its validity. The way in which a written text is weaned from its origin is quite different from the way in which any expression can be severed from its meaning through the form of "iterability" that is exemplified by quotation. The two phenomena operate on quite different principles. The principle according to which we can wean a written text from its origin is simply that the text has a permanence that enables it to survive the death of its author, receiver, and context of production. This principle is genuinely "graphematic." But the principle according to which quotation (citation) allows us to consider an expression apart from its meaning is simply this: since any system of representation must have some representing devices whether marks, sounds, pictures, etc., it is always possible to consider those devices quite apart from their role in representation. We can always consider words as just sounds or marks[2] and we can always construe pictures as just material objects. But again this possibility of separating the sign from the signified is a feature of any system of representation whatever; and there is nothing especially graphematic about it at all. It is furthermore quite independent of those special features of the "classical concept" of writing which are supposed to form the basis of the argument. The type-token distinction, together with the physical realization of the signs makes quotation possible; but these two features have nothing to do with previously mentioned special features of graphemes. I conclude that Derrida's argument to show that all elements of language (much less, experience) are really graphemes is without any force. It rests on a simple confusion of iterability with permanence.

I have left the most important issue in this section until last. Do the special features of writing determine that there is some break with the author's intentions in particular or with intentionality in general in the forms of communication that occur in writing? Does the fact that writing can continue to function in the absence of the writer, the intended receiver, or the context of production show that writing is not a vehicle of intentionality? It seems to me quite plain that the argument that the author and intended receiver may be dead and the context unknown or forgotten does not in the least show that intentionality is absent from written communication; on the contrary, intentionality plays exactly the same role in written as in spoken communication. What differs in the two cases is not the intentions of the speaker but the role of the context of the utterance in the success of the communication. To show this ask yourself what happens when you read the text of a dead author. Suppose you read the sentence, "On the twentieth of September 1793 I set out on a journey from London to Oxford." Now how do you understand this sentence? To the extent that the author said what he meant and you understand what he said you will know that the author intended to make a statement to the effect that on the twentieth of September 1793, he set out on a journey from London to Oxford, and the fact that the author is dead and all his intentions died with him is irrelevant to this feature of your understanding of his surviving written utterances. But

John R. Searle

suppose you decide to make a radical break—as one always can—with the strategy of understanding the sentence as an utterance of a man who once lived and had intentions like yourself and just think of it as a sentence of English, weaned from all production or origin, putative or otherwise. Even then there is no getting away from intentionality, because a *meaningful sentence is just a standing possibility of the corresponding (intentional) speech act.* To understand it, it is necessary to know that anyone who said it and meant it would be performing that speech act determined by the rules of the languages that give the sentence its meaning in the first place.

There are two obstacles to understanding this rather obvious point, one implicit in Derrida, the other explicit. The first is the illusion that somehow illocutionary intentions if they really existed or mattered would have to be something that *lay behind* the utterances, some inner pictures animating the visible signs. But of course in serious literal speech the sentences are precisely the realizations of the intentions: there need be no *gulf* at all between the illocutionary intention and its expression. The sentences are, so to speak, fungible intentions. Often, especially in writing, one forms one's intentions (or meanings) in the process of forming the sentences: there need not be two separate processes. This illusion is related to the second, which is that intentions must all be conscious. But in fact rather few of one's intentions are ever brought to consciousness as intentions. Speaking and writing are indeed conscious intentional activities, but the intentional aspect of illocutionary acts does not imply that there is a separate set of conscious states apart from simply writing and speaking.

To the extent that the author says what he means the text is the expression of his intentions. It is always possible that he may not have said what he meant or that the text may have become corrupt in some way; but exactly parallel considerations apply to spoken discourse. The situation as regards intentionality is exactly the same for the written word as it is for the spoken: understanding the utterance consists in recognizing the illocutionary intentions of the author and these intentions may be more or less perfectly realized by the words uttered, whether written or spoken. And understanding the sentence apart from any utterance is knowing what linguistic act its utterance would be the performance of.

When we come to the question of context, as Derrida is aware, the situation really is quite different for writing than it is for speech. In speech one can invoke all sorts of features of the context which are not possible to use in writing intended for absent receivers, without explicitly representing these features in the text. That is why verbatim transcripts of conversations are so hard to interpret. In conversation a great deal can be communicated without being made explicit in the sentence uttered.

Derrida has a distressing penchant for saying things that are obviously false. I will discuss several instances in the next section but one deserves special mention at this point. He says the meaningless example of ungrammatical French, "le vert est ou," means (*signifie*) one thing anyhow, it means an example of ungrammaticality. But this is a simple confusion. The sequence "le vert est ou" does not MEAN an example of ungrammaticality, it does not mean anything, rather it IS an example of ungrammaticality. The relation of meaning is not to be confused with instantiation. This mistake is important because it is part of his generally mistaken account of the nature of quotation, and his failure to understand the distinction between use and mention. The sequence "le vert est ou" can indeed be *mentioned* as an example of ungrammaticality, but to mention it is not the same as to *use* it. In this example it is not used to mean anything; indeed it is not used at all.

II. DERRIDA'S AUSTIN

Derrida's discussion of Austin is designed to show that all the difficulties encountered by Austin in his theory of speech acts have a common root: "Austin has not taken account of what—in the structure of *locution* (thus before any illocutory or perlocutory determination)— entails that system of predicates I call *graphematic in general* . . ." (p. 187). Thus in what follows Derrida ties his discussion of Austin to his preceding discussion of writing; in both he emphasizes the role of the iterability and citationality of linguistic elements. I believe he has misunderstood Austin in several crucial ways and the internal weaknesses in his argument are closely tied to these misunderstandings. In this section therefore I will very briefly summarize his critique and then simply list the major misunderstandings and mistakes. I will conclude with an—again all too brief—discussion of the relation between intention and iterability in speech acts.

Derrida notes that Austin distinguishes between felicitous and infelicitous speech acts but does not sufficiently ponder the consequences arising from the fact that the possibility of failure of the speech act is a necessary possibility. More to the point, according to Derrida, Austin excludes the possibility that performative utterances (and *a priori* every other utterance) can be quoted. Derrida makes this extraordinary charge on the grounds that Austin has excluded fictional discourse, utterances made by actors on a stage, and other forms of what Austin called "parasitic" or "etiolated" speech from consideration when setting out the preliminary statement of his theory of speech acts. Furthermore, according to Derrida, Austin saw these forms of discourse as a kind of *agonie* of language "qu'il faut fortement tenir à distance." They are not, according to Derrida's version of Austin, even part of "ordinary language." But, asks Derrida, does the possibility of this parasitism surround language like a ditch (*fossé*), an external place of perdition, as Austin seems to think; or it is not rather the case that this risk is the internal and positive condition of language itself? He points out ominously that "it is as just such a 'parasite' that writing has always been treated by the philosophical tradition" (p. 190). And he concludes his sequence of rhetorical questions with the following: "For, ultimately isn't it true that what Austin excludes as anomaly, exception, 'non-serious,' *citation* (on stage, in a poem, or a soliloquy) is the determined modification of a general citationality—or rather, a general iterability—without which there would not even be a 'successful' performative" (p. 191). According to Derrida (and contrary to what he supposes is Austin's view) a performative can succeed only if its formulation repeats a coded or iterable utterance, only if it is identifiable in some way as a citation. Once we have a typology of such forms of iteration we can see that there is "an essential absence of intention to the actuality of the utterance," and that Austin was wrong to exclude "parasitic" forms from ordinary language.

Before beginning a discussion of Derrida's charge I should point out that I hold no brief for the details of Austin's theory of speech acts, I have criticized it elsewhere and will not repeat those criticisms here.[3] The problem is rather that Derrida's Austin is unrecognizable. He bears almost no relation to the original.

1. Derrida has completely mistaken the status of Austin's exclusion of parasitic forms of discourse from his preliminary investigations of speech acts. Austin's idea is simply this: if we want to know what it is to make a promise or make a statement we had better not *start* our investigation with promises made by actors on stage in the course of a play or statements made in a novel by novelists about characters in the novel, because in a fairly obvious way such utterances are not standard cases of promises and statements. We do not, for example, hold the actor responsible today for the promise he made on stage last night in the way that we normally hold people responsible for their promises, and we do not demand of the author how he knows that his characters have such and such traits in a way that we normally expect the maker of a statement to be able to justify his claims. Austin describes this feature by saying that such utterances are "hollow" or "void" and "nonserious."

Furthermore, in a perfectly straightforward sense such utterances are "parasitical" on the standard cases: there could not, for example, be promises made by actors in a play if there were not the possibility of promises made in real life. The existence of the pretended form of the speech act is logically dependent on the possibility of the nonpretended speech act in the same way that any pretended form of behavior is dependent on nonpretended forms of behavior, and in that sense the pretended forms are *parasitical* on the nonpretended forms.

Austin's exclusion of these parasitic forms from consideration in his preliminary discussion is a matter of research strategy; he is, in his words, excluding them "at present"; but it is not a metaphysical exclusion: he is not casting them into a ditch or perdition, to use Derrida's words. Derrida seems to think that Austin's exclusion is a matter of great moment, a source of deep metaphysical difficulties, and that the analysis of parasitic discourse might create some insuperable difficulties for the theory of speech acts. But the history of the subject has proved otherwise. Once one has a general theory of speech acts—a theory which Austin did not live long enough to develop himself—it is one of the relatively simpler problems to analyze the status of parasitic discourse, that is, to meet the challenge contained in Derrida's question, "What is the status of this parasitism?" Writings subsequent to Austin's have answered this question.[4] But the terms in which this question can be intelligibly posed and answered already presuppose a general theory of speech acts. Austin correctly saw that it was necessary to hold in abeyance one set of questions, about parasitic discourse, until one has answered a logically prior set of questions about "serious" discourse. But the temporary exclusion of these questions within the development of the theory of speech acts, proved to be just that—temporary.

2. Related to the first misunderstanding about the status of the exclusion of parasitic discourse is a misunderstanding of the attitude Austin had to such discourse. Derrida supposes that the term "parasitic" involves some kind of moral judgment; that Austin is claiming that there is something bad or anomalous or not "ethical" about such discourse. Again, nothing could be further from the truth. The sense in which, for example, fiction is parasitic on nonfiction is the sense in which the definition of the rational numbers in number theory might be said to be parasitic on the definition of the natural numbers, or the notion of one logical constant in a logical system might be said to be parasitic on another, because the former is defined in terms of the latter. Such parasitism is a relation of logical dependence; it does not imply any moral judgment and certainly not that the parasite is somehow immorally sponging off the host (Does one really have to point this out?).

John R. Searle

Furthermore it is simply a mistake to say that Austin thought parasitic discourse was not part of ordinary language. The expression "ordinary language" in the era that Austin gave these lectures was opposed to technical or symbolic or formalized language such as occurred in mathematical logic or in the technical terminology of philosophy. Austin never denied that plays and novels were written in ordinary language; rather his point is that such utterances are not produced in ordinary *circumstances*, but rather, for example, on stage or in a fictional text.

3. In what is more than simply a misreading of Austin, Derrida supposes that by analyzing serious speech acts before considering the parasitic cases, Austin has somehow denied the very possibility that expressions can be quoted. I find so many confusions in this argument of Derrida that I hardly know where to get started on it. To begin with, the phenomenon of citationality is not the same as the phenomenon of parasitic discourse. A man who composes a novel or a poem is not in general *quoting* anyone; and a man who says his lines on a stage while acting in a play while he is indeed repeating lines composed by someone else, is not in general quoting the lines. There is a basic difference in that in parasitic discourse the expressions are being *used* and not *mentioned*. To Derrida's rhetorical question, "For, ultimately, isn't it true that what Austin excludes as anomaly, exceptions, 'non-serious' *citation* (on stage, in a poem, or a soliloquy) is the determined modification of a general citationality—or rather, a general iterability—without which there would not even be a 'successful' performative?" (p. 191), the answer is a polite but firm "No, it isn't true." To begin with most of the instances of parasitic discourse are not cases of citation at all. They are, to repeat, cases where expressions are *used* and not mentioned. But, more important, parasitic discourse of the kind we have been considering is a determined modification of the rules for performing speech acts, but it is not in any way a modification of iterability or citationality. Like all utterances, parasitic forms of utterances are instances of, though not modifications of, iterability, for—to repeat—without iterability there is no language at all. Every utterance in a natural language, parasitic or not, is an instance of iterability, which is simply another way of saying that the type-token distinction applies to the elements of language.

Derrida in this argument confuses no less than three separate and distinct phenomena: iterability, citationality, and parasitism. Parasitism is neither an instance of nor a modification of citationality, it is an instance of iterability in the sense that any discourse whatever is an instance of iterability, and it is a modification of the rules of serious discourse. Stated in its most naked form, and leaving out the confusion about citationality, the structure of Derrida's argument is this: Parasitism is (an instance of) iterability; iterability is presupposed by all performative utterances; Austin excludes parasitism, therefore he excludes iterability; therefore he excludes the possibility of all performative utterances and *a priori* of all utterances.

But this argument is not valid. Even had Austin's exclusion of fictional discourse been a metaphysical exclusion and not a part of his investigative strategy, it would not follow from the fact that Austin excludes parasitic discourse that he excludes any other forms of iterability. Quite the contrary. He sets aside the problems of fiction in order to get at the properties of nonfictional performatives. Both are instances of iterability in the trivial sense that any use of language whatever is an instance of a use of iterable elements, but the exclusion of the former does not preclude the possibility of the latter.

On a sympathetic reading of Derrida's text we can construe him as pointing out, quite correctly, that the possibility of parasitic discourse is internal to the notion of language, and that performatives can succeed only if the utterances are iterable, repetitions of conventional—or as he calls them, "coded"—forms. But neither of these points is in any way an objection to Austin. Indeed, Austin's insistence on the conventional character of the performative utterance in particular and the illocutionary act in general commits him precisely to the view that performatives must be iterable, in the sense that any conventional act involves the notion of the repetition of the same.

4. Derrida assimilates the sense in which writing can be said to be parasitic on spoken language with the sense in which fiction, etc., are parasitic on nonfiction or standard discourse. But these are quite different. In the case of the distinction between fiction and nonfiction, the relation is one of logical dependency. One could not have the concept of fiction without the concept of serious discourse. But the dependency of writing on spoken language is a contingent fact about the history of human languages and not a logical truth about the nature of language. Indeed, in mathematical and logical symbolism the relation of dependence goes the other way. The spoken, oral version of the symbols is simply an orally communicable way of representing the primary written forms.

5. A leitmotif of Derrida's entire discussion is the idea that somehow the iterability of linguistic forms (together with the citationality of linguistic forms and the existence of writing) militates against the idea that intention is the heart of meaning and communication, that indeed, an understanding of iteration will show the "essential absence of intention to the actuality of the utterance." But even if everything he said about iterability were true it would not show this. Indeed, I shall con-

clude this discussion by arguing for precisely the converse thesis: The iterability of linguistic forms facilitates and is a necessary condition of the particular forms of intentionality that are characteristic of speech acts.

The performances of actual speech acts (whether written or spoken) are indeed events, datable singular events in particular historical contexts. But as events they have some very peculiar properties. They are capable of communicating from speakers to hearers an infinite number of different contents. There is no upper limit on the number of new things that can be communicated by speech acts, which is just another way of saying that there is no limit on the number of new speech acts. Furthermore, hearers are able to understand this infinite number of possible communications simply by recognizing the intentions of the speakers in the performances of the speech acts. Now given that both speaker and hearer are finite, what is it that gives their speech acts this limitless capacity for communication? The answer is that the speaker and hearers are masters of the sets of rules we call the rules of language, and these rules are recursive. They allow for the repeated application of the same rule.

Thus the peculiar features of the intentionality that we find in speech acts require an iterability that includes not only the type we have been discussing, the repetition of the same word in different contexts, but also includes an iterability of the application of syntactical rules. Iterability—both as exemplified by the repeated use of the same word type and as exemplified by the recursive character of syntactical rules—is not as Derrida seems to think something in conflict with the intentionality of linguistic acts, spoken or written, it is the necessary presupposition of the forms which that intentionality takes.

NOTES

1. I am indebted to H. Dreyfus and D. Searle for discussion of these matters.

2. This of course is not the normal purpose of quotation, but it is a possible purpose.

3. See J. R. Searle, "Austin on Locutionary and Illocutionary Acts," *Philosophical Review* (1968), and "A Taxonomy of Illocutionary Acts," *Minnesota Studies in the Philosophy of Science* 6 (1975).

4. For a detailed answer to the question, see J. R. Searle, "The Logical Status of Fictional Discourse," *New Literary History* 5 (1975).

NOTES ON CONTRIBUTORS

PAUL DE MAN is professor of French and comparative literature at Yale University. His present contribution to *Glyph* is the concluding chapter of a book on Rousseau to be published in the near future. He is the author of *Blindness and Insight: Essays in the Rhetoric of Contemporary Criticism* and is currently completing a book-length study of Nietzsche.

JACQUES DERRIDA teaches philosophy at the Ecole Normale Supérieure in Paris. He is best known for his theory and practice of "deconstruction," which he elaborates in such texts as *La voix et le phénomène, De la grammatologie, L'écriture et la différence, La dissémination*, and *Marges*. His more recent work has dealt with writers such as Genet and Hegel (*Glas*), Kant, Maurice Blanchot, and Francis Ponge.

RODOLPHE GASCHÉ teaches French in the Department of Romance Languages at the Johns Hopkins University. He is the author of *Di hybride Wissenschaft*, the French translation of which will appear shortly. He has published essays on Nietzsche, Freud, Artaud, and Bataille and has translated major works by Derrida and Lacan into German.

LOUIS MARIN, born in Grenoble in 1931, studied at the Ecole Normale Supérieure in Paris, where he received his academic degrees: Licence-ès-lettres, Agrégation (philosophy), and Doctorat d'Etat (philosophy);

his thesis, *La critique du discours: Etudes sur la logique de Port-Royal et les "Pensées" de Pascal*, was published in 1975. Now a professor of Romance languages at the Johns Hopkins University, he has taught at the Sorbonne, the Ecole Pratique des Hautes Etudes, and the University of California at San Diego. He is also the author of *Etudes sémiologiques* and *Utopiques*.

WALTER BENN MICHAELS teaches English at the Johns Hopkins University. He has published articles on Ezra Pound and on T. S. Eliot and is currently completing a book on Henry James.

JOHN R. SEARLE is professor of philosophy at the University of California, Berkeley. He is the author of *Speech Acts: An Essay in the Philosophy of Language* and has edited *Philosophy of Language*. His essay "A Classification of Illocutionary Acts" recently appeared in *Language in Society*.

JAMES SIEGEL is associate professor of anthropology and Asian studies at Cornell University. He has published *The Rope of God*. In his current work he is examining Sumatran epics.

HENRY SUSSMAN is Andrew Mellon Scholar in the Humanities at the Johns Hopkins University. His essay in the current volume of *Glyph* is part of a book-length study on the metaphor in Kafka. His essays and reviews have appeared in *PMLA* and in *Modern Language Notes*, on whose staff he serves as comparative literature editor.

SAMUEL WEBER (founder of *Glyph*), is associate professor of comparative literature at the Johns Hopkins University. From 1967 to 1975, he taught comparative literature and critical theory at the Free University of Berlin (West). "The Divaricator" will be published later this year as part of a book entitled *Die Legende Freuds*.

THE JOHNS HOPKINS UNIVERSITY PRESS

This book was composed in Linotype Primer text and Permanent display type by the Maryland Linotype Composition Co., Inc., from a design by Susan Bishop. It was printed and bound by The Maple Press Company.